LEADERSHIP
[*for*]
TEACHER
LEARNING

Visit www.learningsciences.com/bookresources to download materials from this book.

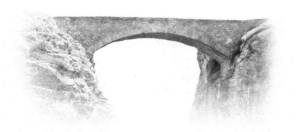

LEADERSHIP
[*for*]
TEACHER
LEARNING

Creating a Culture Where All Teachers
Improve so That All Students Succeed

DYLAN WILIAM

LearningSciencesInternational
LEARNING AND PERFORMANCE MANAGEMENT

1400 Centrepark Blvd, Suite 1000
West Palm Beach, FL 33401
717-845-6300

email: pub@learningsciences.com
learningsciences.com

21 20 19 18 17 16   2 3 4 5 6

Publisher's Cataloging-in-Publication Data
Wiliam, Dylan.
Leadership for teacher learning / Dylan Wiliam.
      pages cm
    ISBN: 978-1-941112-26-7 (pbk.)
  1. Effective teaching. 2. Educational leadership. 3. Educational tests and measurements.
4. Academic achievement.   I. Title.
  LB1025.3 .W47 2015
  371`.26—dc23
                              [2015946927]

Table of Contents

Acknowledgments

A book of this kind is inevitably the result of contributions from hundreds of people with whom I have discussed ideas relating to education and leadership over the years. These interactions have shaped my thinking in various ways, both consciously and unconsciously, and it is impossible to acknowledge them all. However, I do want specifically to thank individuals who made comments on drafts of the book: Daisy Christodoulou, David Didau, Tammy Heflebower, Laura McInerney, Roo Stenning, and Marc Tucker. In most cases, I have accepted the advice offered by others, but in other cases, I have not, sometimes because the comments were contradictory, and sometimes because I thought I knew better. Any errors that remain in the book are, therefore, entirely my responsibility.

As ever, my greatest thanks go to my partner, Siobhán Leahy, who as well as providing detailed comments on the entire content of the book, has also ensured that, even as it has explored some fairly esoteric aspects of research, the book does not stray too far from the enormously challenging work of leading real schools.

Learning Sciences International would like to thank the following reviewers:

John F. Ash
2014 Tennessee Middle School Principal of the Year
Central Magnet School
Murfreesboro, Tennessee

Jayne Ellspermann
2015 National Principal of the Year
West Port High School
Ocala, Florida

Jill Gildea
2014 NASS Superintendent of the Year finalist
Fremont School District 79
Mundelein, Illinois

Arch Ruth
2014 Nevada Assistant Principal of the Year
Pine Middle School
Reno, Nevada

Jared C. Wastler
2014 Maryland Assistant Principal of the Year
Liberty High School
Eldersburg, Maryland

Gregory Zenion
2012 Rhode Island Middle School Principal of the Year
Chariho Regional Middle School
Wood River Junction, Rhode Island

About the Author

 Dylan Wiliam, PhD, is a leading authority on the use of assessment to improve education. He has helped successfully implement classroom formative assessment in thousands of schools all over the world, including in the United States, Canada, Singapore, Sweden, Australia, and the United Kingdom. A two-part BBC series, *The Classroom Experiment*, tracked Dr. Wiliam's work at one British middle school, showing how formative assessment strategies empower students, significantly increase engagement, and shift classroom responsibility from teachers to their students so that students become agents of and collaborators in their own learning.

Dylan Wiliam is a professor emeritus of educational assessment at University College London. After a first degree in mathematics and physics and one year teaching in a private school, he taught in urban schools for seven years, during which time he earned further degrees in mathematics and mathematics education.

From 1996 to 2001, Wiliam was the dean and head of the School of Education at King's College London, and from 2001 to 2003, he served as assistant principal of the college. In 2003, he moved to the United States and became the senior research director at the Educational Testing Service in Princeton, New Jersey. In 2006, he returned to the United Kingdom as deputy director (provost) of the Institute of Education, University of London. In 2010, he stepped down as deputy director to spend more time on research and teaching.

Over the past fifteen years, Wiliam's work has focused on the profound impacts of embedding classroom formative assessment on student learning. In 1998, he coauthored, with Paul Black, a major review of the research evidence on formative assessment, together with a guide to the research for policy makers and practitioners, entitled *Inside the Black Box*. This booklet and subsequent booklets on formative assessment for practical application in the classroom and individual subject areas are available from Learning Sciences International. He is the author of *Embedded Formative Assessment* and coauthor, with Siobhán Leahy, of *Embedding Formative Assessment*.

Introduction

The argument of this book is simple: the main job of school leaders is to improve the work performance of those they lead. The *Mabinogion* is a collection of myths and legends compiled, from earlier oral traditions, in the 12th and 13th centuries in the Welsh language. One of the legends concerns a giant named Bendigeidfran (Brân the Blessed) who is leading his army across the countryside when they come across a chasm. At the bottom of the chasm is a river, which is too deep for the soldiers to wade through, and there are rocks in the river that are so close together that the soldiers are unable to use the small boats they have brought with them. After some discussion, the giant decides that he will lay his body across the chasm, so the soldiers can walk across his back to the other side. As he lays himself down, he says, "One that would be a leader must be a bridge."

This, it seems to me, is a powerful and fitting metaphor for leadership in schools, and neatly encapsulates the main argument of this book—that the main job of school leaders is to improve the work performance of those they lead. Other things that leaders do will, of course, have an impact on the learning of the students in the schools they lead, such as creating policies on grouping students for instruction, but the size of the impacts are small in comparison to the impact of developing the classroom practice of teachers in those schools (Educational Endowment Foundation, 2015).

There are, in addition, many things that affect educational outcomes for young people over which school leaders have little or no control. There is some evidence that the quality of school buildings can influence how much students learn (Commission for Architecture and the Built Environment, 2002), although the impact of the school environment on student achievement appears to be rather small (PricewaterhouseCoopers, 2003). On the other hand, there are many other factors, again over which leaders have little or no control, that have significant impacts on student achievement, such as poverty, teacher preparation, and teacher compensation.

Of course poverty should not be an excuse for low educational achievement, but there is now a huge body of evidence that teaching children growing up in poverty is more challenging than teaching more affluent students (Dickerson & Popli, 2012; Taylor, 2010). Reducing the number of children growing up in poverty will substantially increase student achievement (Carnoy & Rothstein, 2013), but school leaders cannot do much to affect those numbers.

In many countries, and particularly in the United States, the pre-service preparation of teachers is only loosely coupled with the needs of schools, and so creating better alignment between teacher training programs and the realities of school life would also have a substantial impact on student achievement (Anderson & Stillman, 2013; Cochran-Smith & Zeichner, 2005). But again, it is hard to see how individual school leaders can do much to make university schools of education more responsive to their needs.

Closer to home, school leaders do have some influence over teacher compensation, by evaluating teachers, for example. However, in most districts, school leaders are rarely consulted about the design of teacher compensation schemes, and there is considerable evidence that these schemes are not well aligned with what matters for student achievement. For example, across the United States, compensating teachers for gaining a master's degree costs well over $8 billion each year (Roza & Miller, 2009) even though there is little evidence that teachers with master's degrees are more effective than those without (Harris & Sass, 2007). The focus of this book is squarely on the bottom right-hand cell of the control-impact matrix shown in Table I.1.

Table I.1. Control-Impact Matrix for Schools

		Control	
		Low	High
Impact	Low	School buildings	Ability grouping
	High	Poverty	Teacher practices

In making the argument presented in this book, I have drawn together evidence from a range of sources in order to provide leaders with arguments and evidence they can use to persuade others of the importance of these ideas in their own local contexts. The result is therefore not a book designed to be read at a single sitting but rather a resource, to which I hope that readers will return from time to time for ideas to use in their own work.

In chapter 1, I argue that in the future, young people will need higher levels of achievement than have ever been needed before, not only to find fulfilling work, but also to empower themselves to thrive in an increasingly complex world. Both routine and non-routine jobs will continue to be automated at an increasing rate, and others will be undertaken by people in other countries, but new opportunities will also be created at an equally extraordinary rate, for those who can see and seize them. This will require higher levels of achievement in the traditional school subjects, but it will also require creativity and entrepreneurship, which are currently being squeezed out of our schools' curricula due to the pressure to improve reading and math scores. Therefore, we need to encourage young people to reach higher levels of achievement in the traditional school subjects in *less* time than we are currently devoting, to leave plenty of time in school for them to find their passions. I also argue that most of the reforms that have been tried so far have either been complete failures or, at best, have had only marginal impacts because they have ignored the crucial importance of teacher quality.

Chapter 2 shows how, over the last forty years, evidence has accumulated that the quality of teachers is one of the most important influences on how much children and young people learn at school. While the quality of teaching is influenced by a range of factors, including the amount of time and support teachers get, the size of the classes they teach, the quality of the curriculum they are using, and so on, there is now very strong evidence that the personal qualities that teachers bring to their work are extremely important. This evidence has led to calls to increase the quality of teachers by increasing the quality of entrants to the profession and by removing less effective teachers. However, as I show in chapter 2, while both of these approaches may improve the situation somewhat, neither approach, either separately or in tandem, has the potential to produce the kinds of improvements in teacher quality that are needed. The major contribution to improving teacher quality must come from improving the quality of the teachers already working in our schools.

Chapter 3 examines the available evidence for the kinds of changes in teacher behavior that are likely to have the greatest impact on student achievement. Inevitably, because it engages with a large body of research literature, some of the arguments get rather technical, and I did consider removing some of the technical details to make the chapter more readable. However, because one aim of this book is to equip leaders with the arguments they need to convince others about the need to focus teacher professional development on classroom formative assessment, I felt it was important to offer clear evidence about the weaknesses of competing claims.

In particular, in recent years, a number of writers and researchers have argued that the best way to aggregate evidence from multiple research studies is through a statistical technique called meta-analysis. In medicine, and a number of related fields, meta-analysis has produced extraordinary breakthroughs in research synthesis that have saved hundreds of thousands of lives, but in chapter 3, I show that meta-analysis has important shortcomings when applied to education. In particular, a number of aspects of meta-analysis appear to be poorly understood by those working in the field, with the result that most of these meta-analyses cannot be relied upon to produce valid syntheses of what the research evidence actually says. For the foreseeable future, I argue, for all its faults, the best way to use research to direct the improvements that teachers make is through "best-evidence synthesis" in which professional judgment is used to weigh the available evidence for its relevance to classrooms. When we use this professional judgment, we find that the currently available evidence suggests that nothing is likely to be more cost effective than improving teachers' use of classroom formative assessment, which is the subject of chapter 4.

Chapter 4 briefly summarizes the research that has been published on the impact of formative assessment on student achievement and then shows how formative assessment can be thought of as a general framework that encompasses current policy priorities, such as differentiated instruction (DI) and response to intervention (RTI). Because the research on initiatives such as DI and RTI is weak, I argue that a focus on formative assessment is the best way of ensuring that DI and RTI are implemented in a way that maximizes the impact on student achievement. I also show that formative assessment is a key aspect of currently used frameworks for the evaluation of teaching. Because such frameworks are, by definition, comprehensive, there is a danger that teachers improve aspects of their practice that have little or no impact on their students' achievement. A focus on formative assessment ensures that teacher development focuses on aspects of teaching that will have the greatest impact on student achievement. Chapter 4 also reviews different approaches to formative assessment, in particular focusing on instructional data teams and formative assessment as approaches to improving classroom practice, and shows how the two approaches are complementary. Finally, chapter 4 also responds to a number of critiques of formative assessment and concludes that although the evidence for using formative assessment, and in particular how it should be implemented, is not as strong as we would like, it is still more likely to have a substantial impact on student achievement than anything else that could be adopted.

Chapter 5 deals with the issue of teacher change, and in particular, why so many efforts to change classroom practice have been relatively unsuccessful. Drawing on the research on expertise in a range of different fields, I show that expertise cannot generally be put into words and also that expertise in teaching shares most, if not all, of the features of expertise in other domains. Attempts to "tell teachers what to do" are therefore bound to fail because they fail to address the kind of knowledge that is needed for expert performance. Instead, what is needed is a focus on what expertise researchers call "deliberate practice." Research on teachers in the United States suggests that they improve rapidly in their first few years, but then, generally, the improvement slows down and, in many cases, stops altogether. Because the variation in teacher quality for more experienced teachers is almost as great as that for novices, it suggests that many teachers are not engaging in the deliberate practice that the expertise research indicates is necessary for elite performance. This, in turn, suggests that we are only beginning to scratch the surface of what is possible for US teachers to achieve, given the right support.

In chapter 6, I focus on what has been learned in ten years of supporting teachers to develop their practice of formative assessment through building-based teacher learning communities. While there is much advice already available on how to lead, and support, instructional data teams, there is much less on how teachers can be supported in changing their "real-time" use of classroom formative assessment. The chapter provides a detailed protocol for teacher meetings and also includes advice on how to select and support leaders of the teacher groups.

Chapter 7 deals with issues of implementation in greater detail, including the importance, for leaders, of deciding what doesn't get done in order to give teachers time to work on practice and how leaders can evaluate the progress being made. A key element of this in-school evaluation is the adoption of a logic model that explains the key processes by which the implementation of classroom formative assessment is presumed to improve student achievement. This allows leaders to identify a number of leading indicators of success, which provide assurance that the steps that will result in increased student achievement are, in fact, in place and developing appropriately. This allows monitoring of formative assessment to be integrated into existing building-level information-gathering systems, such as walk-throughs or learning walks. The chapter also includes ideas for how the development of classroom formative assessment can be integrated into teacher evaluation programs, allowing the work to be taken forward in a coherent and aligned way.

Although the book is written to have a clear argument from one end to the other, depending on your interests, certain chapters may be skipped or skimmed without losing the main thread of the argument. For example, if you are happy to accept that teacher quality matters and is highly variable, but cannot currently be measured with acceptable accuracy for individual teachers, then you could skip chapter 2. Similarly, if you agree that meta-analysis has not yet been developed to the point where it provides reliable guides for action in education and that professional judgment is needed in synthesizing results from different studies, then you could skip chapter 3. If you are already convinced that classroom formative assessment is a more cost-effective way of improving student achievement than anything else we know about right now, then you could skip parts of chapter 4, although you may still find the evidence collected there useful in persuading others. Finally, if you already believe that expertise in teaching is like expertise in other fields, that expertise is largely (but not entirely) a matter of practice rather than talent, and that most people currently teaching could be as good as the very best teachers if they work at it, then the main argument of chapter 5 will be familiar to you, although some of the examples given there may still be interesting or useful.

In this regard, chapters 6 and 7 are rather different from those that precede them, as they draw together, for the first time, all that I and my various colleagues have learned over the last fifteen years about supporting teachers in their development of classroom formative assessment. As well as providing detailed guidance for the creation of building-based teacher learning communities, these chapters detail what we have learned about the problems of actually making all this work, in real schools, where pressure to increase test scores can feel overwhelming.

[*Chapter 1*]

Why We Need to Raise Student Achievement, What's Been Tried, and Why It Hasn't Worked

The idea that our schools need to get better has been around for a very long time, but of course before we can decide how to make our schools better, we need to be clear about what we are making them better *for*. In many countries, it would be thought absurd to design an education system without having a clear statement of the purpose of education, but in the United States, like many English-speaking countries, there is a widespread distrust of philosophy. This practical approach can be very useful in avoiding long debates, but there is also a danger that differences in unexamined assumptions make meaningful debate impossible. In this opening chapter, I argue that there are many reasons to educate young people, and any education system has to pull off a delicate balancing act between these. However, preparation for work deserves special attention, not because it is the most important purpose of education, but it is where things are changing fastest. In the second half of the chapter, I review some of the main measures proposed to improve education and conclude by looking at whether comparing the United States with other countries is helpful.

Why We Need to Raise Achievement

One of the problems with debates about education is that often people talk past each other because they differ in their beliefs about why education is important. There isn't space here for a lengthy discussion of the philosophy of education, but the main reasons that have been proposed over the years for educating young people can be grouped into four broad categories:

1. *Personal empowerment*—enabling young people to take greater control over their lives

2. *Transmission of culture*—passing on the "great things that have been thought and said" from one generation to the next

3. *Preparation for citizenship*—preparing young people to take an active role in society and to make a difference in the world

4. *Preparation for work*—ensuring that young people are able to find fulfilling and rewarding employment

It is obvious that all of these are important. No education system can focus on just one, or even a few of these, and the balance between these four broad kinds of goals may vary from place to place, will change over time, and will also vary according to the age of the student. However, what does seem to be the case is that the demands of the world of work require particular attention, not because those demands are more important than the other categories, but because it is in the world of work that things are changing fastest. After all, the great things that have been thought and said are not changing particularly quickly. It is likely that in one hundred years' time, we will still believe that students should study Shakespeare. There are, of course, changes taking place in what tools students need to use to take greater control over their lives and to participate in a democratic society, but these changes are dwarfed by the changes in the world of work.

The Changing Nature of Work

In 1900, 41 percent of the US workforce was employed in agriculture. A century later, the proportion was down to 2 percent (Autor, 2014). Because the US working population in 1900 was around 28,000,000 (Lebergott, 1957), we can estimate that despite a four-fold increase in the US population, around one-fourth as many people work in agriculture today as did so in 1900.

Other industries have changed even more. In the United States in 1900, over 100,000 people were employed as carriage and harness makers, and another 100,000 worked as cobblers, while today the total of each is approximately zero (Cox & Alm, 2008). Similar fates have befallen telegraph operators, boilermakers, and watch-makers (down from 75,000, 74,000, and 101,000, respectively, in 1920 to zero today). These figures may not be surprising, as the jobs being done have largely disappeared, but even where the work continues, in many cases, the number of individuals employed has reduced drastically. For example, US railroad companies employed over 2 million people in 1920; today, it is around 110,000. Even as late as 1970, over 400,000 were employed as telephone operators, while today the total is about 120,000. Since 1980, 40 percent fewer people are working as secretaries, and 60 percent fewer are working as metal or plastic machinists (Cox & Alm, 2008).

Perhaps the starkest decline in employment in recent years has been in manufacturing, which has lost as many jobs since 2000 as were lost in agriculture in the last century. According to data published by the Bureau of Labor Statistics (2014), in 2013, 5.25 million fewer people were employed in manufacturing in the United States than in 2000. Or, to put it another way, since 2000, the United States has lost over 1,000 manufacturing jobs *every single day*. Many people attribute this to the fact that "we don't make stuff in America anymore," but this is simply not true.

It is true that China overtook the United States as the world's largest manufacturing nation in 2010 (depending on how this is measured), but the real-terms value of goods manufactured in the United States has never been higher than it is now, as shown in Figure 1.1 (United Nations Statistics Division, 2013). We still make stuff in America. We just don't use as many people to do so as we used to. This idea is neatly encapsulated by the joke about an automobile factory being run by one man and a dog. The man's job is to feed the dog, and the dog's job is to make sure the man doesn't go near any of the controls, because the robots have it all figured out.

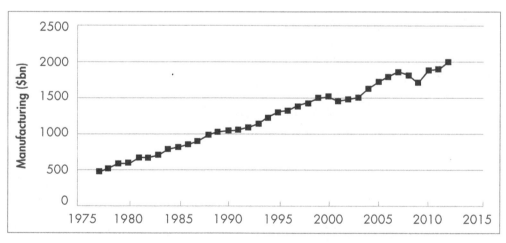

Figure 1.1. US manufacturing (in current US dollars): 1977 to 2012.

The idea of finding work for the millions of workers displaced by changes in technology has always seemed overwhelming to many. They believe that there is only a certain amount of work to go around—what is sometimes called the "lump of labor" fallacy by economists (Schloss, 1891). And while there is no doubt that the kinds of changes described previously are painful to those involved, at the broader level, it seems as if the number of new jobs being created is enough to replace the jobs that are lost (Autor, 2015).

A summary of some of the most significant positive changes in the US labor market is shown in Table 1.1 (Cox & Alm, 2008). More recently, Mandel (2013) estimates that around 750,000 full-time equivalent jobs were created in the "App Economy" in the United States alone in the six years after the appearance of Apple's first iPhone in 2007.

Table 1.1. Job Creation in the United States: 1900 to 2002

Job creation	1900	1970	2002
Airplane pilots and mechanics	0		255,000
Auto mechanics	0		867,000
Engineers	38,000		2,028,000
Medical technicians			1,879,000
Truck, bus, and taxi drivers	0		4,171,000
Electricians	*		882,000
Professional athletes			95,000
Computer programmers/operators/scientists		160,613	2,648,000
Actors and directors		34,643	155,000
Editors and reporters		150,715	280,000
Medical scientists		3,589	89,000
Dietitians		42,349	74,000
Special education teachers		1,563	374,000
Physicians		295,803	825,000
Pharmacists		114,590	231,000
Authors		26,677	139,000
TV, stereo, and appliance salespersons		111,842	309,000
Webmasters			500,000

*Fewer than 5,000 people

As Autor, Katz, and Krueger (1998) have shown, one of the key changes in the US labor market in recent years has been the increasing use of sophisticated technology and, in particular, computers. In 1984, only about 25 percent of workers used a computer during the course of a typical working day. Just seven years later, it was almost 50 percent. It is this, they argue, that has fueled the demand for more educated workers and, in particular, for college graduates: "Rapid skill upgrading . . . accounts for most of the growth in the relative demand for college workers, particularly since 1970" (p. 1169).

This observation partially explains the apparent paradox between the increasing capabilities of US school-leavers and the dissatisfaction of employers with the quality of applicants. There is no doubt that young Americans today are smarter than their parents and grandparents. No one is really sure why, but American IQs have been rising steadily, by around three points per decade, for the last eighty years (Flynn, 1984, 2012). In addition to higher IQs, the long-term trends in the National Assessment of Educational Progress show steady long-term improvements in math and reading (Loveless, 2010). So why are employers unhappy? Because the demands of the world of work are increasing faster than the improvements in education—what Jan Tinbergen described as "a race between education and technology" (Goldin & Katz, 2009, p. 30).

America became the world's leading manufacturer in the second half of the 20th century by massively expanding the proportion of students who enrolled in, and completed, high school in the period between 1910 and 1940. At the time, most countries in Europe provided education beyond the age of fourteen or fifteen only for the 5 to 10 percent of students who were likely to attend institutions of higher education. In contrast, most US states saw high school as being for everyone. Now some of the reasons behind this expansion of high schooling for all were not particularly noble (for example, some saw the expansion of high schools as a way of keeping young people out of a depressed labor market). But whatever the motivations, the change was dramatic. In 1910, only around 10 percent of American eighteen-year-olds completed high school. By 1940, it was over 50 percent (Goldin & Katz, 2009). The result was a highly educated general population that was able to adopt new technology as it became available and to use it effectively. However, since then, while educational achievement has continued to improve, the rate at which it has done so has slowed. The need for higher-level skills is increasing at what appears to be an accelerated rate as well.

As noted previously, the adoption of technology has been a major factor in changes to the US labor market in recent years. In some cases, the adoption of technology removes the need for humans completely. In many states, road tolls are now collected by electronically reading in-car transponders, with billing done automatically, so the number of toll-booth attendants has declined drastically. When credit cards were first used, physical copies of vouchers were sent to (human!) data-processing centers for keying, whereas now the information is captured at the point-of-sale.

In other cases, technology does not replace workers but allows individual workers to become more productive. Many restaurants now allow guests to select and order their food from electronic devices, thus reducing the number of servers that are needed. In many municipalities, homeowners are asked to place their recycling or garbage in dedicated bins and to orient them in a specific way when they put them out in the street, so that the work of an entire collection truck crew can now be done by the driver.

However, it is important to realize that the key factor in making jobs suitable for automating is not that they are manual or low skill. It is that they are *routine* (Autor, Levy, & Murnane, 2003). One of the starkest illustrations of this is a study that compared the performance of computers with board-certified urologists in the diagnosis of prostate cancer in men whose blood tests had revealed more than four nanograms of prostate-specific antigen (PSA) per milliliter of blood. An artificial neural net—a computer program that can learn from its experiences and refine its future performance—was first "trained" by feeding it with the outcome of biopsies together with the following data on a group of men: age, maximum PSA concentration over all visits, average PSA concentration over all visits, maximum digital rectal examination over all visits (0, 1, or 2), maximum transrectal ultrasonography results over all visits (0, 1, or 2), and change of PSA value between visits.

Once the neural net had been trained, it was then given the same data on a different set of 1,787 men, and the neural network then predicted whether the individual had prostate cancer or not. The positive predictive value (percentage of those predicted who had positive biopsies) for expert urologists had been established in an earlier study to be 34 percent (Catalona, Smith, Ratliff, & Basler, 1993). For the neural net, it was 77 percent (Snow, Smith, & Catalona, 1994). A task can require many years of training for humans to become good at it, but it can still be relatively routine, thus making it relatively straightforward to automate.

This is just one example of a much more general principle, which is that many of the things that we thought would be easy to automate turn out to be rather complex, while many of the things that we thought would be hard to automate turn out to be reasonably simple. We think playing chess is one of the high points of human intellect, and yet, for a few dollars, one can buy a chess-playing app for a smartphone that will beat just about every human being on the planet. On the other hand, recognizing objects is something that infants (and indeed almost all animals) find easy, but currently computers find difficult. Perhaps the most graphic illustration of this is the recent attempt by Google to produce the largest artificial neural net yet developed. In one study, a network of over 1,000 different computers was exposed, over a three-day period, to over 10,000,000 images drawn from the Internet. At the end of the exercise, the artificial neural net managed to correctly categorize around 16 percent of objects (Le et al., 2012).

This observation—that high-level reasoning seems to require very little in the way of machine power, while many low-level sensorimotor skills appear to require huge computational resources—is known as Moravec's paradox, named after Hans Moravec, who pointed out that "it is comparatively easy to make computers exhibit adult-level performance on intelligence tests or playing checkers, and difficult or impossible to give them the skills of a one-year-old when it comes to perception and mobility" (Moravec, 1988, p. 15).

Moravec's paradox explains why computer programs have replaced humans in assessing the suitability of applicants for mortgages (Levy & Murnane, 2004) but shelf stacking in the grocery store is still done by humans. However, as Brynjolfsson and McAfee (2014) point out, computing power is growing so rapidly that problems that were simply infeasible a few years ago can become straightforward very quickly.

Most people have heard of Moore's law. In an article in *Electronics* magazine, Gordon Moore (1965) proposed the idea that the number of components in an integrated circuit would double every year for at least the next ten years, and possibly longer, although he later revised this estimate to once every two years. When Moore wrote his article, the typical integrated circuit contained about 50 transistors. It is a testimony to Moore's genius (or luck!) that half a century later, the (modified) rule still seems to work reasonably well, even though today's most powerful central processing units contain around 2.5 billion transistors. While people understand the idea of Moore's law, they often fail to appreciate what the kind of exponential growth entailed in Moore's law means in practice.

Ray Kurzweil (1999) illustrates this by describing the invention of the game of chess. There are many different versions of the legend, with some having chess being invented in India and others placing it in Persia, but in all versions, a ruler of some region is so pleased with the game of chess that he asks the inventor to name a reward. The inventor says that he would like one grain of rice (or wheat) for the first square on the board, two for the second, four for the third, and so on, with the number of grains doubling each time. The ruler agrees, but quickly becomes angry when the consequences of the agreement are clear. After thirty-two squares, the running total is just over eight billion grains of rice, which is the yield of two large fields, and is perhaps reasonable. But each square requires adding more rice than has been added so far (this is the inevitable consequence of exponential growth), and the total amount of rice needed for the reward would be more than the total amount of rice ever produced in the world up until the present day (Brynjolfsson & McAfee, 2014).

Kurzweil uses this idea of "the second half of the chessboard" to illustrate how difficult we find it to understand the long-term consequences of exponential growth. Aspects of machine intelligence that are currently not well developed can improve rapidly if the processing power is doubled every two years.

As a concrete example, consider the issue of driverless cars. In 2004, Levy and Murnane wrote, "But executing a left turn against oncoming traffic involves so many factors that it is hard to imagine discovering the set of rules that can replicate a driver's behavior" (p. 20). Just six years later, in October 2010, Google announced that Toyota Prius cars modified to run Google's Chauffeur software were fully autonomous (Brynjolfsson and McAfee, 2014).

Now, it is important to realize that Google's self-driving cars are not really able to drive themselves very well because they require extremely detailed GPS mapping to operate. To stay inside lanes on highways, cars operating Google's Chauffeur program do not observe lane markings but rather rely on the fact that the parts of California where they operate have been mapped in great detail (i.e., to the nearest inch or so). In this sense, they are more like trains than cars. They also, currently at least, struggle with four-way streets, where driving includes an element of social negotiation— self-driving cars that prioritize avoiding risk give way to more impatient (human!) drivers. However, most researchers in the field believe that driverless taxis and delivery trucks will be commonplace, and perhaps even universal, within twenty or thirty years. The important lesson in all of this is that changes that seemed, even a few years ago, to be only remote possibilities may actually become reality in the near future, as we move into the second half of the chessboard.

To try to understand what proportion of current jobs might be automated in the future, Frey and Osborne (2013) undertook a sophisticated analysis of 702 occupations. They examined in particular three kinds of "bottlenecks" to automation: perception and manipulation (dexterity, awkward or inaccessible work positions); creative intelligence (generating unusual or ingenious solutions); and social intelligence (social perception, persuasiveness, negotiation, caring for others). Then, for each of the occupations, they estimated the likelihood the occupation could be automated over the next ten to twenty years (i.e., in the early stages of the working lives of students now in school). As might be expected, some jobs had a low probability of automation (e.g., choreographers, surgeons, athletic trainers, clergy), while others had a high probability of automation (e.g., telemarketers, watch repairers, legal secretaries, cooks). However, what was less obvious was their overall estimate that 47 percent of all current US jobs (i.e., around 70 million) might be automated within the next twenty years or earlier.

Now of course, as we saw previously, this is nothing new. Indeed, data from the US Bureau of Labor Statistics' *Job Openings and Labor Turnover Survey* suggest that there has always been a great deal of "churn" in the US labor market. For example, in October 2014, the US economy added around 300,000 jobs, but what this doesn't show is the fact that 4.8 million people left their jobs and 5.1 million people started new jobs. Of the 4.8 million people who left their jobs, 1.7 million were laid off or discharged (Bureau of Labor Statistics, 2014). In other words, each year, around 20 million jobs—or about 15 percent of the total—are lost in the US economy. What is new, however, is that the kinds of jobs that are being created are very different from the kinds of jobs that are being lost.

One clear trend is that many of the new jobs being created require relatively high levels of education. For example, according to Carnevale, Jayasundera, and Cheah (2012), those with just a high school diploma lost 5.6 million jobs in the recent recession (2008 to 2010) and lost another 230,000 jobs in the recovery (2010 to 2012). Those with an associate's degree lost 1.75 million jobs in the recession but gained 1.6 million jobs in the recovery. Those with at least a bachelor's degree actually gained 187,000 jobs in the recession and gained another 2 million jobs in the recovery.

However, it is also important to note that changes in the US workforce are not one-way traffic with higher and higher levels of skill being required for employment. Rather, what seems to be taking place is a process described by Goos and Manning (2003) as "job polarization." Because so many middle-skill jobs are routine, these are being automated rapidly, and because many of the people who were doing these jobs are not able to move up to the high-skill jobs, they compete with those doing low-skill jobs, thus depressing wages. The result is an expansion in employment in both low-education, low-wage occupations and in high-education, high-wage occupations—or "lousy and lovely jobs" (Goos & Manning, 2003, p. 1). Similar arguments are made by Tyler Cowen (2013) in his recent book, *Average Is Over*.

As well as losing jobs to technology, wealthier countries are also, of course, losing jobs to countries with lower labor costs. At first, they were low-skill jobs, such as data processing, food packaging, and call-center jobs that were offshored. Then, the adoption of technology allowed jobs requiring much higher levels of skills, such as radiology, to be offshored. However, in recent years, US companies have become far more adept at separating the various components of jobs into those that can be offshored and those that cannot. So for lawyers, for example, much of the review of legal documents can be outsourced to lower-cost workers in India, but court appearances, depositions, and meetings with clients are conducted face to face. The result is that offshoring changes, rather than completely destroys, jobs.

The result is that it is far from straightforward to estimate the extent to which offshoring is destroying jobs in the United States. However, despite much of the hype, compared to technology, offshoring appears to have been a much less significant source of job loss in the United States than automation.

Public perception has been shaped by books like *The World Is Flat*, by Thomas Friedman (2005), which have argued that the world is becoming increasingly interconnected and have talked about "the death of distance." However, as Pankaj Ghemawat (2011) has shown, location matters far more than we generally realize. Only around 1 percent of physical mail and 2 percent of telephone minutes cross a national boundary. Only 10 percent of people will ever cross a national boundary in their lives, and between 2006 and 2008, only around 17 percent of Internet traffic was routed across a national border (Ghemawat, 2011).

It turns out that there are many subtle and complex barriers to trade. For example, Ganong Brothers is Canada's oldest candy maker and is based in Saint Stephen, New Brunswick. Because of the North American Free Trade Agreement, there are no tariffs on Canadian goods imported into the United States, but in order to sell its jelly beans on Main Street in Calais, Maine, just a mile and a half from Ganong Brothers' factory, they have to label their products differently. In Canada, nutritional information has to include a space between the quantity and the unit (e.g., "5 mg"), but in the United States, no space is permitted (so the label has to read "5mg"). Additionally, the two countries specify different methods for calculating the percentage of daily nutritional requirements, so that "a serving from a box of assorted chocolates meets 4 per cent of the daily requirement for iron for a Canadian but only 2 per cent for an American" (Thompson, 2007). The result is that Ganong Brothers actually manufactures jelly beans for the US and Canadian markets in different production runs, with different packaging, thus reducing economies of scale.

As Joseph Stiglitz (2007) said, "Not only is the world not flat: in many ways it has been getting less flat" (p. 57). Perhaps the best description of the world is "still mostly round, with some flat bits."

As a result, despite what many people have believed, offshoring has been almost irrelevant to US employment (Mankiw & Swagel, 2006). It may be, of course, that in the future, offshoring is a greater factor in job destruction, but in this context, as far as we can tell, only around 25 percent of current US jobs are at risk of being offshored (Blinder & Krueger, 2011).

The important conclusion from the preceding analysis is that we should not worry very much about our perceived industrial competitors. The major threat to jobs in the United States in the future will be the same as what it has always been—what Joseph Schumpeter (1942) called the "creative destruction" that is an inevitable part of economic development. However, what is different about recent changes is the impact on different sectors of the economy. Previous "skill-biased technology change," as it is called by economists, tended to have a similar effect on all workers. Whether this was because US workers were already educated well enough to use the emerging technology or for some other reason, the fact is that for the second half of the 20th century, wages increased steadily across the board. This is no longer happening. Because of the hollowing out of the job market, the rewards for those at the top are increasing far faster than for those at the bottom. For example, in the United States, the median weekly wage for thirty-five- to forty-four-year-old male high school graduates has been flat, in real terms, since 1990, while for those with a bachelor's degree, it has risen by around 12 percent. For female high school graduates, median weekly wages have improved a little—around 6 percent—but for those with a bachelor's degree, the real-terms increase since 1990 is almost 30 percent (Levy & Murnane, 2013).

Given these extraordinary changes in the world of work, it is not surprising that many have argued that we need higher levels of educational achievement, particularly in so-called "STEM" subjects (science, technology, engineering, and mathematics). However, it is far from clear that we know what kinds of skills will be needed in the future. The earliest computers were humans who performed arithmetic calculations. One of the earliest uses of the term in print comes from an advertisement in the *New York Times* on May 2, 1892:

> Washington, May 1st.—A civil service examination will be held May 18 in Washington, and, if necessary, in other cities to secure eligibles for the post of computer in the Nautical Almanac Office, where two vacancies exist—one at $1,000 and one at $1,400. . . .
>
> The examination will include the subjects of algebra, geometry, trigonometry, and astronomy. Application blanks may be received from the United States Civil Service Commission. (New York Times, 1892)

Such individuals were in great demand during the Second World War, especially in the Manhattan Project, to help scientists by performing calculations necessary to the solution of equations related to nuclear fission, as part of the development of the first atomic bombs. A shortage of "computers" at that time would have led to calls for more training of students in mathematics and, especially, computation. However, within a few years, the demand for human computers was eliminated by the development of the first electronic computers, programmed largely by those who had been employed as human computers.

A sobering fact is that children in kindergarten this year will still be working in the final quarter of the 21st century, and we simply have no idea what kinds of jobs will be available or what skills will be needed. What this means is that any attempt to predict in any kind of detail what we should be teaching in schools is likely to be disastrous for our young people. I believe there are really only two things that are clear. The first is that higher levels of achievement will be needed in the future than in the past, and the second is that the curriculum that young people experience in school needs to be balanced and broadly based.

The reason we need higher levels of academic achievement has already been discussed at length previously. There will be a large number of service jobs in the future, but the associated wages are likely to be low. Of course, it could be that in the future, we decide to share more equally the extraordinary profits that are being made from the spread of information technology, but in the United States at least, hoping that this happens does not seem to be a particularly sensible strategy. Higher levels of achievement are also likely to be necessary for effective participation in a democratic society. In addition to higher levels of achievement, the achievement itself needs to be broadly based, for at least three reasons.

First, and to me, most important, the reason that we need education to be broadly based is that a broadly based curriculum can provide young people with sources of fulfillment into adulthood. I am constantly amazed, and more than a little saddened, by the number of adults who tell me that they wished that they had learned to play a musical instrument when they were younger. Art, music, dance, and drama are things that adults choose to do when they have the time, but, as Ken Robinson (2009) points out, these aspects are being marginalized in many, and perhaps most, of our schools. It seems to me that a good guiding principle for the design of elementary schooling is that it should help children find their passion—the thing they love to do. For me, the whole idea of school is that it exposes children to things that they would not otherwise come across. Schooling should, literally, broaden the mind.

Second, as is now becoming clear, education that is narrowly focused is less effective even in terms of what is being focused on. Engagement in the arts improves learning in mathematics and reading (President's Committee on the Arts and the Humanities, 2011) and, for example, makes individuals more successful as innovators even in STEM subjects (LaMore et al., 2013).

Third, increasingly, the arts are becoming sources of new jobs. In the United States, the traditional circus had been in steady decline for years, but then in 1984, a group of stilt walkers from Baie-Saint-Paul, Quebec, formed Cirque du Soleil, which now employs 5,000 people at eight permanent shows in Las Vegas, Nevada, and has twelve other shows touring the world (Economist, 2014). Less than one-third of these are performers. Others are lighting engineers, sound engineers, musicians, construction specialists, and so on—jobs requiring specialist knowledge well beyond what could be learned in school but not requiring degrees.

Indeed, new digital tools mean that there has never been a better time for young people to make their living by pursuing their passion. Amazon's Kindle Direct Publishing allows budding authors to create original works in Microsoft Word and upload them to Kindle Direct. The author decides in which countries the book is to be published and how much to charge. Amazon keeps track of the number of copies that have been downloaded and, each month, deposits the proceeds into the author's bank account.

Valve—a computer games maker—allows users to design "mods" (i.e., modifications) to their games, and if Valve decides to make the mods an official part of the game, the designer of the mod gets paid. In January 2015, Valve announced that 1,500 individuals shared a payout from Valve of $57 million (i.e., an average of around $38,000 each) for the mods they had designed (BBC News, 2015).

Three-dimensional printers can now be bought for less than $500. Free software allows people to design whatever they like and to print it in plastic at home. Of course, there is a limit to what usefully can be produced in plastic, but what is fascinating is the infrastructure that has grown up around three-dimensional printers. Those interested in restoring vintage motorcycles can design replacement gearbox parts online, print them in plastic at home, try them out in the gearbox, and then, when they are happy with the design, send the design to a company called Shapeways, in New York, which will print the part in titanium steel and send it back within a week or two. Others design jewelry, prototype them in plastic on their home three-dimensional printers, and then send the finished design to Shapeways to be printed in silver.

All this creates a real problem for our current models of schooling. Over the last twenty years or so, there has been increasing pressure on teachers, schools, and districts to get higher scores in reading and mathematics. The result has been that other school subjects have been squeezed out in the quest for higher math and reading scores. Now of course, math and reading are important, but they are not more important than science and social studies, and they are not more important than art, music, dance, and drama. In the mid-1980s, when my colleagues and I asked a group of business people to identify the skills they really wanted from school-leavers, after a significant amount of debate, they came up with a list. We then looked at the school curriculum and found that only one school subject encompassed it all—drama. The business people had identified communication skills, confidence, collaboration, creativity, self-control, discipline, problem-solving, tolerance, and empathy—all capabilities that were developed in good drama teaching.

This means that, in education, we are faced with a double whammy. We need higher student achievement in math and reading, but we have to achieve this in less time so that balance can be restored to our curricula, particularly in elementary and middle schools.

What's Been Tried

Over the years, a number of methods have been proposed for increasing student achievement. Some have argued that technology is the answer. There have been some notable successes, such as Carnegie Learning's Cognitive Tutor for Algebra (Ritter, Anderson, Koedinger, & Corbett, 2007), but overall, the huge investments in information technology in schools have had little payoff in terms of student achievement (Wenglinsky, 2005/2006), although this appears to be in large part due to weak implementation (Penuel, 2006; Tamim, Bernard, Borokhovski, Abrami, & Schmid, 2011). Others have proposed changes in the nature of the teacher workforce, such as increasing the use of teachers' aides, although such studies show that the effects of these policies are small and may even be negative (Blatchford et al., 2009).

Particularly in the United States, structural reforms such as vouchers and charter schools have been the subject of much experimentation. The idea of using funds that would otherwise go to public schools to allow parents to reduce, or offset entirely, the cost of private schools is attractive, especially to those who believe that publicly provided services are unlikely to be as effective as those provided by the private sector. They point to the fact that on the triennial tests administered by the Organisation for Economic Co-operation and Development's (OECD's) Programme for International Student Assessment (PISA), students attending private schools in the United States outscore those attending public schools by around twenty-five points. However, interpreting this result is rather difficult because the students who attend private schools in the United States are not representative of those who attend public schools. What is interesting about the PISA data set is that it contains a number of indices of socioeconomic status, such as the number of books in the family home. Once the effects of social class are taken into account, it turns out that students attending public schools in the United States actually outperform those attending private schools by around ten points (Schleicher, 2008).

The number of charter schools in the United States has risen steadily from fewer than 2,000 in 1999 to over 6,000 in 2014. Over the same period of time, the number of students served by charter schools has risen from around 350,000 to over 2.5 million (National Alliance for Public Charter Schools, 2015). However, it is important to note that the impact of charter schools on student achievement, both now and in the future, is likely to be small. First, charter schools currently serve fewer than 5 percent of US school-age children, and even if they expand at the current rate, it would take about a hundred years for charter schools to serve even half the school population. Second, while the quality of charter schools has been improving slowly, the average quality of charter schools is similar to comparable public schools (Center for Research on Education Outcomes, 2013). In some respects, this is a significant achievement, because just four years earlier, the average charter school was significantly less effective than comparable schools in the area (Davis & Raymond, 2009). In broad terms, approximately one-half of charter schools currently are not significantly different from comparable public schools, about one-fourth are better, and about one-fourth are less effective, in terms of student progress in math and reading (Center for Research on Education Outcomes, 2013). It is not an overstatement to say that vouchers and charter schools are completely irrelevant to the scale of the challenge that education in the United States is facing—the equivalent of rearranging the deck chairs on the *Titanic*.

Most recently, there has been an enormous amount of interest in the idea of benchmarking the performance of students in the United States with those in other countries, and particularly those of our industrial competitors. I conclude this chapter with a discussion of why this kind of "policy tourism" is unlikely to be helpful in improving the US education system.

The Danger of Trying to Copy Others

Hardly a day goes by without some comparison being made between the performance of students in the United States and that of our industrial competitors. It is true that the scores gained by US fifteen-year-olds are lower than those in many, perhaps most, of the world's leading industrial nations. As a result, many writers have claimed that we ought to be learning about how to improve education in the United States by looking at what other, more successful countries are doing. This is a really bad idea.

It's a really bad idea because the assumption that we should base our education system on particular features of what more successful systems are doing is based on two fundamental flaws. The first flaw is that the features we select as being responsible for the success of other countries may not be the right ones. The second is that even if we are right about the causes of success in other countries, we are assuming that the same thing would work in the same way in the United States.

The first error is so common that it has its own Latin tag—*post hoc ergo propter hoc* (after the event therefore because of the event)—and yet it remains a staple of much policy making in education and indeed elsewhere. We start by identifying people, organizations, or institutions that are successful and then try to discover the secrets of their success. A classic example in the business world is *Good to Great: Why Some Companies Make the Leap . . . and Others Don't* in which Jim Collins (2001) sought to identify what allowed some companies to go from being average performers to being great performers (defined as financial performance several times better than the market average over a sustained period of time). However, as Michael Mauboussin (2012) points out, by focusing only on those companies that are still around, we create an element of what economists call "survivorship bias." The classic example of this bias is the attempt by researchers working at Columbia University's Statistics Research Group during the Second World War to identify how to improve the effectiveness of the armor on US aircraft using the patterns of bullet damage found on returning aircraft. Some researchers had suggested armoring the most damaged areas because that was where planes seemed to get hit, but Abraham Wald pointed out that the parts of the aircraft that needed more armor were those that were *not* damaged on the returning aircraft, because damage in those areas had presumably resulted in those aircraft not returning (Wald, 1943).

Mauboussin (2012) points out that if companies pursue high-risk strategies, then some will fail and others will do well. If we only look at the survivors, we think the strategy is a good one because we do not take into account those companies that are no longer around. It is also worth noting that investments in the companies identified by Jim Collins as "great" in 2001 would actually have performed worse over the subsequent seven years than investments that simply tracked the S&P 500 index (Levitt, 2008).

In education, when the first international comparisons came out, Germany was held up as an example to emulate. Unfortunately, the reason for Germany's apparent success was the practice of grade retention. The early international comparisons selected a certain age group to study (e.g., fourteen-year-olds) and then sampled students from classes where most fourteen-year-olds were being taught. In the United States, this resulted in a reasonably random sample of fourteen-year-olds because although the United States has a grade-based system, most districts tend to promote students to the next grade on the basis of age, not achievement. In Germany, however, by the time they are fourteen, about 25 percent of all students have repeated a grade. The low-achieving students are no longer with their peers but are, instead, with students a year or even two years younger. The first administration of the PISA, carried out by the OECD in 2000, corrected this deficiency in the sampling method, and the performance of German students was found to be below the international average (Programme for International Student Assessment, 2001).

Perhaps predictably, attention then switched to Finland, whose students placed first in reading, third in science, and fourth in mathematics in the first round of PISA in 2000 and topped all other OECD countries in all three subjects in 2003 (Programme for International Student Assessment, 2004). Over the next few years, politicians and their advisers visited Finland to find out the magic ingredient. A delegation of politicians from England concluded that the cause of Finland's success must be the fact that most Finnish teachers had master's degrees and so decided that all teachers in England should have master's degrees too. The resulting program was called the Master of Teaching and Learning, rather than the more obvious Master of Learning and Teaching, because politicians were worried that someone who failed to achieve a pass at master's level would be awarded a "BLT" (really!).

Others saw Finland's highly selective entry into teacher education programs as the solution. There are ten applicants for every place on a course to be a school teacher (Organisation for Economic Co-operation and Development, 2014), and at the more prestigious institutions, it's twenty. The reasons for this are complex, but despite the fact that teacher salaries are not particularly high in Finland (Dolton & Marcenaro-Gutierrez, 2011), teaching has high social status, at least on some measures (Organisation for Economic Co-operation and Development, 2014).

Still others have highlighted trust in teachers (Richardson, 2013), the lack of pressure on students (Levine, 2011), the lack of standardized testing, except at the end of high school (Sahlberg, 2014), the Finnish commitment to equity (Partanen, 2011), or political stability, at least as far as education policy is concerned (Sahlberg, 2011). None of these seem implausible, but the arguments in favor of each are not strong.

In some cases, it is the characterization of the system that is in question. While many anecdotal reports mention the high status of teachers in Finland, one well-designed and systematic survey found that the social status of teachers was in fact below average in Finland, and much lower than in Greece (Dolton & Marcenaro-Gutierrez, 2013).

In other cases, it is the presence of counterexamples that weakens the argument. In the Republic of Ireland, for example, entry into teacher preparation programs is even more competitive than in Finland (International Review Panel on the Structure of Initial Teacher Education Provision in Ireland, 2012), but Ireland's scores on PISA are indistinguishable from the international average. Finland does have a very inclusive system, with little grouping of student by ability, but Japan and Singapore do even better than Finland and have highly selective school systems.

However, the danger of this kind of policy tourism is perhaps most clearly demonstrated by what has happened to Finland in recent years. Finland again topped the

OECD countries in science and math in 2006, coming second in reading, but since then, results have declined steadily, as Figure 1.2 shows clearly.

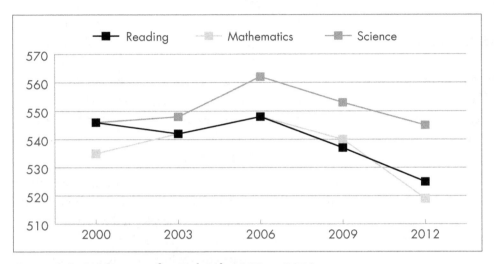

Figure 1.2. PISA scores for Finland: 2000 to 2012.

Now, as might be expected, the explanations for Finland's rapid fall from grace are as numerous as were the explanations for the original growth. All are likely to have some grain of truth, but the fact is that we simply do not know the reasons for Finland's extraordinary success in 2006, nor do we know what caused the decline in the two administrations of PISA since then. Guesses about what Finland did right up to 2006, or did wrong after that, are unlikely to be helpful guides for educational improvement. It is also worth remembering that Finland's results in 2006 were the accumulation of ten years of education for students who started their compulsory schooling in 1998, and were therefore the results of policy decisions made in the early 1990s.

After the publication of results of the PISA surveys conducted in 2009 and 2012, many writers switched attention to the systems in the western Pacific Rim—Japan, Taiwan, Hong Kong, Singapore, and Shanghai. While the first four of these had done well in previous international comparisons, the high performance of Shanghai came as a surprise to many. While US fifteen-year-olds averaged a score of 492, which was not significantly different from the international average of 500, students in Shanghai averaged 587.

Again, predictably, attention then shifted from Finland to Shanghai, even though comparing a single, admittedly large, metropolitan area with a whole country is not particularly informative. This was partly, no doubt, because China had overtaken the United States to become the world's leading manufacturer (in terms of value) in 2010.

Now, it is important to be clear that in many ways, Shanghai's education system is doing a lot of things right. Although teachers are not, in general, drawn from the highest achievers, as is the case in Finland or Singapore, esteem for teachers in China is very high—in a study of twenty-one education systems around the world, esteem for teachers was higher in China than in any of the other countries studied (Dolton & Marcenaro-Gutierrez, 2013). And, compared to others, teachers in China are well paid. Typically teachers in China earn a salary well over double per-capita gross domestic product (GDP), while in the United States, teacher salaries are on average well below per-capita GDP (Dolton & Marcenaro-Gutierrez, 2013). In Shanghai, teachers typically spend only about three hours a day teaching, and the rest of the time, they meet with subject peers to plan high-quality lessons. They also meet with colleagues teaching students in the same grade, and it is common for teachers to meet on a daily basis with a mentor who has observed a lesson the teacher has taught so they can discuss potential improvements. The Shanghai system is also well aligned, in that incentives for teachers are tightly tied to what the system needs (Kaplan & Norton, 2006). For example, there are thirteen salary points on the scale for regular teachers. To get to the higher points on the scale, teachers have to spend a certain amount of time working in hard-to-staff schools, and they also have to mentor other teachers, with the reports from those they mentor about the quality of support received counting toward decisions on salary advancement.

The measures being taken to improve Shanghai's schools seem to be eminently sensible, but before we look at what Shanghai is doing right, we should first check that the performance of fifteen-year-olds in Shanghai really is as high as their PISA scores indicate. When we look carefully at Shanghai's performance on PISA, there are considerable grounds for skepticism. Two factors appear to be especially significant—inadequate sampling and student motivation—discussed in turn as follows.

Inadequate Sampling

Over the years, PISA has sought to ensure that the students who actually take PISA tests are—as far as can reasonably be achieved—a random sample of the fifteen-year-olds in the country. In many countries, schools that have been selected to participate are able to choose whether to do so. The important point is that if a large number of schools decline to participate, one cannot assume that those who do participate are representative of those who do not. For example, in 2003 in England, only 64 percent of schools and 77 percent of students selected to participate in PISA did so, compared to an OECD average of around 90 percent (Micklewright & Schnepf, 2006). As a result, England's results were excluded from the international report. However, it does not appear as if such strict criteria have been applied to Shanghai.

In their submission to the PISA organizers, the Shanghai authorities indicated that in 2012, there were 108,056 fifteen-year-olds residing in Shanghai, with 90,786 attending schools at grade 7 or above (Programme for International Student Assessment, 2013). However, these numbers are grossly misleading because of the Chinese *hukou* system of household registration that determines where individuals can receive government services. *Hukou* is hereditary, and so children born in Shanghai to parents who have moved from another province can only attend high school and take the national university entrance examination (the *gaokao*) in the province in which they are registered. The result is that no one really knows how many fifteen-year-olds live in Shanghai, but the number is almost certainly greater than 200,000 (Economist, 2013) and is probably more like 300,000 (Loveless, 2014). Because we cannot assume that the achievement of those not sampled is similar to that of those who were sampled, the average score achieved by those who did participate in PISA is difficult to interpret.

Student Motivation

Although PISA goes to great lengths to ensure that its tests are administered under the same conditions in all participating countries, it is difficult to establish the extent to which this is achieved. It is well established that students do better on tests when they care about the result (Duckworth, Quinn, Lynam, Loeber, & Stouthamer-Loeber, 2011), and many rumors have circulated about different ways that countries participating in PISA have sought to make the students take the test seriously. In an interesting attempt to get its young people to take the PISA tests more seriously, Scotland produced a motivational video, shown to all the students selected to take part in PISA, in which athletes who had been selected to represent Scotland at the forthcoming Olympic Games in London talked about what an honor it was to represent one's country (Smarter Scotland, 2012). The important point here is that students in most countries in the world take tests that are highly consequential for them, but not for their teachers and schools, while in the United States, the reverse is the case. Students in grades 3 through 8 take tests that are consequential for their teachers and schools, but not for them. This presents at least a prima facie case that differences in PISA scores between countries are influenced by factors not relevant to the quality of the education students have received.

Even if the impact of these two factors were not substantial, and the performance of students in Shanghai really was as high as indicated by their PISA scores, this does not mean that we can conclude that it is the difference in the quality of the education system that is the cause of these differences. Again, this is for two reasons—the effects of private tuition and culture.

The Effects of Private Tuition

China's one-child policy was introduced in 1979 to address problems of overpopulation. The name of the policy has always been misleading because from the outset, there were many exceptions to the policy. It was never intended to apply to minority ethnic communities in China, and in the last decade, the policy has been relaxed considerably. Nevertheless, most families in urban China have a single child, and the result is that parents allocate a greater share of the family's resources to ensure that their one child does well in school, through the provision of private tuition. Statistics on the extent of private tuition in China in general, and in Shanghai in particular, are hard to come by, but one study in the urban parts of Chongqing found that around three-quarters of ninth-grade students received private tuition (W. Zhang, 2014). Given that Shanghai is much more affluent than Chongqing, it seems safe to assume that the rate of private tuition in Shanghai would be at least this high, and perhaps substantially higher.

Of course, the prevalence of private tuition is irrelevant if it does no good. So, does private tuition increase student achievement? Some studies (Y. Zhang, 2011) have found that students receiving more private tuition do worse on examinations, but of course, parents may be willing to spend more to support children who are struggling academically. Because of this, these kinds of snapshot studies are not helpful. It is also important to look at what, exactly, "private tuition" means, because in some contexts, it may mean having an individual tutor, while in others, it may mean attending an after-school class along with around forty other students. In Korea, where the government has for some time tried to reduce the prevalence of private tutoring, one study showed that removing private tuition reduced the scores of students on PISA by around fifty points (Choi, 2012). Put another way, without the effects of private tutoring, Korea could be performing below the United States in PISA scores.

Culture

Perhaps the most important finding to emerge from secondary analysis of PISA data comes from John Jerrim, who found that the performance of students of Chinese heritage born and educated in Australia was actually higher than the performance of students in Shanghai, even though the average performance of Australian fifteen-year-olds is only about twenty points higher than those in the United States (Jerrim, 2014). Therefore, it is at least plausible that none of the features of the Shanghai education that have been extensively discussed in recent years has very much to do with the success of Shanghai's students. It could be entirely attributable to the culture of Chinese families. In particular, it could be the importance attached to and the support for education in families of Chinese heritage, wherever they happen to be, that makes the difference. This means that even if we could identify, with reasonable certainty, features of the education systems of other countries that were causing them to be successful, it is far from clear that the same features would be effective in another country.

To sum up, it seems likely that if the PISA sample for Shanghai had been drawn from all fifteen-year-olds living in Shanghai, rather than just those with Shanghai household registration, then Shanghai's performance would be much lower, and possibly below the international mean. It seems plausible that the motivation of students in Shanghai (and indeed in other countries in the Far East) was higher than for those in the United States, and this also may have increased their scores. We cannot, therefore, even be sure that Shanghai's fifteen-year-olds are doing that well. And even if they are, it seems that the amount of private tuition and the effects of culture have a far greater impact than most people realize.

Now this is not intended to disparage the performance of students from Shanghai in recent rounds of PISA—it could be that they are doing very well indeed—nor is it intended to suggest that such kinds of international comparisons are not useful. What the foregoing arguments do show is that it is highly unwise to cherry-pick particular features of the Shanghai education system (or indeed those of other successful systems) and use those as levers for reform. The success of competitors may not be real, may be unrelated to factors of the education system that appear to be distinctive, or may not be reproducible elsewhere.

To understand how we can improve the educational outcomes of young people in the United States, we need to understand the role of teacher quality in education, and specifically, what it is, why it matters, and how to increase it.

[*Chapter 2*]

Teacher Quality: Why It Matters, What It Is, and How to Get More of It

For many years, policies in education tended to treat teachers as commodities. By this I don't mean that policies treated teachers as machines. Rather, I am using the term in its economic sense. To an economist, a commodity is a special kind of good whose quality does not vary from supplier to supplier. In the economics jargon, it "is supplied without qualitative differentiation across a market" (O'Sullivan & Sheffrin, 2003, p. 152). In the same way that 24-carat gold is assumed to be the same no matter where you buy it, it was often assumed that as long as teachers had reached some standard (usually by completing a required program of training), they were all equally good.

Understandably, such a view was popular with teacher unions because it helped to create a sense of solidarity among members. It also was popular with parents. In a nationwide poll conducted in 2000, Americans ranked "ensuring a well-qualified teacher in every classroom" second only to ensuring schools were safe from violence in importance for improving schools (89 percent and 90 percent agreeing, respectively; Haselkorn & Harris, 2001). It was also popular with politicians because it allowed them to avoid issues of quality. As Senator Edward Kennedy said, "We want a well-qualified teacher in every classroom" (Kennedy, 2002, p. 9357).

In recent years, however, it has become clear that teachers are not really interchangeable. Some teachers are better than others, and the difference is significant. In this chapter, I show that teacher quality is variable, that it matters for students, and that most of the measures being proposed in the United States to increase teacher quality will have little, if any, impact on student achievement. Perhaps most important, however, I show that while it is possible to demonstrate that teachers in general differ greatly in their effectiveness, we cannot currently identify individual good teachers with any precision.

Teacher Quality Versus Teaching Quality

The quality of instruction that students receive obviously depends on a number of variables, such as the quality of the curriculum, the amount of time teachers have to prepare instruction, the kinds of resources available, the number of students in a class, the skill of the teacher, and so on. In some systems (e.g., Japan, Finland), the number of hours that teachers will spend actually teaching students is below 700 hours per year, while in others (e.g., United States, Chile), it is well over 1,000 (Organisation for Economic Co-operation and Development, 2013). Moreover, as Darling-Hammond (2014) points out, these issues interact in complex ways. There is really no point in developing highly skilled practitioners if we then deploy them to work in conditions that do not allow them to use the skills they have. In this context, it is worth noting that Pasi Sahlberg, former deputy director of education for Finland, has suggested that Finnish teachers would not be particularly effective if they taught in, say, Indiana, because education policies in the United States would limit the ability to use their skills effectively (Sahlberg, 2013).

For these reasons, it is difficult, and perhaps impossible, to entirely disentangle *teacher* quality from *teaching* quality. However, a number of studies have attempted to understand the impact of teachers and teaching by examining to what extent the amount that students learn depends on which teacher is teaching them. The approach taken in most such studies is broadly similar. Some baseline measurement of student achievement is taken at the beginning of the school year (or at the end of the previous year) and compared with another measure of achievement at the end of the year. The difference between these scores is taken as a measure of the progress made by students.

Now of course, such a measure of progress is far from perfect. The second measurement may not accurately encompass all the things that are important in student achievement, nor even in what they have been learning, and the first baseline assessment may not capture all the things that are important in determining progress. Moreover, both assessments will be affected by what is called *measurement error*. No measurement is perfectly accurate, so there is always some degree of variability in a student's result on a test. Students have good and bad days. Even with multiple-choice tests, there are differences in how accurately scanners of the bubble sheets record erasures and ambiguous responses, and when humans assess students' responses, there are often large differences in the scores awarded to the same piece of work by different raters. More surprisingly, the same rater can give the same piece of work a different score at different times of the day.

This becomes particularly important when we use before and after measurements to determine the progress made by a student, because both the before and the after measurements have a certain amount of inaccuracy. For some students, their before assessments will be lower than they would get on average, and their after assessments will be higher than they would get on average. These students will appear to make substantial progress. For other students, their before assessments will be higher than they would get on average, and their after assessments will be lower than they would get on average. These students will appear to have made relatively little progress. For individual students, therefore, the change in scores is not a particularly reliable guide to their progress. Over twenty to thirty students, however, these variations will tend to average out (i.e., for every student who is reported as making more progress than he or she has actually made, there is likely to be another who is reported as making less progress than he or she has actually made). The average of the progress measures of all the students in a class, therefore, is likely to be a reasonably reliable estimate of the actual progress made by the students in the class, within the limitations of the tests being used.

If the quality of teachers and teaching were approximately similar in different classes, then we would find that the amount of progress varied little from class to class. This is not what we find in practice. In fact, we find that students in some classes make much more progress than others—a phenomenon first demonstrated in a school district in California over forty years ago by Eric Hanushek (1971).

For example, Aaronson, Barrow, and Sander (2007) looked at the progress made by ninth-graders in math in Chicago Public Schools (CPS). For the before measurement, they used the Iowa Test of Basic Skills taken by all CPS eighth-grade students, and for the after measurement, they used the Test of Achievement and Proficiency taken by CPS students in ninth grade. Taking into account a range of demographic variables, they found that students taught by an effective teacher (i.e., one in the top one-third of effectiveness) would, on average, make 40 percent more progress per year than those taught by an average teacher. Those taught by a less effective teacher would make 30 percent less progress. In other words, students taught by a more effective teacher make twice as much progress as those taught by a less effective teacher (140 percent of average progress versus 70 percent).

To check that these differences were not just the result of random year-to-year variation, Aaronson, Barrow, and Sander then looked at whether teachers who were rated as being more effective were also more effective the next year. They divided the teachers into four equal-sized groups: most effective, above average, below average, and least effective. They then looked at whether teachers placed in a particular category in a particular year would be placed in the same category the following year, teaching different students. What they found is shown in Table 2.1 (Aaronson et al., 2007).

Table 2.1. Stability of Teacher Effectiveness Estimates

		Rating in the following year			
		Most effective	Above average	Below average	Least effective
Rating in a given year	Most effective	36	29	26	10
	Above average	24	31	32	12
	Below average	20	32	23	24
	Least effective	8	12	23	57

There is no simple interpretation of the data in Table 2.1. One way to explore the evidence in the table is to note that if the results were truly random, then all the numbers in the table would be approximately 25. If how good a teacher was this year told you nothing about how good he or she was likely to be next year, then the teacher would be equally likely to end up in each of the four categories. This is clearly not what we observe.

For example, the least effective teachers in any given year tend to be least effective in the following year: 57 percent of those who were least effective in a given year were placed in the same category the following year. At the other extreme, while the most effective teachers in a given year are more likely to be rated in the same category than would be expected by chance, the effect is not strong. Across the whole table, only around 16 percent more of the teachers were placed in the same category than would be expected by chance alone. Similar findings were noted by Ballou (2005) in Tennessee and by McCaffrey, Sass, Lockwood, and Mihalyi (2009) in Florida.

However, as McCaffrey et al. (2009) pointed out, one of the reasons that teachers who are regarded as effective in one year may not appear so effective the next year is related to the preceding point about the consequences of measuring student achievement with reliability that is less than perfect. Some students appear to have made more progress than they really have, and some appear to have made less progress than they really have. Although these effects tend to average out over a large number of students, the estimate of how much progress the students have made (what is sometimes called *value added* by the particular teacher) in a given year is still not that reliable. However, when the estimate of a teacher's quality is based on data over several years, the estimate is much more reliable.

For example, using the data reported by McCaffrey et al. (2009) and again dividing teachers into four groups, as was done by Aaronson et al. (2007) previously, we would find that based on just one year's data, only around 10 percent more teachers would be classified in the same way next year than we would expect by chance. But when the classification is based on multiple years of data, this figure rises to 40 percent, indicating that there is something about some teachers that persists over time and that these differences are substantial.

In another study, Rockoff (2004) looked at the results from two school districts over a twelve-year period and found that, compared to those taught by an average teacher, elementary school students taught by an effective teacher would make 50 percent more progress in math and around 40 percent more progress in reading each year. One important point about Rockoff's analysis is that because the same teachers were observed on multiple occasions, it is more likely that the observed variation in performance was attributable to the individual teachers, rather than just chance variation.

Of course, because the preceding analyses tend to look over time at the same teachers in the same schools, they shed little light on the debate about teaching quality versus teacher quality. It could be that teachers are effective because of the particular contexts in which they work and the particular students they teach.

To address this, a number of studies have looked at the effectiveness of the same teachers as they move to other schools. Chetty, Friedman, and Rockoff (2014) examined changes in teacher effectiveness as teachers moved from school to school and also in terms of changes of grade assignment (e.g., what happens when a teacher moves from teaching fifth grade in one school to teaching fourth grade in another). They found that when an effective teacher moved from one school to another, the achievement in the school the teacher left went down, and the achievement in the school he or she moved to went up. Even when teachers moved to schools with a different proportion of socioeconomically disadvantaged students (i.e., when teachers moved from rich to poor schools or vice versa), effective teachers tended to stay effective, and less effective teachers tended to stay less effective (e.g., Sanders, Wright, & Langevin, 2008; Xu, Özek, & Corritore, 2012).

One problem with all such analyses is that it could be that different teachers are assigned to teach different kinds of classes. Some teachers may just happen to be assigned to teach students who will make a lot of progress, while others are assigned to teach students for whom progress will be more difficult. This is a significant issue in the United States because there is certainly evidence that less experienced teachers are more likely to be assigned to teach in schools with more socioeconomically disadvantaged students (Sanders et al., 2008). But even when teachers are randomly assigned to groups of students, we still find that some teachers are consistently more effective than others.

A particularly important study of this kind was carried out by Thomas Kane and his colleagues (2013) as part of the Bill and Melinda Gates Foundation's Measures of Effective Teaching (MET) project involving teachers from New York City (NY), Charlotte-Mecklenburg (NC), Hillsborough County (FL), Memphis (TN), Dallas (TX), and Denver (CO). In the study, they measured how effective a group of 1,591 teachers were during the 2009–2010 school year and then randomly assigned these teachers to groups of students in the 2010–2011 school year. The study found that the teachers who were more effective than average in 2009–2010 were more effective than average when assigned to a different school the following year (Kane, McCaffrey, Miller, & Staiger, 2013).

To summarize the argument so far, there is now considerable evidence that there are substantial differences in the relative effectiveness of different teachers. There is something about the more effective teachers that makes them more effective than others, even when they change grade assignment, when they change schools, and when they teach different kinds of students. Therefore, while there is certainly value in looking at both *teacher* quality and *teaching* quality, it does seem clear that a significant proportion of the difference in the quality of instructional experiences received by students is attributable to the individual qualities of the teacher in the class.

Moreover, the differences between teachers are substantial. If we divide teachers into three equal-sized groups—effective, average, and less effective—then as noted previously, students taught by an effective teacher learn twice as much per year as those taught by less effective teachers. If instead, we compare the very best with the least effective, the differences are even starker. For example, if we take a group of fifty teachers all teaching the same subject, then the students taught by the most effective teacher in that group will learn in six months what those taught by the average teacher will take a year to learn. And those taught by the least effective teacher in the same group will take two years to learn the same material. In other words, the most effective teachers are four times as effective as the least effective.

In fact, this may be an underestimate because Fitzpatrick, Grissmer, and Hastedt (2011) estimated that one-third of the progress made by seven-year-olds is a result of maturation, rather than the quality of the teaching, so it is likely that the most effective teachers are in fact at least five times as effective as the least effective. This observation may also explain why, typically, the quality of the teacher seems to make much more difference in learning mathematics than in learning how to read. Students are developing their language skills all the time, inside and outside school, while for most children at least, mathematics tends to be developed primarily in mathematics lessons.

Moreover, in both elementary (Hamre & Pianta, 2005) and secondary schools (Slater, Davies, & Burgess, 2008), the most effective teachers are disproportionately effective for the lowest achievers. In other words, while all students benefit from more effective teachers, the gains are greater for the lowest achievers, and therefore, increasing the number of effective teachers in our schools will raise the achievement of all students but will also close the gaps in achievement between different groups of students.

Now, of course, this does not mean that we should focus only on teacher quality. Ensuring that teachers have the resources they need to do their job is important. They need time, material resources, and the support of leaders and colleagues to do their best work. But the magnitude of the differences between teachers in their effects on student learning means that it is hard to envisage any effective way of improving the quality of educational outcomes for young people that does not involve a sustained effort to improve teacher quality.

Improving Teacher Quality

Improving the quality of teachers can be done in two ways: by replacement and by improvement. We can replace existing teachers with better ones, and we can improve the teachers who are already working in our schools. Both of these mechanisms have roles to play, but the important issue is how we divide our attention between the two.

Many labor economists have focused on replacing existing teachers with better ones, primarily because they argue that efforts to improve the effectiveness of existing teachers have been relatively unsuccessful. They have a point. Professional development for serving teachers has been a standard feature of the education system in the United States for at least three decades, and yet evidence of the impact on student achievement is hard to find (TNTP, 2015). Moreover, the evidence that does exist suggests the impact of teacher professional development is limited. For example, Harris and Sass (2007) found that the average of fifty hours of professional development received by teachers each year improved performance by only around 10 to 25 percent of the improvement made by a novice teacher in his or her first year.

However, absence of evidence is not evidence of absence. The fact that previous attempts to improve teachers' effectiveness have not worked does not mean that it is not possible to improve the effectiveness of existing teachers. In fact, given that there is now considerable evidence that the typical kinds of professional development being provided to teachers in the United States are known to be ineffective (Darling-Hammond, Wei, Andree, Richardson, & Orphanos, 2009), the failure of previous efforts is hardly surprising. What is rather surprising is that teachers continue to be offered professional development that is known to have little impact on student achievement. This might be understandable if there was no evidence about the kinds of professional development that were likely to be more effective, but in fact, as we shall see, there is now considerable evidence that there are ways of making existing teachers significantly more effective. Unfortunately, these measures are not easy to implement at scale.

However, no matter how difficult it is to improve the effectiveness of existing teachers, we need to do what we can, because as we shall see, the kinds of improvements in average teacher quality that we can secure by replacing existing teachers with better ones are likely to be small, for three reasons. First, it turns out to be extremely difficult to reliably identify less effective teachers. Second, a considerable amount of political capital would need to be expended to remove ineffective teachers even if we can identify them. Third, there is little evidence that there are better teachers out there being prevented from entering the profession. The improvement in educational achievement needed to give our students a decent shot at a good life is so large that we need to ensure that we do everything we can to achieve it.

Replacing existing teachers with more effective ones can be done in a number of ways. First, we can simply raise the bar for hiring. For example, we could increase the requirements for entry into the profession so that only those teachers who are more effective than the average of existing teachers are certified. We could also do this for every hiring decision, so that for any post, we hire only those more effective than average. Second, we can increase the number of vacancies by removing the least effective. Even if those removed were replaced by teachers somewhere in the middle on the effectiveness scale, this would increase the average quality of teachers. Third, we can make sure that the most effective teachers do not leave the profession by paying the most effective teachers more, for example. Each of these replacement examples is discussed as follows.

Raising the Bar

The idea that we can improve educational outcomes just by improving the quality of entrants into the profession is attractive, even if it would take a long time to achieve. Eric Hanushek (2004) has shown that if, each year, the new teachers we hired were just slightly better than the teachers already working in our schools, the improvement in teacher quality over a generation would be substantial. For example, over a thirty-year period, it would be possible to improve the scores of US fifteen-year-olds on PISA by fifty points—to approximately the level achieved by those in Singapore—simply by replacing teachers who retired with ones who were at the 54th percentile of effectiveness (Hanushek, 2004). With a more aggressive policy applied to all teacher transfers (i.e., applying the same criteria to all those who change schools and not just entrants to the profession), the same outcome would be achieved in just fifteen years and, in thirty years, would result in PISA scores comfortably ahead of those posted by Shanghai. The difficulty with this solution, attractive as it is, is that for most jobs, it appears to be remarkably difficult to identify in advance how good someone will be.

For example, Bliesener (1996) reviewed 116 studies of the accuracy of predictions of job performance based on biographical data. He found that it was, on average, possible to use biographical data to improve personnel selection, but not by much. Faced with two candidates for a single post, flipping a coin would get you the person who eventually turned out to be the better worker 50 percent of the time. Using biographical data would improve the odds of getting the right person to 57 percent, but you would pick the wrong person 43 percent of the time. Or, to put it another way, using the biographical data would improve the result only once in every fourteen hires.

Turning to teaching in particular, Harris and Sass (2007) used a set of administrative records from Florida that included details of all the test scores of students from third to tenth grade over a six-year period from 1999–2000 to 2004–2005. A particular feature of this data set was that for each student, in each year, it was possible to identify the teacher who had been primarily responsible for teaching that student that year. Because they had details on the qualifications of the teachers, they were able to systematically examine the relationship between student progress and the academic preparation of their teachers. Their findings are summarized in Table 2.2 (Harris & Sass, 2007), which shows whether the variable in question has a positive or negative correlation with student progress (empty cells indicate no statistically significant relationship with student achievement).

Table 2.2. Relationship Between Teachers' Qualifications and Student Progress

	Mathematics			Reading		
	Elem.	Middle	High	Elem.	Middle	High
General theory of education courses					−	
Teaching practice courses				−	+	
Pedagogical content courses	+	+				
Advanced university courses			−			+
Aptitude test scores			−			

There are a number of surprising things about this table. First, there are relatively few significant relationships of any kind—twenty-two of the thirty cells (over 70 percent) are empty. Second, and perhaps even more surprisingly, there are as many negative as positive relationships. Third, even those significant relationships that do exist are rather difficult to understand. The fact that college courses in pedagogical content improve the effectiveness of math teachers in elementary and middle schools—but not high schools—does not seem particularly surprising, but the fact that they do not do so for reading at any level seems odd. Perhaps even more surprising is the fact that those with higher aptitude test scores are worse than those with lower aptitude scores at teaching high school math. When one considers that with thirty cells in the table, one or two of the values would be expected to be significant just by chance, one is led to the conclusion that the table is probably just statistical noise.

In fact, this is not an isolated result. Indeed, the lack of any simple relationship between formal qualifications and the effectiveness of teachers is one of the most well-established findings in the research literature (see Table 1 in Harris, 2009, for a summary). There is evidence that what Lee Shulman (1986) called "pedagogical content knowledge"—the kind of knowledge that is needed for teaching but not for advanced work in a subject—does in fact matter, but the effects are smaller than most imagine. For example, Hill, Rowan, and Ball (2005) found that elementary school students taught by teachers with greater mathematical knowledge for teaching did make more progress, but the effect was small. Students taught by teachers with strong mathematical knowledge for teaching made about one month's more progress per year than those taught by teachers with weak mathematical knowledge for teaching. This is an important difference but clearly only a small part of teacher quality. It does seem that specific pedagogical content knowledge is more important in high school, but even here, mathematical knowledge for teaching accounts for only about one-third of the variation in teacher quality (Baumert et al., 2009).

To sum up the argument so far, we know that teachers make a difference, but we don't know what makes the difference in teachers. Physicists talk about dark matter, which is a kind of matter that they believe exists because its gravitational impact can be felt (or at least inferred from its impact on traditional matter) but is not matter in any form that we understand. We might talk about the dark matter of teacher quality in the same way.

In an article titled "Most Likely to Succeed," Malcolm Gladwell (2008) likened picking teachers to drafting quarterbacks in the National Football League (NFL). Performance in football at the college level predicts performance in professional football reasonably well at most positions, but at quarterback, there is little relationship between success in college and success in the NFL. At one point, it was thought that this might be because offenses and defenses were more complex in professional football, and so those who are drafted into the NFL are now asked to take the Wonderlic Cognitive Abilities test. Despite its continued use, however, it appears that there is absolutely no correlation between a player's score on the Wonderlic and his ability to play quarterback (Lyons, Hoffman, & Michel, 2009; Mirabile, 2005). Even when the Wonderlic is used as a benchmark rather than as a predictor (e.g., when a team decides to draft only those quarterbacks with a score of 27 out of 50 on the Wonderlic, at least twenty-seven starts in college, and a completion percentage of 60 percent), it is not particularly effective. Such a rule would have teams passing on Brett Favre (Wonderlic score of 22), Terry Bradshaw (16), Dan Marino (15), and Donovan McNabb (14).

Because college preparation and other measures of performance have such a weak relationship with teacher effectiveness, a number of school districts have explored the use of screening tools to improve the chances of selecting the most effective teachers. One of the most interesting is that used by Spokane Public Schools in Washington, which was studied by Goldhaber, Grout, and Huntington-Klein (2014).

Spokane Public Schools uses a three-stage selection procedure. In the first stage, applications are reviewed by human resource professionals who are asked to rate applicants on three dimensions: experience (1 to 6), depth of skills (1 to 6), and quality of recommendations (1 to 9), resulting in a score from 3 to 21.

In the second stage, a principal wishing to fill a vacancy will ask for a list of applicants who meet a specific level, such as a score of at least 17 on the 21-point profile (the average across all applicants is 16). The principal then gives each listed applicant a rating from 1 to 6 on ten dimensions: certificate and education, training, experience, classroom management, flexibility, instructional skills, interpersonal skills, cultural competency, specific qualifications for the particular post, and letters of recommendation. Those scoring highest on the 60-point profile are then invited for interviews.

A particularly important feature of the study by Goldhaber et al. (2014) was that the available data allowed a comparison of the effectiveness of teachers who were selected to teach in Spokane with those who were not, but who ended up teaching in other schools in the state of Washington. They found that using the screening tools improved the likelihood of choosing the better candidate of two from the 50 percent that would have been achieved by flipping a coin to 67 percent in math and 62 percent in reading. To see what this might mean in practice, assume that each year, 7 percent of teachers retire, and 7 percent change schools (these are the rates for 1994–1995 given in Hanushek, 2004). If we applied a screening process such as that used by Spokane Public Schools to all replacements, and had enough applicants so that those with screening scores in the lower quartile (i.e., those scoring in the bottom 25 percent) were not considered, over the next thirty years, each student would experience an increase in teacher quality that would, over the first ten years of his or her education, result in fifteen-year-olds scoring about thirty points higher on PISA. Therefore, improved selection tools certainly have a role to play in improving teacher effectiveness, but given the arguments in the previous chapter about the rate at which automation and offshoring are destroying jobs and the level of education that is likely to be required in the future for effective citizenship, then by itself, improving the quality of entrants to the profession will not be enough. In the following section, I discuss how the improvement of teacher quality might be accelerated by removing less effective teachers.

Removing the Least Effective Teachers

If we could remove less effective teachers and replace them with average teachers, this would undoubtedly have a significant impact on the achievement of young people. Chetty, Friedman, and Rockoff (2011) estimated that if we could replace teachers who were in the bottom 5 percent of effectiveness with average teachers, the impact on achievement would increase the lifetime income of the students in an average US classroom by $250,000 (net present value). They would also be less likely to be teenage parents, and they would save more for retirement. However, removing less effective teachers is both politically and technically difficult.

In the 2007–2008 school year, according to the national Schools and Staffing Survey, across the United States, only 2 percent of teachers were dismissed or did not have their contracts renewed (Aritomi, Coopersmith, & Gruber, 2009). In California, over the last ten years, just 22 out of a total of 275,000 permanent teachers were dismissed for unsatisfactory performance (Students Matter, 2014). And yet, a number of surveys have suggested that the number of ineffective teachers in US schools is greater than this (Chait, 2010; Weisberg, Sexton, Mulhern, & Keeling, 2008). It is therefore hardly surprising that there have, over recent years, been calls for increasing the rate at which ineffective teachers are removed. Most recently, in a landmark ruling in the case of *Vergara v. State of California*, Judge Rolf M. Treu struck down five statutes in the California Education Code relating to the state's arrangements for teacher tenure, dismissal, and the use of "last-in, first-out" policies in determining which teachers should be dismissed in school closures and reorganizations (Treu, 2014).

A detailed discussion of the costs and benefits of teacher tenure arrangements across the 14,000 school districts in the United States is beyond the scope of this book. Here, I want to focus simply on the evidence about whether it is possible to reliably identify which teachers are less effective, and I want to look at three particular ways we might do this: value-added analyses, teacher observation, and student perception surveys.

Value-Added Analyses

Asking whether we can identify good teachers may seem odd, because earlier in this chapter, I presented a number of studies showing that there are large differences in teacher performance based on differences between students' scores at the beginning and the end of the school year. However, these analyses show that teachers on average make a difference, which is not the same as identifying how effective an individual teacher is. An analogy may be helpful here.

If we had weighing scales that could measure someone's weight only to an accuracy of ±50 pounds, we would not be able to say very much about the weight of any particular person. But, provided the errors in measuring weight were random, we would be able to conclude that in a group of fifty men and fifty women, the males were heavier than the females. Similarly, when we try to measure how good an individual teacher is from the progress made by his or her students, the precision of those estimates is rather low, even though we can see such an effect on average.

To start with, the assumptions made in the data analysis have a huge impact on which teachers are rated as effective. For example, Goldhaber, Goldschmidt, and Tseng (2013) examined the impact of different modeling assumptions on estimates of teacher effectiveness. They used two different, equally defensible models (a traditional random-effects model and a fixed-effects model) to classify high school teachers into five categories, or quintiles (i.e., most effective, above average, average, below average, and least effective). The results are shown in Table 2.3 (Goldhaber et al., 2013).

Table 2.3. Percentages of Teachers Placed in Different Quintiles of Effectiveness With Two Equally Plausible Value-Added Models

		Student fixed-effects model				
		1	2	3	4	5
Traditional model	1	38	22	24	16	0
	2	26	28	15	20	11
	3	20	20	20	24	16
	4	13	24	26	13	24
	5	9	5	12	28	47

Perhaps the most surprising feature of the data in Table 2.3 is that 9 percent of the teachers who are rated as the *least* effective with the traditional random-effects model are actually rated as the *most* effective with the fixed-effects model.

Even when we use the same models from year to year, the estimates of effectiveness of teachers vary considerably from one year to the next. McCaffrey et al. (2009) found that between 4 and 15 percent of teachers who were rated in the top fifth one year were rated in the bottom fifth the next year.

The problem with value-added models, when they are applied to the evaluation of individual teachers, is that, as Harris (2009) points out, there are a large number of assumptions that have to be made, which may be reasonable across a large group of teachers, but may not be justified for individual teachers.

For example, if we are drawing conclusions about individual teachers, we have to assume that the support of school administrators and teamwork among teachers do not improve student achievement. As noted earlier, we have to assume that measures of previous achievement account for all the differences in students that are relevant to progress, and this is unlikely to be the case. In Florida, for example, at the end of third grade, students are tested in math and reading, but at the end of fourth grade, students are tested in math, reading, and writing. A fourth-grade teacher who inherits a class that has done no writing in third grade will look less effective than an equally good teacher who inherits a class where the third grade teacher has spent a lot of time on writing. As another example, if some teachers spend time investing in building autonomy and resilience—what Angela Duckworth calls "grit" (Duckworth & Gross, 2014)—then that year's test scores may well be lower than they would otherwise have been, but teachers teaching those students in the future will benefit. Moreover, this is not just a hypothetical argument. Master, Loeb, and Wyckoff (2014) found that achievement of students taught by teachers with weaker academic credentials decayed more quickly than the achievement of students taught by teachers with stronger academic credentials. In other words, students with the same amount of progress in a given year, as determined by value-added measures, might do very differently in the future. This appears to be a particular concern where teachers are under the greatest pressure to raise test scores. In fact, Rothstein (2010) found that good teachers benefit students for three years after they stop teaching them. In other words, good teachers make the teachers who teach their students in future years look better than those teachers really are.

In addition, some teachers may be more effective with some kinds of students than others, so value-added estimates will be higher if teachers are teaching the kinds of students with whom they are more effective and lower if they are teaching the kinds of students with whom they are less effective. In addition, many value-added models assume the effects are linear, so that one additional point on a test represents the same quality of contribution by the teacher, regardless of the student's initial level of achievement. With many measures of progress, high achievers make faster progress than low achievers (which is of course why they are high achievers in the first place), so teachers who are assigned to teach classes with more high-achieving students will look better than others even though they are in reality no more effective.

Even if we ignore the impact of these assumptions, the resulting estimates of teacher effectiveness are so imprecise that they are almost useless for teacher evaluation (Jacob & Lefgren, 2005). Using conventional standards of statistical significance, it is possible to distinguish highly effective teachers from very ineffective teachers, but that's about it. Specifically, we can be reasonably sure that a teacher who appears to be very, very weak is unlikely to be very, very good, and we can be reasonably sure that a teacher who appears to be very, very good is unlikely to be very, very weak, but finer distinctions are simply not possible at the levels of reliability that would be needed to command public confidence.

The consequences of the imprecision of teacher effectiveness estimates were demonstrated in a study by Winters and Cowen (2013). They note that because of the unreliability of teacher effectiveness estimates, any plausible policy of removing teachers on the basis of value-added estimates would have to be based on more than a single year's data. They matched math and reading test scores of 227,014 students to 15,152 teachers in Florida (96 percent of students were matched to teachers), and then they examined the consequences of two different policy options based on removing teachers whose performance fell below some threshold (weakest 5 percent, 10 percent, or 25 percent). The first policy option was to remove teachers whose performance fell below the threshold in *each* of two consecutive years. The second policy option was to remove teachers whose *average* performance across two years fell below the threshold.

If all teachers scoring in the least effective 5 percent for two consecutive years were removed, then this would result in the removal of just thirty-one teachers across the entire state. If teachers scoring in the least effective 5 percent on average over a two-year period were removed, this would result in the removal of 292 teachers across the state—just four teachers in each county. Of course the policy could be applied more aggressively, for example, by removing teachers ranked in the lowest 10 percent or even the lowest 25 percent, but of course this would also result in the removal of some highly effective teachers, which would be politically difficult to sustain.

Moreover, the impact on average student achievement would not be particularly large. Table 2.4 shows how many additional weeks of learning would result depending on the severity of the policy applied (i.e., at what percentile teachers would be removed) and whether the rating is based on the performance in consecutive years or averaged over two years. The analysis presented in Table 2.4 also assumed that teachers who are removed are replaced by average teachers (i.e., those at the 50th percentile, Winters & Cowen, 2013).

Table 2.4. Additional Weeks of Learning Produced by Different Teacher-Removal Policies

Policy	Severity (percentile)	Additional weeks of learning per student per year
Consecutive years	5th	0
	10th	0.1
	25th	0.3
Two-year average	5th	0.3
	10th	0.4
	25th	0.7

Some writers have taken the limitations of value-added analyses of teacher effectiveness previously outlined as evidence that they should not be used at all. Robert Solow (1970) rightly criticized any such extreme positions in the social sciences as absurd: "It is as if we were to discover that it is impossible to render an operating-room perfectly sterile and conclude that therefore one might as well do surgery in a sewer" (p. 101).

Value-added analyses have an important contribution to make to the improvement of teaching—and it is important to remember that value-added analyses represent a huge improvement on attempts to evaluate teachers on the basis of the scores achieved by their students. But, value-added modeling remains a very fragile technology, so the value-added estimates for individual teachers depend strongly on the assumptions that are made in the modeling and vary considerably from year to year and from context to context. Many of these difficulties would be ameliorated if value-added analyses were conducted exclusively at the level of the school, as they are in other countries (Ray, McCormack, & Evans, 2009), but the use of value-added estimates as measures of the effectiveness of individual teachers cannot currently be justified (American Statistical Association, 2014; Baker et al., 2010). Indeed, some scholars doubt that value-added models, on their own, will ever provide the precision needed to make high-stakes decisions about the removal of teachers. That is why many, including those collaborating in the MET project, funded by the Bill and Melinda Gates Foundation, have suggested supplementing teacher value-added analyses with direct observations of teaching and student-perception surveys. These two approaches to evaluating the effectiveness of teachers are discussed in the next two sections.

Teacher Observation

Because value-added analyses are unlikely to provide us with usable indications of which teachers are more effective and which teachers are less effective, a number of schools, districts, and states have adopted more direct measures of classroom practice, such as observing teachers. Perhaps the best known such system of classroom observation is the Framework for Teaching, developed by Charlotte Danielson (1996). Of course, such frameworks have been around for many years, but the important feature of the Danielson framework is that it has been rigorously researched, and most important, it has been shown that students taught by teachers who are rated highly on the framework do, in fact, make more progress.

The Framework for Teaching identifies twenty-two components of teaching, which are grouped into four domains of teaching responsibility:

Domain 1   Planning and preparation

 1a   Demonstrating knowledge of content and pedagogy

 1b   Demonstrating knowledge of students

 1c   Setting instructional outcomes

 1d   Demonstrating knowledge of resources

 1e   Designing coherent instruction

 1f   Designing student assessments

Domain 2   The classroom environment

 2a   Creating an environment of respect and rapport

 2b   Establishing a culture for learning

 2c   Managing classroom procedures

 2d   Managing student behavior

 2e   Organizing physical space

Domain 3   Instruction

 3a   Communicating with students

 3b   Using questioning and discussion techniques

3c   Engaging students in learning

3d   Using assessment in instruction

3e   Demonstrating flexibility and responsiveness

Domain 4   Professional responsibilities

4a   Reflecting on teaching

4b   Maintaining accurate records

4c   Communicating with families

4d   Participating in the professional community

4e   Growing and developing professionally

4f   Showing professionalism

For each of the twenty-two components, a scoring rubric is provided that identifies four levels of achievement, which are labeled unsatisfactory, basic, proficient, and distinguished (Danielson, 2014).

Sartain et al. (2011) investigated whether there was any association between the progress made by students in different classrooms in Chicago Public Schools and the ratings their teachers were given on a slightly modified version of the Framework for Teaching. Perhaps surprisingly, they found no significant relationship between the progress made by students and their teachers' ratings on domains 1 and 4. Of course, this does not mean that these aspects of teaching are unimportant. What the analysis showed was that variation in the ratings given to teachers for domains 1 and 4 did not seem to be systematically related to variations in the achievement of students. Or to put it another way, students taught by teachers who were rated higher on domains 1 and 4 did not learn more. However, for domains 2 and 3, there was a systematic relationship between the progress made by students and the ratings given to their teachers, and this is shown in Figures 2.1 to 2.3 (Sartain et al., 2011).

Figures 2.1 and 2.2 show the additional teacher value-added on the ten components of domains 2 and 3 in the Framework for Teaching. The vertical axis in both Figures 2.1 and 2.2 are the nominal value-added ratings used by Sartain et al. As can be seen, there is a clear relationship between the rating on the Framework for Teaching and the teacher value-added. However, these nominal ratings of teacher value-added are not particularly easy to interpret, and so Figure 2.3 condenses the information from Figures 2.1 and 2.2 into a single average composite for each subject and re-scales the graph so that the vertical scale represents the percentage change in the rate of learning found in classrooms taught by teachers at different levels of the Framework for Teaching based on measures of annual progress for students of different ages given by Bloom, Hill, Black, and Lipsey (2008).

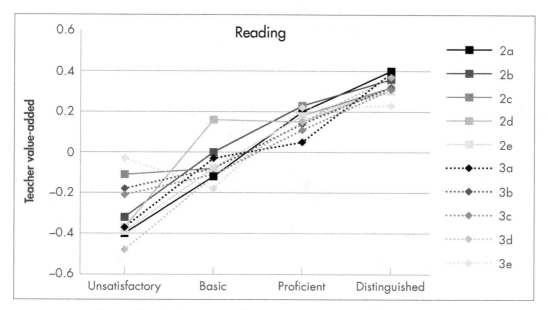

Figure 2.1. Relationship between teacher value-added for reading and teacher ratings on domains 2 and 3 of the Framework for Teaching.

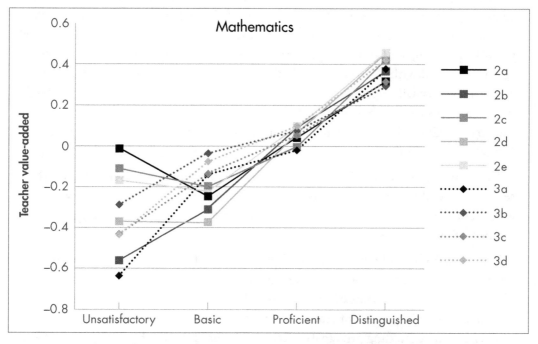

Figure 2.2. Relationship between teacher value-added for mathematics and teacher ratings on domains 2 and 3 of the Framework for Teaching.

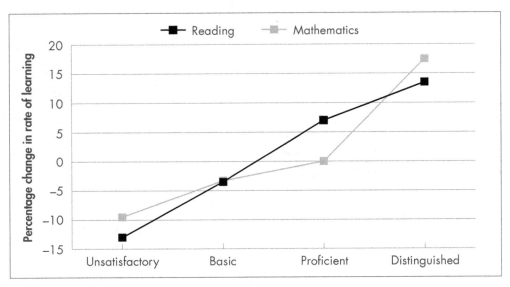

Figure 2.3. Relationship between teacher value-added for reading and mathematics and teacher ratings on domains 2 and 3 of the Framework for Teaching

From Figure 2.3, we can see that in both reading and mathematics, compared with an average teacher (i.e., the mean performance of all teachers in the study), students taught by a teacher who is rated as distinguished will progress about 14 percent faster per year in reading and about 18 percent faster in mathematics. At the other extreme, again compared with an average teacher, students taught by a teacher who is rated as unsatisfactory will progress about 14 percent slower per year in reading and about 9 percent slower in mathematics. In other words, on average, a teacher rated as distinguished will be almost 30 percent more productive than one rated unsatisfactory (actually 28 percent more in reading and 27 percent more in math).

This is an important finding. For the first time, it is possible to relate things that teachers actually do in classrooms to outcomes for their students. However, it is important to note that the power of the Framework for Teaching to identify effective teachers is rather limited.

First, although the Framework for Teaching identifies four categories for teachers, the vast majority of teachers are assigned to the middle two categories. Trained observers placed 95 percent of teachers as either basic or proficient, while building principals rated 80 percent of teachers in these categories—the main reason for the difference is that building principals rated 17 percent of the teachers as distinguished, while only 3 percent of trained observers did so (Sartain et al., 2011).

Second, the Framework for Teaching captures only a small part of the differences that we know to exist in teacher effectiveness. As noted previously, students taught by a teacher rated as distinguished will make almost 30 percent more progress than those taught by a teacher rated as unsatisfactory. Or, to put it another way, an increase in one category in the teacher's rating would improve the rate of student learning by 10 percent. But as we saw earlier, teachers in the top one-third of effectiveness are at least twice as effective as those in the lowest third. Indeed, as we did earlier, if we group teachers into four equal-sized categories (most effective, above average, below average, and least effective), then an increase in one category in actual teacher effectiveness would increase the rate of student learning by over 40 percent while an increase in teacher rating on the Danielson framework is associated with an improvement of only 10 percent in student achievement. In other words, the Framework for Teaching captures less than one-third of the variation in teacher effectiveness.

This matters a great deal because the Framework for Teaching is being widely used across the United States for teacher evaluation, with sanctions (e.g., termination) and rewards (e.g., increases in compensation) tied to the outcomes. If the Framework for Teaching captured most of the variation in teacher effectiveness, then this would not be a problem, because higher ratings on the Framework for Teaching would indicate increased teacher effectiveness. But because the Framework for Teaching captures so little of the variation in teacher effectiveness, it is entirely possible for teachers to game the system by adopting the features of effective teaching identified in the Framework and, at the same time, actually become *less* effective teachers.

None of this is intended as a criticism of the Framework for Teaching. As noted previously, the Framework for Teaching represents an extraordinary advance in our ability to relate observable features of classroom practice to changes in student outcomes. However, the fact that the Framework identifies only four levels of achievement, combined with the fact that most teachers are allocated to the middle two levels, places inherent limitations on its use for identifying effective teachers. It is also important to note that in the study by Sartain et al. (2011) discussed previously, most teachers were observed on only one occasion and observed by a principal or an assistant principal and an external expert rater.

This is an important limitation because the ratings given to the same teacher can vary by lesson. Many middle school and high school teachers have had the experience of delivering the same lesson to one section in period 1 and to another, supposedly parallel, section in period 2, and finding that the first lesson goes well and the second is a disaster. An observation of the first period would result in a high rating, and an observation of the second lesson would result in a low rating, and yet it's the same teacher. Now of course, this is just the teacher/teaching issue that was discussed at the beginning of this chapter. Some teachers are, on average, more effective than others, but performance is highly variable from lesson to lesson. Just how variable was powerfully illustrated by Heather Hill and her colleagues (2012) in a study of the

variability of ratings of teaching performance across different lessons and when evaluated by different raters. Their findings are shown in Figure 2.4, which shows how
the reliability of the rating changes when more raters assess the same lesson and when
the rating of a teacher is based on a greater number of different lessons observed. (The
paper by Hill et al. actually uses the idea of generalizability rather than reliability,
but, for the purpose of the argument here, the generalizability coefficients cited can
be thought of as reliability coefficients for an assessment.)

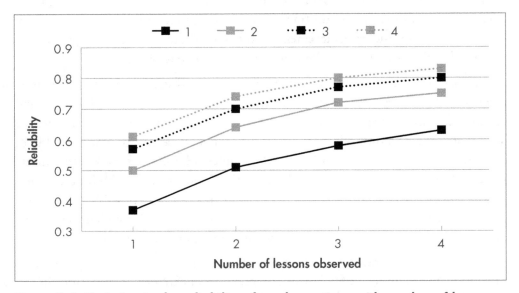

**Figure 2.4. Variation in the reliability of teacher ratings with number of lessons
observed and number of raters.**

As can be seen, the reliability of the rating increases when more raters judge the
quality of a piece of teaching and when the same teacher is observed over multiple
lessons. However, perhaps the most surprising feature of Figure 2.4 is how slowly the
reliability of the teacher ratings increases with the number of raters and the number
of lessons observed. There is no magic number for a reliability coefficient that can
be taken as a benchmark, but for comparison purposes, the two major assessments
used for selection to higher education—the College Board's SAT and the ACT college readiness assessment—have reliabilities in excess of 0.90. The reliability of the
English and math SAT scores are 0.92 and 0.91, respectively, while those for the
ACT are 0.92 and 0.93, respectively (ACT, 2014; College Board, 2014). Given that
these are the levels of reliability that we feel are necessary for the selection of students
to higher education institutions, it seems that a comparable level of reliability would
be a necessity for making judgments about the effectiveness of teachers.

If we did decide that we would want a reliability of 0.90 for our teacher observations, the analysis by Hill et al. (2012) discussed previously suggests we would need to have each teacher observed teaching six different classes and have each lesson observed by five independent judges—a total of thirty independent observations of teaching practice.

In addition to the Framework for Teaching discussed above, the MET project has examined a number of other approaches to teacher observation, including the Classroom Assessment Scoring system (Pianta, La Paro, & Hamre, 2008), the Protocol for Language Arts Teaching Observations (Grossman et al., 2010), and the Mathematical Quality of Instruction (Hill et al., 2008). However, none of these frameworks has found as strong a relationship with student growth as the Framework for Teaching (Polikoff, 2013). At the moment, the Framework for Teaching would appear to represent the best we can do in relating student progress to classroom observations. Perhaps even more surprisingly, an additional study of 327 of the teachers participating in the MET project found little relationship between how well the teacher's curriculum was aligned to the tests being used and the achievement gains made by students and no relationship at all with the measures of teacher effectiveness (Polikoff & Porter, 2014).

Now again, this should not be taken as implying that observations of teaching have no value—they clearly do. Rockoff and Speroni (2011) have shown that teacher observations identify different aspects of teacher quality from those identified in value-added analyses, and Grissom and Loeb (2013) have shown that regular observations of teaching by school leaders can improve outcomes for students, provided the leaders use that information to guide the teacher's development. However, the number of observations of teachers that would be required for defensible evaluations of teacher effectiveness is much greater than is normally assumed and probably greater than could reasonably be implemented.

Student-Perception Surveys

A third source of evidence about the effectiveness of teaching is, of course, the perceptions of students in the classrooms. As with value-added analyses and teacher observations, students' perceptions of their experiences in classrooms can provide valuable insights into the quality of teaching and helpful support for teachers about how they might improve their teaching.

One of the most promising approaches to surveying students has been the Tripod project developed by Ronald Ferguson (2008). The project's name comes from its focus on three attributes that are posited as being essential to the creation of effective learning environments for students, namely content knowledge, pedagogic skills, and relationship-building skills. In the version adopted by the Gates Foundation's MET project, students are asked to indicate—on a 1 (totally untrue) to 5 (totally true) scale—the extent of their agreement with thirty-seven statements about their classroom (thirty-five in the secondary school version) that are grouped into seven clusters. The seven clusters, and indicative examples of relevant statements, are shown in Table 2.5 (Bill and Melinda Gates Foundation, 2012a).

Table 2.5. Clusters and Indicative Example Statements From the Tripod Student Survey

Cluster	Elementary example	Secondary example
Care	My teacher seems to know if something is bothering me.	My teacher seems to know if something is bothering me.
Clarify	My teacher knows when the class understands and when we do not.	My teacher knows when the class understands and when we do not.
Challenge	In this class, my teacher accepts nothing less than our full effort.	My teacher doesn't let people give up when the work gets hard.
Control	My classmates behave the way the teacher wants them to.	My classmates behave the way the teacher wants them to.
Captivate	School work is interesting.	I like the way we learn in this class.
Confer	My teacher wants us to share our thoughts.	My teacher wants us to share our thoughts.
Consolidate	When my teacher marks my work, s/he writes on my papers to help me understand.	The comments I get help me know how to improve.

There is no doubt that the responses to such surveys can be immensely valuable to teachers and administrators where the primary aim is to improve teaching performance. However, where such surveys are used to evaluate the quality of teaching, the value is less clear.

As would be expected, there is a positive relationship between the responses of students to the Tripod survey and their progress in math and reading—after all, each of the examples in Table 2.5 is widely regarded as a feature of effective classrooms. However, the correlation between the students' responses and the growth in their achievement is not strong.

For example, the MET project compared the performance of students whose teachers received Tripod scores in the top 25 percent with that of students whose teachers received Tripod scores that placed them in the bottom 25 percent. They found that in the classrooms of the teachers with the higher Tripod scores, students made 4.6 months' more progress in mathematics than those in the classrooms taught by teachers with Tripod scores in the lowest quartile. For English language arts, the benefit of being in the classroom of a high-scoring teacher was about half as great. In other words, high-scoring teachers are around 45 percent more effective than low-scoring teachers (Bill and Melinda Gates Foundation, 2012a). However, as noted earlier in the discussion of the Danielson Framework for Teaching, the most effective 25 percent of teachers are around 120 percent more effective than the least effective 25 percent. This suggests that, like the Framework for Teaching, the Tripod survey captures only around one-third of the variation of teacher quality.

Now of course, as further research provides insights into the features of learning environments that are most important for student learning, it will be possible to improve student surveys so that they have greater explanatory power and will provide greater insights for teachers and leaders into how teaching can be improved. However, there are two inherent features of student-perception surveys that fundamentally limit their use for identifying effective teachers for high-stakes purposes.

First, it is well known that students do not always know when they are learning. One of the most famous illustrations of this is the so-called Doctor Fox experiment conducted in 1970 at the University of Southern California School of Medicine. In the experiment, a character actor, Michael Fox, delivered a lecture on "Mathematical Game Theory as Applied to Physician Education" to three groups of psychiatrists, psychologists, psychiatric social workers, social work educators, grade school educators, and educational administrators. The actor had been introduced to the groups as "Dr. Myron L. Fox, an authority on the application of mathematics to human behavior" (Naftulin, Ware, & Donnelly, 1973, p. 631). The lecture was based on a paper that had appeared in *Scientific American* eight years earlier, titled "The Use and Misuse of Game Theory" (Rapaport, 1962), but the actor had been coached by one of the researchers "to present his topic and conduct his question and answer period with an excessive use of double talk, neologisms, non sequiturs, and contradictory statements . . . interspersed with parenthetical humor and meaningless references to unrelated topics" (pp. 631–632). After the lecture, participants were asked to rate their experience of the lecture, and the ratio of positive to negative comments was approximately six to one.

In a subsequent experiment, 207 students were randomly allocated to view one of six lectures that varied in the quality of the content (high, medium, or low quality) and the manner of delivery (engaging or not) delivered by the same actor who had been used in the earlier experiment (Ware & Williams, 1975). After viewing the lecture, participants were asked to rate their satisfaction with the lecture and were tested on their understanding of the content. The results showed that both the content of the lecture and the way it was delivered affected students' achievement. In terms of achievement, the quality of the content mattered much more to students who had seen the lecture delivered in an engaging style. In contrast, those who had seen the less engaging lectures scored uniformly lower on the achievement test. In terms of student ratings of the lecture, however, students who had seen more engaging lectures were much less sensitive to the content of the lectures—the ratings they gave to the low-content lecture were no different than the ratings given to the high-content lecture, even though the latter contained six times as much academic content. In their conclusion, the authors note:

> To the extent that the current study findings hold true for the many facets of teaching and for the duration of a course, the use of student ratings to make decisions regarding faculty retention, tenure, and promotion may be invalid. Faculty who master the "Doctor Fox Effect" may receive favorable student ratings regardless of how well they know their subjects and regardless of how much their students learn. (Ware & Williams, 1975, p. 155)

Of course, these are just two studies, with their attendant limitations, but subsequent research has consistently demonstrated the existence of the Dr. Fox effect. For example, in a systematic review of the research, Abrami, Lenventhal, and Perry (1982) found that the expressiveness of the lecturer had a substantial impact on student ratings but a small impact on student achievement, while lecture content had a substantial impact on student achievement but only a small impact on student ratings. In other words, students cannot always tell when they are learning.

The second reason that student ratings of teachers may be of limited usefulness is that they can change the behavior of teachers. In higher education, where students' rating of their teachers is widespread, there have been concerns that using student evaluations of faculty to inform decisions about tenure and promotion has resulted in teachers omitting more challenging or controversial material from their courses. The extent to which this actually happens is still a subject of debate (see Greenwald, 1997, and other articles in the same issue of the journal). However, there is evidence that some teachers do teach in ways that maximize short-term learning gains, and student ratings, but that leave students less prepared for advanced courses in the same area (Carrell & West, 2010).

The available research evidence suggests that as long as student-perception surveys are used to identify how teaching might be improved, they have an important role to play. However, if they are used, either on their own or in combination with classroom observations and value-added measures, to determine the effectiveness of teachers, then they are likely to lose their value. This is yet one more illustration of Campbell's law: "The more any quantitative social indicator is used for social decision making, the more subject it will be to corruption pressures and the more apt it will be to distort and corrupt the social processes it is intended to monitor" (Campbell, 1976, p. 49).

Combinations of Measures

As noted earlier, the MET project has looked at whether it is possible to identify effective teachers from value-added measures, from classroom observations, and from student-perception surveys. In addition, they have explored whether weighted combinations of these three forms of evidence can provide better estimates of teacher effectiveness than might be obtained by any one of the sources alone.

They explored four different weighting schemes, shown in Table 2.6 (Bill and Melinda Gates Foundation, 2012b). In the first model, the weights for the three components were selected to maximize the accuracy in predicting the results of student performance on state tests, the second model placed half the weight on the value-added measures and weighted the other two sources equally, the third placed half the weight on the teacher observations and weighted the other two sources equally, and the fourth weighted the three sources equally.

Table 2.6. Weights Used in Different Models to Explore the Predictive Power of Combinations of Different Sources of Evidence

Model	Value-Added Measures	Observations	Student Surveys
1	81%	17%	2%
2	50%	25%	25%
3	25%	50%	25%
4	33%	33%	33%

They then examined how well the composite measure of teacher effectiveness predicted the actual gains made by students. They expressed their results in the form of a correlation coefficient, shown in Table 2.7 (Bill and Melinda Gates Foundation, 2012b, p. 12).

Table 2.7. Predictive Power of Measures of Effective Teaching Using Different Weights for Value-Added, Observation, and Student Surveys

	Model			
	1	**2**	**3**	**4**
Correlation with state test gains	0.69	0.63	0.43	0.53
Correlation with higher-order tests	0.29	0.34	0.32	0.33
Reliability	0.51	0.66	0.75	0.76

Astute readers will have noticed that although I have been talking about the relationships among variables, I have avoided the use of correlation coefficients until Table 2.7. This is partly because correlation coefficients take some explaining, and this chapter is pretty heavy going as it is. It is also partly because researchers often use correlation coefficients without taking time to explain how to interpret them.

Most people know that a correlation coefficient is a number between -1 and 1. A correlation of 1 between two variables means that if we plotted the two variables on a scatter plot, the points would lie in a straight line. With a correlation of 1, knowing the value of one of the variables would enable you to calculate exactly what the value of the other variable was for that data point. At the other extreme, a correlation of -1 would also mean that the points lie in a straight line, but now, an increase of the value of one of the variables would correspond to a *decrease* in the value of the other. A correlation of zero would mean that there was no relationship between the variables. In other words, knowing the value of one variable would tell you nothing about the value of the other. For example, in his study of Columbia undergraduates over a century ago, Clark Wissler (1901) found a correlation of -0.02 between a student's rank in the class and his reaction time. Specifically, knowing a student's reaction time would tell you nothing about his or her class rank. However, he found a correlation of 0.75 between class rank and the student's score in Latin and Greek. So, if you knew someone was above average in Latin and Greek, then he or she would be likely also to be above average in class rank (and vice versa). On the other hand, the correlation between class rank and French was only 0.30—a much weaker relationship—which means that someone who was above average in French would still be likely to be above average in class rank, but the chances of this not being so would be far less than if they were above average in Latin and Greek.

To illustrate what the correlations in Table 2.7 mean in practice, the six panels of Figure 2.5 (page 58) illustrate the results of a simulation of 1,000 teachers, showing how accurate the prediction of their value-added would be depending on the correlation between the two variables (actual effectiveness and predicted effectiveness). Model 1 in Table 2.7 provides an estimate of teacher effectiveness that correlates 0.7 with their true effectiveness. That sounds good until you look at panel (f) of Figure 2.5 and see that while, on average, those with higher true effectiveness do get higher predictions, the relationship is far from perfect. Some teachers who are truly average get high ratings, while some of those who are outstanding get modest ratings. It is almost possible to distinguish the least effective from the most effective, but even the best correlations identified by the MET project are an unsound basis for making high-stakes decisions about teacher effectiveness.

A particularly interesting feature of the analysis conducted by the MET project was that they also investigated whether the ratings of teacher effectiveness would successfully identify teachers who were more effective at increasing students' achievement across a broader profile than just state-mandated accountability tests. To this end, students taught by the participating teachers completed two additional assessments: the Stanford Open-Ended Reading Assessment published by Pearson and the Balanced Assessment in Mathematics (Balanced Assessment, 2007). These assessments were chosen because they include more cognitively challenging items, students are required to compose and write answers rather than selecting a correct response, and the assessments require analysis and application of concepts, and thus assess higher-order thinking skills. As such, they are likely to be closer to the kinds of assessments being developed by the Partnership for Assessment and Readiness for College and Careers and Smarter Balanced Assessment Consortium for the Common Core State Standards. As can be seen from Table 2.7, the results are rather disappointing. Even using all three sources of evidence, the prediction is not quite noise, but it is very weak.

Finally, the MET project researchers calculated the reliability of the predictions that would be made using this approach—in other words, the extent to which the composite would produce consistent results from year to year for a given teacher. As we saw earlier, for high-stakes decisions on students, we would want an assessment with a reliability of at least 0.85, and ideally over 0.90. The values shown in Table 2.7 are well below what would be considered acceptable for even a moderate-stakes assessment of a student (American Educational Research Association, American Psychological Association, & National Council on Measurement in Education, 2014).

At the risk of repeating myself, none of this is intended as a criticism of this work. Indeed, in my view, the work being done by the MET project is some of the most important and exciting research in education to have appeared in the last half-century. The work holds real promise for helping teachers and leaders look at classroom practice and for helping identify fruitful directions for future development.

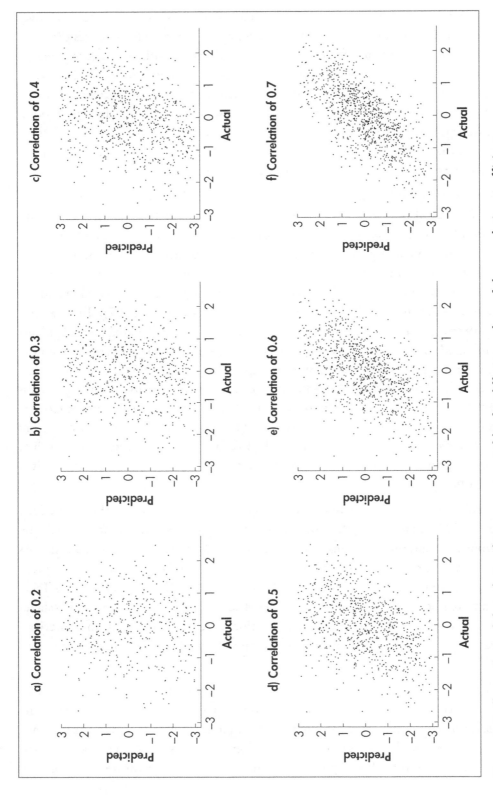

Figure 2.5. Illustrations of the relationships among variables for differing values of the correlation coefficient

Furthermore, engaging students in the process is a real step forward in putting the student at the heart of the learning process. However, the evidence is clear that the available methods of teacher evaluation—value-added analyses, classroom observation, and student surveys—are right now simply unable to identify the differences between teachers that we know exist. The tools available can (just about) reliably distinguish between the most effective and the least effective teachers, but finer distinctions are simply not defensible.

Retaining the Best Teachers

Much of the preceding discussion also applies to the issue of rewarding the best teachers. Just as it is almost impossible to reliably identify the worst teachers, it is also impossible to reliably identify the best. Teacher-compensation arrangements that pay teachers more on the basis of their performance are likely to reward many average and below-average teachers and are also likely to fail to reward the very best. More important, the evidence from experimental trials is not encouraging. Many of the studies that are cited in support of the benefits of merit pay for teachers have been conducted in settings that are very different from those in the United States, and whether they have any relevance is questionable. For example, in many low- and middle-income countries, just getting teachers to turn up for work is difficult. It is not therefore surprising that incentive schemes that use cameras to monitor daily teacher attendance improve attendance and student achievement (Duflo, Hanna, & Ryan, 2012). However, if teachers are in fact turning up for work, such incentive schemes are unlikely to have any impact.

The logic of most teacher incentive schemes in the United States is that teacher quality is made up of two components—teacher talent and teacher effort—where it is assumed that teacher talent is relatively fixed. Increasing teacher quality therefore requires increasing teacher effort. The assumption is that if teachers only tried harder, their students would learn more.

Now it is important to acknowledge that there are almost certainly a substantial number of teachers who could make a greater effort than they are making currently, so for those teachers, incentive pay schemes may improve effort. However, there are two problems with this. The first is that there appear to be relatively few teachers who are not working as hard as they can right now. The second is that increased effort may not actually result in better teaching. As Daniel Pink (2009) points out, extrinsic rewards can, and generally do, increase performance in low-complexity, low-creativity areas of human performance. If I have a stack of boxes that I need moved from one room to another, and I tell the staff that they will get a $20 bonus if the task is completed within the next hour, then that extrinsic reward may indeed improve performance. However, on high-complexity, high-creativity tasks, extrinsic rewards tend to degrade performance because people get locked into pursuing ineffective strategies more aggressively in pursuit of the reward.

The negative effects of extrinsic rewards were neatly demonstrated in a study of twenty-three professional artists carried out by Amabile, Phillips, and Collins (1994). Each of the artists was asked to submit ten randomly chosen commissioned works and ten randomly chosen noncommissioned works. The resulting 460 works of art were assessed by expert judges who were told, for each piece of work, only the name of the artist. In other words, the judges did not know whether each piece of work they judged was commissioned or not. When the ratings were analyzed, Amabile and her colleagues found that there was no difference in the ratings of the technical quality of the commissioned and noncommissioned works, but the commissioned work was judged less creative than noncommissioned work. Moreover, where artists had experienced constraints undertaking the commission, the resulting artwork was judged less creative. If teaching is, as I believe it to be, a high-complexity, high-creativity task, then extrinsic rewards are likely to make performance worse, not better.

Whatever the reasons, the empirical evidence is that teacher incentives appear to have only a modest impact on student achievement. Some, such as a scheme in New York, have been abandoned before they were finished because the evidence that the schemes were ineffective was clear before the scheduled end of the study. Those that have been completed have, in the main, found no effects. Perhaps the best designed study of teacher pay conducted to date, in Nashville Public Schools, found that bonuses of up to $15,000 per teacher per year had no impact on student achievement (Springer et al., 2010).

Some teacher incentive programs have had an effect on student achievement, perhaps most notably the IMPACT program in Washington, DC. Under the program, every teacher in DC is given, each year, a score from 100 to 400. For those teaching students in fourth through eighth grade, the teacher's individual value-added is weighted at 50 percent, and the results of five observations of teaching performance receive a weighting of 35 percent. For those not teaching students taking district-wide standardized tests, the observations of teaching performance are weighted at 75 percent, and a rating of the extent to which the teacher has met administrator-assigned goals is weighted at 10 percent. For all teachers in the district, a rating of the teacher's contribution to the school and community is weighted at 10 percent, and the school's value-added score is weighted at 5 percent. The impact score is then adjusted to take into account attendance, punctuality, respect for supervisors, and adherence to school and district policies.

A score between 100 and 175 results in immediate dismissal, while a score between 175 and 249 results in a warning to improve, followed by dismissal if the following year's rating is not 250 or higher. Those with a score of 350 or higher receive bonuses of $5,000, plus $5,000 if the IMPACT score includes an individual value-added element, with an additional $2,500 if the teacher teaches a high-need subject. Moreover, these bonuses are doubled if the teacher works in a high-poverty school. A teacher who gets a score of 350 or higher for two consecutive years is immediately paid as if he or she has a master's qualification and is given three years' seniority credit (five in high-poverty schools), and these additional bonuses are retained until the teacher stops teaching in the district.

The program was effective in moving some teachers out of the district—half of those scoring between 175 and 249 chose to leave the district—and the high-performing teachers improved by around one-quarter of a standard deviation. But the total cost, over the next fifteen years, of the incentives for those who scored 350 or higher for two consecutive years was over $185,000 for each teacher (in current dollars). Even when they work, therefore, incentive schemes do not appear to represent good monetary value.

In her more recent work, Teresa Amabile has sought to identify what does, in fact, motivate people in the world of work, and perhaps surprisingly, the answer is what she and her colleagues term *small wins*—getting a spreadsheet to do what it is meant to do, getting people who have been sniping at each other to work cooperatively together (Amabile & Kramer, 2011). And that is why performance-related pay is unlikely to be effective in education. Teachers already have incentives built in to every working day because every interaction with a student is an opportunity for a small win.

What all this means is that while improving teacher quality is essential to improving educational outcomes for young people, the contributions that will be made by replacing existing teachers with better ones will be small. We should, of course, try to increase the quality of entrants into the profession, but we also need to be aware that because our ability to predict who will be the best teachers is so limited, any attempt to make entry into teaching more selective risks excluding those who would be excellent teachers. Similarly, we should also try to remove the least effective teachers from our schools, but again, because we are not able to determine reliably who the least effective teachers are, the impact will be small. If we employ a strict burden of proof, then few teachers will be identified as ineffective. If we employ less stringent criteria, highly effective teachers will, by chance, be identified as ineffective, with all the political costs that label would entail. And similarly, because it is impossible to identify the best teachers reliably, any attempt to reward those with higher achievement is likely to be a waste of money and will serve only to alienate those who do not get the rewards. The only way to substantially improve teacher quality is to invest in the teachers we already have serving in our schools—what my friend Marnie Thompson calls the "love the one you're with" strategy.

Conclusion

Despite its length, the argument of this chapter is actually quite simple. Teachers vary considerably in their effectiveness in promoting growth in student achievement, so improving the quality of teachers is essential to improving student achievement. Improving the quality of the teachers in our schools can be done by replacing existing teachers with better ones and by improving the quality of teachers already serving in our schools. The question, then, is how do we distribute attention between these two approaches in order to maximize the impact on teacher quality? Those who have looked at the lack of success of previous attempts to improve the effectiveness of existing teachers conclude that replacing existing teachers with better ones must be the main approach to improving teacher quality. While the efforts made by the MET project and others have yielded important insights into the factors that influence the effectiveness of teachers, the current "state of the art" suggests that not only is it impossible to reliably distinguish effective and ineffective teaching, but also that we are unlikely to get much better at this in the foreseeable future. Unless we can improve the effectiveness of the teachers already working in our schools, we can expect that the improvements in student achievement will be marginal at best.

Of course we can improve the teachers working in our schools in many ways. The following chapter examines how we can use research to make sure that our teachers improve in ways that have the maximum benefit for students.

[*Chapter 3*]

Learning From Research

If a couple were shopping for a new refrigerator in an electrical goods store and were told that there were two models that fit their specifications, one costing $800 and the other costing $1,200, their next question would be utterly predictable. Any reasonable person in that situation would ask, "What's the difference between the two models?" In most of our lives, the idea that there are trade-offs between costs and benefits seems to be hardwired into our thinking; we naturally engage in such thinking without being told it is necessary. And yet, when we think about the improvement of educational outcomes for young people, our critical faculties seem to get suspended. Researchers find that something works in raising achievement, and people immediately jump on the bandwagon without stopping to think about important issues such as, "Are we already doing this?" "Could this new idea be implemented in this context?" "By how much will achievement improve?" and "What will it cost?" At the other extreme, some people completely ignore any research evidence that is published because they believe that nothing that has been done anywhere else would have any relevance for their own practice.

The argument of this chapter is that neither of these extreme positions is defensible. Those who want to determine what works in education are doomed to fail, because in education, "What works?" is rarely the right question, for the simple reason that in education, just about everything works somewhere, and nothing works everywhere. At the other extreme, those who want to improve their practice but think that educational research is a waste of time are likely to get nowhere because, unless they are very lucky, they will spend time improving aspects of their practice that do not benefit their students.

The argument of this chapter is that research evidence is essential to the task of improving outcomes for young people, but research will never be able to tell teachers what to do, because the contexts in which teachers work are so variable. What research can do is identify which directions are likely to be the most profitable avenues for teachers to explore.

Some of the blind alleys are obvious. For example, Brain Gym is founded on the idea that "moving with intention leads to optimal learning" (Brain Gym International, 2011c). The main idea behind Brain Gym is that getting students to engage in one or more of the twenty-six Brain Gym movements will enhance their learning. In support of this, the Brain Gym International organization lists thirty-eight studies on its website that claim to provide quantitative evidence of the impact of Brain Gym on student achievement. Three of the studies are unpublished, and the other thirty-five were published in a magazine titled *The Brain Gym Journal* (Brain Gym International, 2011a). In other words, there is not a single study in an academic journal showing any impact of Brain Gym on student achievement. Now, of course, as I have said before, absence of evidence does not imply evidence of absence. The fact that there is no evidence of the impact of Brain Gym does not mean that there will be no evidence in the future. However, this seems unlikely because the entire scientific basis of Brain Gym is unsound (Hyatt, 2007).

In other cases, the fact that something is likely to be unproductive is harder to establish. For example, over the past fifty years, a number of writers have proposed the idea that students have preferences for particular ways of learning and that, further, the students will learn better if the way they are taught is a match for their preferences. This is at the heart of the whole idea of differentiated instruction, which is discussed in greater detail in chapter 4.

In their review of the research on learning styles, Coffield, Moseley, Hall, and Ecclestone (2004) identified seventy-one different models of learning styles and descriptions of the most commonly used that can be found in Adey, Fairbrother, Wiliam, Johnson, and Jones (1999). A particular problem with the research on learning styles is that researchers often propose new ways of classifying learning styles without relating them to those that have been proposed by others. As a result, the extent to which new ways of classifying learning styles are really different from previous models, or just represent the same model with different labels, is often not clear. Some models seem to be popular because they resonate with deeply held beliefs about how people learn (e.g., that there are visual, auditory, and kinesthetic learners), while others are based on views about personality types (e.g., the Myers-Briggs Type Indicator, or MBTI, is based on the psychology of Carl Jung). However, while it may not be clear how the various models of learning styles relate to each other, the one thing that does seem to be clear is that there is very little evidence that teaching students in ways that take account of their learning styles helps students learn.

We know this because a distinguished group of psychologists was asked by the Association for Psychological Science to review whether the idea of taking learning styles into account in teaching was supported by scientific evidence. In framing their review, the group decided that they would consider only studies where students were divided at random into at least two groups, where students in different groups were taught in different ways but were assessed in the same way. Learning styles would be accepted as having some utility if it was the case that

> Students with one learning style achieve the best educational outcome when given an instructional method that differs from the instructional method producing the best outcome for students with a different learning style. In other words, the instructional method that proves most effective for students with one learning style is not the most effective method for students with a different learning style. (Pashler, McDaniel, Rohrer, & Bjork, 2008, p. 105)

Pashler et al found that there *was* evidence that, for some learning-style models, students had stable preferences in how they said they liked to learn. In other words, the responses given by students to a learning-style questionnaire on one day were similar to responses given on another day, although for others, most notably the Myers-Briggs Type Inventory, responses seemed to vary quite markedly from one occasion to another (Pittenger, 2005). However, they were unable to find any evidence for what they called the "meshing hypothesis"—the idea that instruction would be more effective if it meshed with the student's preferred learning style. They concluded:

> The contrast between the enormous popularity of the learning-styles approach within education and the lack of credible evidence for its utility is, in our opinion, striking and disturbing. If classification of students' learning styles has practical utility, it remains to be demonstrated. (p. 117)

Now, of course, it could be that at some point in the future, we might find that one particular way of looking at learning styles may allow us to improve teaching, but despite its widespread appeal, it appears that schools would almost certainly be wasting their time trying to improve students' achievement by matching instruction with students' preferred learning styles.

I want to make clear that I am not suggesting that teachers are especially gullible. Indeed it appears that medical practitioners are at least as guilty of basing their practice on weak or nonexistent evidence by prescribing for their patients treatments that are at best unproven and at worst proven to be ineffective (Goldacre, 2012). Indeed, one survey found that almost half of family practice physicians admitted prescribing antibiotics for a viral infection even though they knew it would be ineffective (National Endowment for Science, Technology and the Arts, 2014).

What I *am* suggesting is that, given the moral imperative to improve educational outcomes for young people, school leaders must strive to make sure that the kinds of changes that their teachers are making in their practice are changes that are likely to be beneficial (I say *likely* because teaching is such a complex task that no innovation can be guaranteed to improve outcomes). This means looking for evidence that indicates that a particular set of innovations is likely to have benefits for students—in other words, by looking at educational research.

The problem, of course, is that research in education really isn't like research in physics (Lagemann, 2000). There is probably not a single result in educational research that can be relied upon to be true everywhere and always. Most important, values intrude into educational research, which is fine (Flyvbjerg, 2001), but researchers rarely acknowledge this in their research. The outcome is that when researchers find conflicting results (e.g., praise works or praise doesn't work), they talk past each other rather than seek to understand the causes of the differences.

This makes things very complicated for educational leaders who want to know how to direct improvement efforts in their schools. It is easy to see that mandating the use of Brain Gym or learning styles in classrooms is unlikely to be effective, but for a whole range of other initiatives, weighing the evidence for and against a particular approach to school improvement is far more difficult.

There isn't space here for me to review all the relevant research on what might and might not help, so in this chapter, I am going to review the evidence for some ideas that have gained serious attention in recent years. I will examine a couple of topics—lesson study and educational neuroscience—that seem to have caught the imagination of educators recently, and then I will look at the idea of systematic reviews of research in education, which appear to be very promising but have particular problems when applied in the area of education. I won't spend any time discussing the costs of different interventions because working out how much something costs turns out to be relatively straightforward in education (Lipsey et al., 2012). The hard thing is generally working out what the benefits will be.

Lesson Study

Lesson study is the conventional translation into English of the Japanese term *jugyo-kenkyu*, which is routinely used to describe a process commonly used in Japanese schools for improving the quality of instruction, particularly in mathematics and science. There is no doubt that much of the interest in lesson study has been generated by the fact that Japan does lesson study, and Japan scores higher than the United States in international comparisons (the logical error of post hoc ergo propter hoc that we encountered in chapter 1).

In fact, the Japanese lead over the United States in mathematics has actually declined over the last fifty years. In the first international comparisons of mathematics achievement conducted in 1964, Japan outscored the United States by the equivalent of ninety points on the Trends in International Mathematics and Science Study (TIMSS) (Husén, 1967). In the TIMSS study in 2011, Japan outscored the United States by only sixty-one points (Mullis, Martin, Foy, & Arora, 2012). Moreover, most of the narrowing occurred after 1995, during the period that lesson study was most intensively implemented in Japan. Between 1995 and 2011, the average score for eighth-grade students in Japan fell from 581 to 570, while that for US eighth graders rose from 492 to 509.

Even more damaging for the idea that lesson study is the cause of Japanese success in mathematics is the fact that the Japanese lead over the international average is actually smaller in mathematics, where lesson study is most intensively used, than it is in reading or science. In the 2012 PISA results, Japan scored 536 in mathematics, 538 in reading, and 547 in science. Now of course such figures are open to a range of interpretations, not least because reading in a letter-based language is a very different process from reading in a character-based language. But the available data, such as they are, certainly do not suggest that lesson study is an important element in the higher performance of students in Japan compared to those in other countries.

Nevertheless, lesson study seems to have captured the imagination of US educators, and over the last twenty years, there have been many groups of teachers all over the country exploring lesson study as a way of improving instruction. And there is much to like about lesson study. As described by the Mills College Lesson Study Group (2014), teachers engaged in lesson study:

> Think about the long-term goals of education—such as love of learning and respect for others;

> Carefully consider the goals of a particular subject area, unit or lesson (for example, why science is taught, what is important about levers, how to introduce levers);

> Plan classroom "research lessons" that bring to life both specific subject matter goals and long term goals for students; and

> Carefully study how students respond to these lessons—including their learning, engagement, and treatment of each other.

These are obviously valuable activities for teachers. It is hard to imagine any of these things having a harmful effect on student achievement. Nevertheless, evidence that having teachers engage in lesson study actually increases student achievement has been hard to find. Recently, the What Works Clearinghouse—a body set up by the US Department of Education to evaluate the quality and trustworthiness of educational research findings—did endorse one investigation of the effects of lesson study as meeting its standards for evidence (Gersten, Taylor, Keys, Rolfhus, & Newman-Gonchar, 2014), but because the only published output from this study is a four-page summary (Perry & Lewis, 2011), it is hard to be sure whether the results are likely to be replicable (and it is also hard to see why the What Works Clearinghouse felt able to endorse this study on such limited evidence).

It may be that, in the future, more and better evidence of the impact of lesson study on student achievement will be forthcoming. However, even if future studies do show that engaging teachers in lesson study is an effective way of improving student achievement, a number of factors would need to be taken into account before its use could be recommended in the United States.

First, lesson study is an extremely time-consuming enterprise. As practiced in Japan, lesson study typically begins with a small group of teachers deciding to collaborate on the planning of a single lesson, such as how to calculate the area of a trapezoid. The teachers will meet together for an hour or more per week to plan a lesson, taking into account what is known about the difficulties that students have with such concepts, and then, after several such meetings, one teacher from the group will teach the lesson to a group of students, with the others observing the lesson and taking notes. Afterward, they will meet, possibly several times, to discuss how the lesson might be improved. The improved lesson would then be delivered to a different class, by another teacher (and possibly by a teacher not in the original group), and this time the lesson might be observed by the entire subject faculty of the building, standing around the edge of the classroom, taking notes on clipboards. Again, at the conclusion of the lesson, there would be a discussion of how the lesson might be improved, and the original group would have further meetings, again possibly on several occasions, to improve the lesson further. A lesson that survived this far might then go on to the final stage of the process—a *research lesson*—in which a classroom is created in a large, open space (e.g., a gymnasium) where one teacher teaches the lesson and is observed by as many as 300 educators, each with a clipboard, and each taking notes on the lesson. At the conclusion of the lesson, those who had observed the lesson meet and spend the rest of the day discussing the lesson and how it might be developed or improved. At the culmination of this process, a report on the lesson would be prepared and would be available to teachers all over the country. It is quite common for teachers to spend six months or more on the development of a single lesson. Therefore, even if lesson study is effective, there is a question about whether the benefits outweigh the costs.

Second, there is little agreement about what, exactly, *lesson study* is. The process described previously does seem to be widespread in schools in Japan, but what is called "lesson study" elsewhere is usually a rather accelerated form of the process, presumably because the idea of spending six months on the development of a single lesson seems to be very difficult for many US teachers to embrace. One attempt to implement lesson study in a school in England focused on two lessons and spent a single meeting on each (Cajkler, Wood, Norton, & Pedder, 2014). Now, of course such collaborative lesson planning may be helpful and may even be more effective than the process typically followed in Japanese schools. But it highlights the importance of understanding that just because two interventions are called "lesson study" (or indeed anything else for that matter) does not mean they are at all similar, and just because two interventions are called by different names, it does not mean they are necessarily different.

Third, it is not at all clear that lesson study, at least as practiced in Japan, would even be viable in the United States. In chapter 2, we saw that the middle school teachers in Japan teach fewer than 700 hours each year, while in the United States, teachers generally teach well over 1,000 hours each year. Lesson study might be feasible when teachers have sufficient noncontact time to attend to all their other responsibilities, such as grading, but when teachers have little time outside their teaching, as is the case in the United States, lesson study may well squeeze out other, and more important, activities.

At the risk of being repetitive, none of this is intended to suggest that lesson study is a bad idea, but currently, despite the widespread interest in lesson study, there would appear to be insufficient evidence of its utility for it to be a priority for schools.

Educational Neuroscience

In recent years, there have been extraordinary advances in techniques for exploring how the human brain works. Acronyms such as CAT (computerized axial tomography), fMRI (functional magnetic resonance imaging), and PET (positron emission tomography) have passed into ordinary language, and it surely can't be long before more recent innovations, such as diffusion tensor imaging, are as common. In particular, neuroscientists are making rapid progress in understanding how the structure of the brain develops in childhood and adolescence (Burnett, Sebastian, Kadosh, & Blakemore, 2011), and this has understandably prompted interest in the idea that our increasing understanding of how the brain works might be used to improve classroom instruction.

Such work is undoubtedly important, but perhaps predictably, the hype surrounding the application of neuroscience to education has proceeded far in advance of the available scientific evidence. Publishers bombard teachers and leaders with books that claim to reveal how to deliver brain-based education (as if there were any other sort of education), capitalizing on what we know about how the brain works, but the sad truth is that such claims are misleading or just wrong.

The mechanisms of the brain are, at present, rather poorly understood. We can use fMRI scans to determine which parts of the brain are active when it is engaged in certain sorts of tasks, but the fact that there is more blood flowing in one part of the brain than another is difficult to interpret. For example, we know that experts complete tasks with less effort than novices (see, for example, Milton, Solodkin, Hlustík, & Small, 2007), so increased blood flow might indicate only that the task is more demanding for that individual. The result is that any claim that a particular mechanism in the brain is responsible for a particular set of capabilities is highly speculative. This was neatly encapsulated by Della Sala and Anderson (2011) in their introduction to a book titled *Neuroscience in Education: The Good, the Bad and the Ugly*:

> While the use of the term "neuroscience" is attractive for education it seems to us that it is cognitive psychology that does all the useful work or "heavy lifting." The reason for this is straightforward. We believe that for educators, research indicating that one form of learning is more efficient than another is more relevant than knowing where in the brain that learning happens. (p. 3)

In other words, because our understanding of the brain is currently rather rudimentary, any ideas from neuroscience about how to improve education need to be validated by showing that they result in improvements in educational outcomes for learners. Neuroscience may provide interesting and promising hypotheses and may also produce explanatory mechanisms for what we observe in learning, but ultimately it is cognitive science, and not neuroscience, that will help us improve education.

As a concrete example, consider the phenomenon of retrieval-induced forgetting—the idea that our brains naturally help us forget something so that we can remember something more important, such as when I forget the room number of a hotel I stayed in last night in order to better remember the number of the room in which I am staying tonight. A recent study published in *Nature Neuroscience* used MRI scanning to track the brain activity associated with particular memories and showed how retrieval of a particular memory suppressed others (Wimber, Alink, Charest, Kriegeskorte, & Anderson, 2015). However, while the study is interesting, it is important to realize that the phenomenon of retrieval-induced forgetting has been known about for over twenty years (Anderson, Bjork, & Bjork, 1994). What the new study provides is a plausible neurological mechanism for a well-understood phenomenon. Put bluntly, exciting though this study is, there do not appear to be any *educational* implications whatsoever. Any ideas on to how to use the phenomenon of retrieval-induced forgetting are likely to come from the cognitive science studies of this phenomenon, not those from neuroscience.

So far, this chapter has examined a number of ideas about how to improve education that have, in some way, caught the attention of teachers and leaders. Some, such as Brain Gym, are so implausible that they can be dismissed immediately. Others, such as learning styles, have been researched extensively without generating any evidence of impact on learning, but of course, it could be that a different model of learning styles that has not yet been investigated may, in the future, be shown to be useful. Still others, such as lesson study, appear to be promising because they are consistent with a great deal of what we know about effective teacher learning, and yet others, such as educational neuroscience, will undoubtedly increase in importance as more research becomes available.

The problem, of course, is that leaders need to make decisions about priorities for teacher development *right now*. One possibility is to go with your gut and prioritize whatever seems to feel most appropriate. This may work out in the long run, but it may not, and if we accept there is a moral imperative to improve outcomes for young people, then that moral imperative surely requires that we use whatever has the greatest chance of working for our students. This requires looking more systematically at the available evidence.

Systematic Reviews of Research

According to its publishers, since its first publication in 1946, Dr. Benjamin Spock's book *The Common Sense Guide to Baby and Child Care* has, in its various editions, sold over 50 million copies worldwide. One piece of advice given in later editions of the book was concerned with whether it was better for babies to sleep on their backs or their stomachs. In the 1955 edition of the book, the advice was that babies should sleep on their backs, but in the 1956 edition of the book, this was changed: "I think it is preferable to accustom a baby to sleeping on his stomach from the start if he is willing. He may change later when he learns to turn over" (p. 164). Now of course at the time, this advice seemed perfectly sensible. As Spock himself pointed out in the 1956 edition, when a baby sleeps on his back, "if he vomits, he's more likely to choke. Also, he tends to keep his head turned to the same side—usually toward the centre of the room. This may flatten the side of his head" (p. 163). The latter point may seem much less important than the first, but it turns out to be correct. There is no evidence that sleeping on the back increases the risk of inhaling vomit

(Hunt, Fleming, Golding, & ALSPAC Study Team, 1997), but children who sleep on their stomachs are more likely to have rounder heads (Persing, James, Swanson, Kattwinkel, & Committee on Practice and Ambulatory Medicine, 2003).

Much more important, however, we now know that the risk of sudden infant death syndrome (SIDS), or "cot death" as it is sometimes called, is much greater when babies sleep on their stomachs than on their backs, even though we know little about the causes of SIDS. Benjamin Spock could not have known this—he gave the best advice he could at the time. However, what is disturbing is that from about 1970 on, there was increasing evidence of the association between SIDS and prone sleeping positions, and yet the proportion of babies sleeping on their stomachs increased steadily during the 1970s and 1980s, reaching 50 percent in many European countries and 70 percent in the United States (Gilbert, Salanti, Harden, & See, 2005).

It wasn't until the 1990s that the evidence about the increased risk of SIDS accumulated to the point that it was clear that it was much better for babies to sleep on their backs. Many countries mounted public information campaigns, such as the UK government's Back to Sleep initiative, and rates of SIDS began to fall sharply. For example, in England and Wales, the prevalence of SIDS fell by 75 percent in just four years, from two cases per thousand live births in 1989 to just 0.5 in 1993 (Gilbert et al., 2005).

The important point here is not to criticize those giving advice that turned out to be wrong. It is to realize that had the evidence about the increased risk of SIDS that was already in existence by 1970 been synthesized, and the appropriate advice been given in 1970, rather than in 1990, then about 60,000 baby deaths in Europe, Australasia, and New Zealand would have been prevented (Gilbert et al., 2005).

As a second example, consider the use of antiarrhythmic drugs in patients suffering heart attacks. In the 1970s, it was thought that drugs that controlled the irregular beating of the heart would improve outcomes for patients suffering heart attacks. In 1983, a systematic review of fourteen randomized controlled trials (RCTs) concluded, "The theoretical potential for a preventive or prophylactic effect of antiarrhythmic drugs (excluding beta blockers) in the treatment of coronary patients with ventricular arrhythmias has not been realized" (Furberg, 1983, p. 32C).

However, despite the lack of evidence in their support, the use of antiarrhythmic drugs in heart attack patients continued, and it wasn't until ten years later that a systematic review of fifty-one RCTs of the use of antiarrhythmic drugs in 23,229 heart attack patients found 571 deaths in the 11,517 patients who had been allocated to the control group but 660 deaths among the 11,712 who had been allocated to receive the antiarrhythmic drugs (Teo, Yusuf, & Furberg, 1993). In other words, the antiarrhythmic drugs *increased* the risk of death by around 14 percent. In fact,

Thomas Moore (1995) estimated that at the peak of their use in the late 1980s, these drugs killed more Americans *each year* than were killed in the entire Vietnam War.

In both of these cases, the evidence showing that widely accepted—and widely implemented—practices were causing tens or even hundreds of thousands of unnecessary deaths was available for at least a decade before policy changes were implemented. The problem wasn't lack of evidence. The problem was in synthesizing the evidence that had already been generated—what Chalmers (2005) called "the scandalous failure of scientists to cumulate scientifically."

The main reason for the failure to accumulate the findings from research was that until quite recently, the vast majority of reviews of research in a given field were narrative reviews. Experts would read relevant studies and would then summarize the main findings, which would then be peer reviewed, and then, if supported by other experts, would be published as a summary of the evidence in the relevant field. One of the main problems with such a review is the subjectivity involved—it is generally impossible to say whether other experts, reviewing the same field, would come to the same conclusions. While some narrative reviews do try to make clear how studies have been selected, it is impossible to be completely transparent about the review process. A second and less obvious issue with narrative reviews is that such reviews become less useful as more studies become available, because the reviewer cannot possibly hold in mind all the issues with all the studies being reviewed (Borenstein, Hedges, Higgins, & Rothstein, 2011).

Beginning in the 1990s, partly due to awareness of the severe impact that failing to accumulate already existing research evidence could have, there was a substantial interest in making more use of systematic reviews of research—attempts to reduce the degree of subjectivity in reviewing research.

The idea of systematic reviews of research was not new. In his review of health services in the United Kingdom, Archie Cochrane (1972) had suggested that one of the greatest failings in medical science was that what was already known was not being synthesized effectively. He summarized his critique a few years later thus: "It is surely a great criticism of our profession that we have not organised a critical summary, by specialty or subspecialty, adapted periodically, of all relevant randomised controlled trials" (Cochrane, 1979, p. 1).

In the four decades since Cochrane's review, narrative reviews of research have increasingly given way to *systematic reviews*, defined by Green et al. (2008) as reviews that attempt "to identify, appraise and synthesize all the empirical evidence that meets pre-specified eligibility criteria to answer a given research question" (p. 6).

In medicine and the health sciences, adoption of systematic reviews as the standard way of generating reliable knowledge about the effectiveness of different interventions was considerably boosted by the work of the Cochrane Collaboration, established in 1993 to "promote evidence-informed health decision-making by producing high-quality, relevant, accessible systematic reviews and other synthesised research evidence" (Cochrane Collaboration, 2014). The Cochrane Collaboration now involves over 30,000 individuals in over 120 countries, and as a result, health professionals all around the world have access to the latest research findings in just about every aspect of health care.

The success of the Cochrane Collaboration understandably led to calls for similar initiatives in the social sciences, and in 2000, the Campbell Collaboration (2014) was established to produce systematic reviews in crime and justice, education, international development, and social welfare. In the decade and a half since its foundation, the Campbell Collaboration has produced over a hundred systematic reviews of research in its areas of interest, but fewer than 10 percent of these have focused on improving mainstream educational processes. The reasons for this are complex, and many of them are not directly relevant to the subject of this book. There are, however, several reasons why systematic research turns out to be much more difficult to conduct well in some areas than in others, and education appears to be one of those areas.

Identifying Relevant Studies

One of the most significant issues is that of finding relevant studies. In medicine, as in many other areas of scientific inquiry, there is substantial agreement about the key words that would be used in entering a study into a database. If we take the example of antiarrhythmic drugs discussed earlier, it is almost certain that any relevant study would have the terms *antiarrhythmic drugs* and *myocardial infarction* in the key words (and probably in the title too). On the other hand, if we were researching the impact of classroom formative assessment on student achievement, it would be difficult to ensure that all relevant studies were included. Some would use the word *assessment*, while others would use *evaluation*, and others might use neither. As an example, three reviews of the impact of assessment on student learning appeared in consecutive years from 1986 to 1988. The first, by Fuchs and Fuchs (1986), was titled "Effects of Systematic Formative Evaluation: A Meta-Analysis"; the second, by Gary Natriello (1987), was titled "The Impact of Evaluation Processes on Students"; and the third, by Terry Crooks (1988), was titled "The Impact of Classroom Evaluation Practices on Students." What is surprising is that while the papers by Natriello and Crooks cited 91 and 241 papers, respectively, only nine references were common to both, and neither cited the review by Fuchs and Fuchs. When Paul Black and I sought to update these reviews a decade later, we found that depending on the search terms used, database searches either missed important studies or included far too many irrelevant studies. In fact, we found that the only way of being sure to not miss important studies was by conducting a manual search of every single issue published over a ten-year period of the seventy-six journals we considered most likely to include relevant studies (Black & Wiliam, 1998).

Criteria for Inclusion

Once potential studies have been identified, it is necessary to decide which studies should be included in the review. The fact that two studies are investigating the impact of cooperative learning on student achievement does not mean that they are studying the same thing (e.g., Antil, Jenkins, Wayne, & Vadasy, 1998) or that two studies investigating different interventions, such as cooperative learning and collaborative learning, are necessarily investigating different things (Panitz, 1999).

A more subtle issue relates to the research methods used in the studies identified. Some systematic reviews include only RCTs—experiments in which participants have been divided into at least two groups at random, with one group getting the intervention and one other not getting it. The argument for using RCTs is very strong. If we just invited schools to participate in a trial of an experimental approach to teaching early algebra to third graders, then it may be that those that volunteer are schools with higher-achieving students or ones where the teachers are more open to innovation. To overcome this problem, most RCTs employ an intention-to-treat study design, in which volunteers are sought first and then divided at random into two groups, with half getting the new program and the other half not (sometimes the control group gets the intervention at some point in the future in what is called a wait-list control design). If the experimental group outperforms the control group by a statistically significant margin, then we can be reasonably sure that it is the intervention that caused the difference.

Now there is no doubt that when RCTs produce statistically significant effects, they produce strong evidence for a causal relationship. If we can perform RCTs in education, we should probably do so. However, if for whatever reason RCTs are not possible, should we say that we simply do not know anything, or should we investigate what we can say?

In this context, it is worth noting that RCTs were not required to establish that smoking causes cancer. If we truly wanted gold-standard evidence that smoking causes cancer, we would have to solicit volunteers for an experiment, divide them into two groups at random, prevent one group from smoking and ensure that all the members of the other group smoked a certain number of cigarettes per day for a significant length of time (say around twenty years) and then compare the prevalence of cancer in the two groups. Needless to say, this was not the approach adopted.

Instead, researchers looked for a way of establishing a causal relationship without an RCT (Hill, 1965).

Even where RCTs are possible, there are a number of factors that make their use in education difficult. The first has to do with clustering effects. If we wanted to compare the achievement of students using cooperative learning with those who were not, it might be assumed that the students should be our unit of analysis. However, most statistical techniques require the researcher to assume that the effect of the cooperative learning intervention on one student is independent of the effect on the other students using cooperative learning. In general, because the students' experiences will depend on how the teacher implements cooperative learning, the experiences of students in the same class will be more similar to each other than, say, between students doing cooperative learning in different classes. In other words, there is some clustering in the data. In such situations, the unit of analysis would more properly be classrooms, rather than individual students. And if teachers talk to each other about what they are doing in the break room, then the unit of analysis should really be the school. In practice, researchers address this problem by recognizing the nested structure of the data (i.e., that, in terms of the intervention, students in the same classroom are more similar than students in different classrooms, and that teachers in the same school are more similar than teachers in different schools), using what is called "multi-level modeling" (Goldstein, 1987) or "hierarchical linear modeling" (Raudenbush & Bryk, 1988). However, when data are clustered, then far more schools and classrooms are required to have a reasonable chance of getting a significant result. For the kinds of effects that are typical in education, over 100 participating schools are needed for the experiment to yield a significant result (Konstantopoulos, 2006). From the point of systematic reviews, it is also important to remember that the issue of clustering in data is poorly understood by many researchers, and analyses that should have used statistical techniques taking clustering into account, in fact, did not. Many published studies that claimed to have found a significant effect would not have found significant results if they had properly recognized the statistical consequences of the clustering in their data.

There are many other reasons that RCTs are difficult to perform well in education. For one thing, it turns out to be quite difficult to get people to implement the programs as designed. A randomized control study of the Compass Learning Odyssey math program found that only *one* out of the sixty participating teachers used the program for the sixty minutes specified each week—the average usage was around thirty-eight minutes per week (Wijekumar, Hitchcock, Turner, Lei, & Peck, 2009). Similarly, an evaluation of Classroom Assessment for Student Learning found that teachers participating in the trial received only around half of the training specified in the program (Randel et al., 2010). The fact that neither of these evaluations found a significant impact on student achievement shows merely that if you do not implement a program, you are unlikely to get its benefits.

Of course, if an intervention is so cumbersome to implement that it is routinely implemented badly or implementation requires levels of teacher skill that are not commonly found, this would raise questions about the usefulness of the intervention, at least as a way of improving education at scale. On the other hand, if the intervention can be implemented faithfully and has the potential to substantially improve students' achievement, but the nature of the intervention is such that RCTs are difficult, or even impossible, to conduct, then given the substantial lifelong benefit of higher achievement (Crawford & Cribb, 2013), there would appear to be a clear moral imperative for researching education even when RCTs are not possible. As Robert Slavin (1987) once observed, "Do we really know nothing until we know everything?" (p. 347).

Finally, an RCT of an intervention might be successful because of the presence of factors that are not present in all educational settings, so generalizability to other settings would not be warranted. Yeast *causes* bread to rise, in the sense that removing the yeast would mean that the bread would not rise, but yeast only *causes* bread to rise in the presence of moisture and heat. In the examples of performance-related pay discussed in the previous chapter, financial incentives *caused* student achievement to improve but only because teachers were not turning up for work. Where teachers are already turning up for work, such an intervention would have no effect. Interventions don't work if they fix a problem that has already been fixed.

This suggests that even where RCTs can be conducted, for their results to be interpretable, they usually need to be accompanied by careful theorizations, which often benefit from careful qualitative observations of the phenomena under study. More developed theorizations of interventions also permit interventions to be optimized, by removing aspects of the intervention that prove to be unnecessary or less effective.

None of the foregoing is intended to suggest that RCTs are a bad idea. Rather, the discussion highlights that if we rely only on such experimental designs, we end up not being able to say very much, and even when we do conduct such experiments, they benefit from research designs that include complementary approaches to inquiry. As the physicist Arthur Eddington (1935/1959) said:

> But are we sure of our observational facts? Scientific men are rather fond
> of saying pontifically that one ought to be quite sure of one's observational
> facts before embarking on theory. Fortunately those who give this advice
> do not practice what they preach. Observation and theory get on best when
> they are mixed together, both helping one another in the pursuit of truth.
> It is a good rule not to put overmuch confidence in a theory until it has

been confirmed by observation. I hope I shall not shock the experimental physicists too much if I add that it is also a good rule not to put overmuch confidence in the observational results that are put forward *until they have been confirmed by theory.* (p. 211; italics in original)

From the viewpoint of systematic reviews of research, the user of research needs to be aware that relying only on RCTs has costs as well as benefits. By relying only on RCTs, we exclude evidence where RCTs are more difficult to conduct and those interventions where the nature of the intervention means that the data are clustered, and therefore, the studies are less likely to yield significant effects (see discussion of statistical power that follows). In particular, it is worth bearing in mind that, as noted previously, if we relied on RCTs as the only way of generating reliable knowledge, we would still not know whether smoking caused cancer.

Meta-Analysis

Once all the relevant studies have been identified, the next task is to find a way of synthesizing the findings from the various studies. As noted previously, traditionally, this has been done by a narrative review, but over the last fifty years, a statistical technique called "meta-analysis" has become increasingly common. Meta-analysis represents an important step forward in generating reliable syntheses of research studies, but in education, conducting meta-analyses and interpreting their results present particular difficulties that are not widely understood. This is the focus of this section of the chapter.

The term *meta-analysis* was first proposed by Gene Glass in his presidential address to the 1976 meeting of the American Educational Research Association. He defined the term as follows:

> Meta-analysis refers to the analysis of analyses. I use it to refer to the statistical analysis of a large collection of analysis results from individual studies for the purpose of integrating the findings. It connotes a rigorous alternative to the casual, narrative discussions of research studies which typify our attempts to make sense of the rapidly expanding research literature. (p. 3)

While there are slight differences in the way that different authors suggest meta-analyses should be conducted, there are a number of generally agreed-upon principles, many of which are common to all systematic reviews. First, the researchers define the research area they are attempting to summarize, such as whether placing students in different groups according to their achievement or ability increases student achievement. Second, the researchers formulate a search strategy. They decide whether to restrict their search to the use of online databases (and if so, which key words they use in their searches) or whether they will also conduct manual searches.

They decide whether to include only studies that appeared in peer-reviewed journals or cast the net more widely. Third, the researchers then formulate inclusion criteria, such as whether they would only include RCTs or whether they would also include studies with different kinds of design. The resulting set of studies is then regarded as the evidence base for the review—a summary of what is known, at least within the limitations of the search strategy and inclusion criteria, about the issue in question.

It is important to note that the process of meta-analysis is not entirely objective. Different researchers might make different decisions about the search strategy or the inclusion criteria, so that different researchers might reasonably end up with different conclusions. One of the key principles in meta-analysis, however, is that the process is transparent so that the reader can see exactly which subjective decisions were taken— something that is rarely available in a narrative review.

As noted previously, not all systematic reviews restrict themselves to quantitative studies, but this is required for meta-analysis, and then all the findings of the different studies are converted to a standard format so that they can be compared. For example, if we collected research studies on grouping students by ability for mathematics instruction in high schools, one study might report the impact of ability-grouping policies on SAT scores, another might report impact on ACT scores, and another might report scores on the AP examinations. If we found that the average scores were one point higher in the schools where the policy was implemented, then that would be a small and perhaps even negligible effect if the measure was SAT scores (which range from 200 to 800), an important effect if the measure was an ACT score (which range from 1 to 36), and an implausibly large effect for AP (where the scores range from just 1 to 5).

To make outcome measures from different studies comparable, researchers standardize their results. There are several ways this could be done, but the most common method is to find the difference in the measure of the outcome of interest between the experimental group and the control group and then to divide that by a measure of how spread out the data are. The range in the data (i.e., the difference between the largest score and the smallest score) is not a particularly useful measure of spread in data, because changes at the extremes (e.g., one particularly high-achieving student turning up at school or not) can have a big effect on the range. That is why researchers in education and psychology tend to use the standard deviation, which is a measure of how far, on average, the data in the set are from the mean. Formally, the *standardized effect size* proposed by Jacob Cohen (1969) and often called "Cohen's *d*," is defined as:

$$\frac{\text{experimental group mean} - \text{control group mean}}{\text{standard deviation}}$$

Ideally, we would use the standard deviation of the whole population from which the control group and the experimental group are drawn, but of course we don't usually know that, so researchers use the standard deviation of both the control group and the experimental group pooled together, or just the control group, whichever the researchers believe will give the best estimate of the population standard deviation. For example, if we wanted to evaluate the impact of a test preparation program on SAT scores, we might randomly select some students to receive the test preparation program and compare their performance on the SAT with those who had not received the program. The mean score of the 1,664,479 test takers who took the SAT in 2012 was 496 in Critical Reading and 514 in Mathematics, with standard deviations of 114 and 117, respectively (College Board, 2012). If we found that the mean performance in Critical Reading of the students who had taken the test preparation program was 525, then the effect size for the test preparation program on Critical Reading would be:

$$\frac{525 - 496}{114} = 0.25$$

Similarly, if the mean performance in Mathematics of the students who had taken the test preparation program was 530, then the effect size for the test preparation program on Mathematics would be:

$$\frac{530 - 514}{117} = 0.14$$

It therefore appears that in this hypothetical situation, the test preparation program was more effective in improving Critical Reading scores than Mathematics scores, although whether the difference is large enough to be taken seriously (i.e., whether it is statistically significant) would depend on the number of students in the experimental group.

One problem with the standardized effect size is that it is not particularly intuitive. It is not obvious how to interpret the values in the example above. Are 0.25 and 0.14 large or small effects? One way to think about the meaning of an effect size is in terms of the difference an effect of a given magnitude would have on the rank order of individuals in a group. In chapter 2, for example, there were a number of discussions of teacher effectiveness. A professional development program that improved an average teacher (i.e., one at the 50th percentile) up to the top one-third of teacher effectiveness (i.e., one at the 86th percentile) would have an effect size of approximately 1.

Jacob Cohen is frequently cited as suggesting that effect sizes below 0.3 should be regarded as small, those from 0.4 to 0.7 as medium, and those over 0.8 as large. This is not, in fact, what he said. The book in which these labels appeared was concerned with how to make estimates of the statistical power of a proposed experiment (see discussion on statistical power that follows). To make an estimate of the power of an experiment (i.e., the chance of the experiment actually yielding a statistically significant result if the effect exists), it is necessary to specify the size of the effect that is expected, and Cohen (1988) was offering advice about what values of d to use in the calculations: "Thus, if the investigator thinks that the effect of his treatment method . . . is small, he might posit a d value such as 0.2 or 0.3. If he anticipates it to be large, he might posit d as 0.8 or 1.0. If he expects it to be medium (or simply seeks to straddle the fence on the issue), he might select some such value as $d = 0.5$" (p. 25).

Moreover, Cohen (1988) was aware that there was "a certain risk inherent in offering conventional operational definitions for these terms" (p. 25), but he thought the risk was justified because "more is to be gained than lost by supplying a common conventional frame of reference which is recommended for use only when no better basis for estimating the ES [effect size] index is available" (p. 25). He pointed out, "The terms 'small,' 'medium,' and 'large' are relative, not only to each other, but to the area of behavioral science or even more particularly to the specific content and research method being employed in any given investigation" (p. 25). In other words, Cohen understood that effect sizes could not be compared without taking into account the different contexts involved. It is also important to note that the importance of an effect size will depend on the costs associated with the intervention. For example, in the READY4K! program, parents of preschool children were sent text messages reminding them to engage in preliteracy activities with their children. The effect size of the intervention on children's literacy was around 0.3 (York & Loeb, 2014), which as we shall see later, for children of this age, represents something like a 20 percent increase in the rate of learning. Whether one regards this as a small, medium, or large effect size is almost irrelevant when one considers that the program costs only a few dollars per child.

Unfortunately, these days, very few people have actually taken the time to read what Cohen said and routinely label effect sizes as either small, medium, or large based simply on the magnitude of the effect size—a practice that Russell Lenth (2006) derided as "T-shirt effect sizes" (i.e., small, medium, and large). In a report for the US Department of Education, Lipsey et al. (2012) wrote:

> In short, comparisons of effect sizes in educational research with normative distributions of effect sizes to assess whether they are small, middling, or large relative to those norms should use appropriate norms. Appropriate norms are those based on distributions of effect sizes for comparable outcome measures from comparable interventions targeted on comparable samples. Characterizing the magnitude of effect sizes relative to some other

normative distribution is inappropriate and potentially misleading. The widespread indiscriminate use of Cohen's generic small, medium, and large effect size values to characterize effect sizes in domains to which his normative values do not apply is thus likewise inappropriate and misleading. (p. 4)

The big takeaway message here is that a report that labels effect sizes as small, medium, or large based solely on the magnitude of the effect size should be treated with deep skepticism and provides at least a prima facie case that the authors do not know what they are talking about.

The difficulty of interpreting standardized effect sizes led McGraw and Wong (1992) to propose a common language effect size, which was used (incorrectly) by John Hattie in his book *Visible Learning* (2008). The idea of the common language effect size is to present the difference between two groups in terms of the chance that a member of one group has an outcome greater than or equal to the mean of the other group. The example McGraw and Wong give in their original paper is that of the heights of young adults.

They begin by citing data that show that in 1987, the average height of young men in the United States was 69.7 inches and, for women, 64.3 inches, with standard deviations of 2.8 and 2.6 inches, respectively. From these data, assuming that heights of males and females are normally distributed, it is possible, using statistical tables, to calculate that the probability of a randomly selected male being taller than a randomly selected female is 0.92. Or, as they put it, "in 92 out of 100 blind dates among young adults, the male will be taller than the female" (McGraw & Wong, 1992, p. 361).

However, despite its ease of interpretation, the common language effect size—and indeed a whole range of other suggestions about how to report effect sizes—has not caught on, and the standardized effect size proposed by Cohen, for all its problems, is still the most commonly used type of effect size in meta-analysis. More serious, there are a number of issues with the use of effect sizes in education that are important to understand to be able to know what the results of meta-analyses are really saying.

Before I get into some of the problems of using standardized effect sizes in education, I want to emphasize that the standardized effect size is a huge improvement on previous ways of reporting the outcomes of educational experiments. Historically, the results of experiments were reported using probability values, or p values, based on the idea of null-hypothesis significance testing. The idea of null-hypothesis significance testing is that one assumes that one's experiment hasn't worked (that's the null hypothesis), so that the means of the experimental and control group are, in reality, identical. One then calculates how likely one was to get the results that were actually observed, and if the probability of this is very low (conventionally, the threshold is taken as 5 percent), then one concludes that the null hypothesis is incorrect and that the means of the experimental and control group are, in fact, different. So when researchers say that a new reading program has a significant impact on student achievement, all they are really saying is that it is unlikely that the impact on student achievement is exactly zero. Null-hypothesis significance testing just asks the question, "How likely is it that there is absolutely no effect?" So if the improvement in student achievement is statistically significant, all you know is that there is likely to be some effect, but the effect could be so small that it is hardly worth noting.

As an extreme example, Lavy, Ebenstein, and Roth (2014) explored the impact of levels of air pollution on student achievement in the Bagrut examination, taken by Israeli students toward the end of high school and used in selecting students for entry into elite universities. They found that a rise in the level of fine particulate matter known as $PM_{2.5}$ (particles smaller than 2.5 micrometers, or one-thirtieth the diameter of a human hair) of five units (typically the difference between air quality in the suburbs and a city center) was associated with a decline in a student's score of 0.023 percent. Put another way, one in every forty-three students would have their score go down by 1 percent if they took their examination in the city center rather than in the suburbs. The researchers tried to claim this was an important finding because the level of $PM_{2.5}$ can vary by as much as eighty units over a few days, but of course, it rarely does, and the chance of this happening on the days that the students are taking their examinations is very small.

In this study, a very small effect produced a statistically significant result because the data set was so large. The size of the data set means that we can be pretty sure the effect is real (i.e., it's unlikely to be a statistical quirk), but that doesn't mean it is important. This is why reporting an effect size, showing the *size* of the difference, is much better, and many scientific journals in education and psychology have adopted policies of preferring effect sizes to probability values. Indeed, the American Educational Research Association—arguably the premier body for educational research in North America—now requires effect sizes to be reported and interpreted for every essential result in all of its journals (American Educational Research Association, 2006), although the compliance with this policy is still patchy (McMillan & Foley, 2006).

Problems With Effect Sizes

As mentioned above, meta-analysis typically involves taking the effect sizes found in a number of studies and combining them. There are a number of ways in which the effect sizes could be combined. They can be averaged, weighting the different effect sizes by the number of subjects in a study so that larger studies can be given more weight, or they can be combined using more sophisticated techniques (see Borenstein et al., 2011, for a readable and up-to-date account of the "state of the art"). However, in educational research, combining effect sizes in this way can result in seriously misleading conclusions, for a number of reasons. In particular, five issues have an important impact on meta-analyses in education: the intensity and duration of the intervention, the file-drawer problem, the age dependence of effect size, the sensitivity to instruction of outcome measures used, and the generalizability of the studies. Each of the issues will be discussed in turn.

The Intensity and Duration of the Intervention

The preceding definition of effect size, and indeed the kinds of effect sizes used by most researchers, is simply the measure of the size of the difference between those who received some intervention and those who did not. This is perfectly sensible. After all, this means that the effect size simply measures the size of the effect. But to have a fair comparison, we should make sure that we were comparing like with like. For example, in a systematic review of the effect of response to intervention (RTI) treatments on student achievement, Burns, Appleton, and Stehouwer (2005) found that even after removing outliers, the effect sizes ranged from 0.18 to 3.04, with a mean of 1.27 and a median of 1.02. However, we have no way of understanding what this means. Some of the approaches to RTI may have been of longer duration than others. If some of the studies were over two or three weeks, while others lasted a semester or more, then the effect sizes would have to be adjusted before meaningful comparisons could be made. Similarly, if some approaches to RTI involved moving at-risk students into groups of eight, and others placed students in groups of four, simply averaging the effect sizes makes little sense. Unless the intensity and the duration of the interventions are taken into account, it is impossible to make sense of the average effect size. Similarly, it makes no sense to average the effects of class-size reduction programs if some of them involve reducing class size by 10 percent and others involve reducing class size by 50 percent (and it is also important to take into account whether the class-size reduction program was accompanied by some training for the teachers in how to take advantage of the smaller classes).

The File-Drawer Problem

As noted above, to decide whether the result of an experiment is just a fluke or evidence of a real effect, we use null-hypothesis significance testing. First, we decide on our baseline assumption, which is typically that there really is no difference between the control group and the experimental group (this is the null hypothesis). We then decide what evidence we will accept as contradicting this. Typically, researchers set a level of 5 percent, so that if the probability that the difference that we actually observed between the two groups could have arisen by chance is greater than 5 percent, we conclude that we don't have enough evidence to reject the null hypothesis. However, if the probability that the difference that we see between the two groups is less than 5 percent, then we reject the idea that the two groups are the same and adopt the alternative, which is that the experimental group is different from the control group. Note that when we reject the null hypothesis, all we are saying is that the experimental group and the control group are unlikely to be identical.

This sounds straightforward enough, but the way that researchers ask their questions can have a substantial impact on the results they get. For example, an evaluation of the Alabama Mathematics, Science and Technology Initiative (AMSTI) investigated whether the program had a significant impact on student achievement in mathematics and science. They concluded that the program did have a significant impact on student achievement on standardized tests in mathematics but not science. However, had the researchers instead asked the question, "Does the program have a significant impact on student achievement?" and then asked "Is the impact different in mathematics and science?" they would have concluded the answer to the first question was "yes" and to the second was "no" (Newman et al., 2012). This apparently paradoxical result arose because the effect size in mathematics was very slightly larger than the effect size in science, and that small difference in effect size was enough to make the result for mathematics significant, while the result for science failed to reach statistical significance. There was no significant difference between the effectiveness of the program in mathematics and science, but the result that got published was that the program worked in math but not science.

When we use null-hypothesis significance testing, there are two main kinds of mistakes we can make. We can conclude that the means of the control and experimental groups are different when they are in fact the same, or we can decide that they are not different from each other when in fact they are. In one of the least helpful pieces of jargon in the field, researchers call these kinds of errors "Type I" and "Type II" errors, respectively, but it may be more helpful to think about these as false positives and false negatives (i.e., getting a significant result when we shouldn't and not getting a significant result when we should).

The probability of a false positive is the threshold we choose for deciding whether a result is significant. As noted above, this is typically 5 percent, but there is nothing magical about this number. Depending on the costs and benefits of false positives and false negatives, there might be good reason for choosing a higher or lower value. If 5 percent is the value chosen, then, once in every twenty experiments, we will conclude that the means of the control and the experimental groups are different, when they are in fact not—the difference arose entirely by chance. If we do just one test of significance on the data from an experiment, that might not be much of an issue, but if we do a number of tests of significance, the likelihood of a spurious result increases. (This idea is brilliantly captured in an XKCD cartoon by Randall Munroe, which you can view at https://xkcd.com/882/.)

Now, obviously, conducting multiple tests of significance on the same set of data is bad scientific practice (what Ronald Coase described as "torturing the data until it confesses" [Tullock, 2001, p. 205]), and there are ways of setting a higher burden of proof, called Bonferroni adjustments, that researchers can use if they plan to conduct multiple significance tests. But these adjustments are not as commonly made as they should be. Indeed, there is now substantial evidence that rerunning analyses in different ways to get a p value below 5 percent to increase the chances of getting the study published (what Simonsohn, Nelson, and Simmons [2014] call "p-hacking") is a substantial issue in both medicine (Ioannidis, 2011) and social science (Simonsohn et al., 2014). So much so, in fact, that one of the leading researchers in this area went as far as to claim that most published research findings are false (Ioannidis, 2005). A particularly amusing example is provided by Bennett, Baird, Miller, and Wolford (2014), who show how failure to correct for multiple significance tests in fMRI scanning of a dead Atlantic salmon generated results that showed clusters of activity in the brain cavity and the spinal column.

So, published studies may not accurately reflect the truth about the effectiveness of the interventions on which they report for a number of reasons but most notably because of the failure to deal appropriately with clustering in the data and the failure to make Bonferroni adjustments when carrying out multiple tests of significance.

These problems are serious, in that they distort the published findings, but can be addressed by better training of researchers and more consistent application of agreed-upon policies by journal editors.

However, there is another problem that is not so easily addressed, which is caused by the fact that it is impossible for a researcher to know how many other people have undertaken the same experiment they are conducting or, in the case of secondary analysis of existing data, how many others have conducted statistical tests on the data they are analyzing. This is the file-drawer problem (Rosenthal, 1979). We simply cannot be sure how many experiments were conducted but failed to yield significant results and, as a result, have not been published and are instead buried away in researchers' file drawers.

Over the years, researchers have attempted to explore whether the file-drawer problem does, in fact, substantially skew the research that is published. In recent years, the evidence is that the file-drawer problem is a substantial issue in both medicine (Goldacre, 2012) and social sciences (Franco, Malhotra, & Simonovits, 2014), although it is not always present (Dalton, Aguinis, Dalton, Bosco, & Pierce, 2012). The reason we should care about this is that the larger the effect size we actually get in any particular experiment, the more likely it is to produce a statistically significant result, and the more likely we are to be able to get our study published. We do not have good figures for education and psychology, but one study of 198 clinical trials in medicine found that studies that produced a statistically significant result were more than twelve times as likely to get published as those that produced results that were not statistically significant (Dickersin & Min, 1993).

So the crucial question is, "How likely are we to get a significant result when we carry out a study?" This is called the *statistical power* of the study. Formally, the statistical power of an experiment is the probability that the experiment will produce a statistically significant result if the effect is as big as the researchers believe it to be. Statistical power is increased

- When we have a larger effect (because there is a greater difference in achievement between the experimental and the control groups)

- When we have more participants in our study (because then it becomes less and less likely that our result is a fluke)

- When we set a less demanding threshold for statistical significance, such as 10 percent rather than the conventional 5 percent (because then we are less likely to regard a particular result as chance variation and take it as evidence that there is a real difference between the experimental and control groups)

Funding agencies worry a lot about statistical power because they don't want to fund a study that has very little chance of producing a statistically significant result even if things go to plan. Although there is no hard and fast rule, most funding agencies would want an experiment to have a power of 80 percent (Cohen, 1992)—in other words, if the effect being investigated is real, the experiment will have an 80 percent chance of producing a statistically significant result.

However, the evidence is that the statistical power of most studies in education and psychology is rarely as high as 40 percent (Sedlmeier & Gigerenzer, 1989), and a recent investigation estimated the typical statistical power of studies in neuroscience at just 20 percent (Button et al., 2013). What this means is that only 40 percent of experiments in education and psychology and only 20 percent of experiments in neuroscience are likely to produce statistically significant findings.

To take one specific example, an analysis of 627 studies that compared the performance of a group receiving simulation-based education for health professionals with those not receiving the intervention found that only 136 studies (22 percent) had an 80 percent chance to detect an effect of 0.8, and only two studies (0.3 percent) had an 80 percent chance to detect an effect size of 0.2 (Cook & Hatala, 2014). Because most effect sizes in education are closer to 0.2 than 0.8 (see the following), it is clear that most educational experiments are extremely underpowered.

The reason this is important for an understanding of meta-analysis is that when studies are underpowered, only the studies that are, by chance, at the upper end of the true range of effect size get published. To see how this affects the effect sizes reported in meta-analyses, for the sake of illustration, consider an intervention such as cooperative learning (Johnson & Johnson, 2009; Slavin, Hurley, & Chamberlain, 2003). In some contexts, it may work well, and in others it may work less well, so there will be a range of effects, but for the sake of the discussion, let's assume that the average effect size of cooperative learning is 0.4 but that the actual effect sizes in different contexts with different groups of students range from 0.0 to 0.8 (for the technically minded, we are assuming that the standard deviation of the effect sizes is 0.2). Now, by definition, the true average effect size of studies in this case is 0.4, but if the studies have low statistical power, then those studies that, by chance, have an effect size toward the upper end of the range are more likely to be significant and therefore more likely to get reported. Table 3.1 presents the results of a simulation showing how the statistical power of studies influences the average effect size of those that get significant results. So, for example, if the average power of a set of studies of cooperative learning is 40 percent, then the actual average of all the studies that generate significant results is 0.59 even though the true effect size of this intervention is 0.4. The results that we see in the meta-analysis are from a biased subset of all those studies that were actually carried out—the ones that were lucky. The others are in the file drawer.

Table 3.1. Relationship Between Statistical Power and the Average Effect Size of Statistically Significant Studies

Average Statistical Power of Experiments	Average Effect Size of Significant Studies
100%	0.40
80%	0.47
60%	0.53
40%	0.59
20%	0.68

In response to this, researchers have developed a number of very powerful techniques, such as funnel plots (Light & Pillemer, 1984), for detecting whether the studies included in a meta-analysis suffer from the file-drawer problem. More important, there are also techniques that allow researchers to make appropriate corrections to the effect size if the funnel plots show that the file-drawer problem is significant

(Borenstein et al., 2011). However, these techniques are rarely used by those conducting meta-analyses in education.

The conclusion here is clear. Because the vast majority of educational experiments are severely underpowered, only those studies that happen to generate results toward the upper end of the true range of possible outcomes will generate statistically significant results. Since studies generating statistically significant results are far more likely to get published, the studies that are published are likely to considerably overstate the true effect sizes of the interventions being investigated. Moreover, the available evidence suggests that this inflation of effect sizes is not merely a theoretical possibility; it is a real, and substantial, effect, so that the published studies considerably overstate the likely impact of the interventions being investigated when they are implemented in real situations.

The Age Dependence of Effect Size

As noted earlier, the formula for the standardized effect size in an experiment is just the difference between the means of the experimental group and the control group, divided by the standard deviation of the population. This sounds straightforward enough, but the situation is complicated by the fact that the standard deviation of achievement of older students tends to be greater than that for younger students.

One of the first to document this was Lambert Adolphe Jacques Quetelet, who in 1835 published a book titled *Sur l'homme et le developpement de ses facultés, essai d'une physique sociale* (On man, and the development of his faculties, an essay on social physics). He pointed out that as children got older, as well as growing in height, they also became more diverse. This is intuitively obvious. It is not unusual to find two eighteen-year-olds where one is twelve inches taller than the other. It is very unusual to find two seven-year-olds where one is twelve inches taller than the other.

For educational achievement, there are ways of measuring it on a grade-by-grade basis that can sometimes remove this effect, but generally, when we look at the same measures of achievement over time, as children get older, the spread—and specifically, the standard deviation—of achievement increases (Wiliam, 1992). This is important because when we do a standardized effect size calculation for older students, we are dividing by a larger number, and so the effect size, for a given difference between experimental and control groups means, is smaller.

To investigate this more carefully, Bloom, Hill, Black, and Lipsey (2008) looked at the annual progress made by students as measured by a number of standardized tests: the California Achievement Test, 5th edition (1991 norming sample); the Stanford Achievement Test, 9th and 10th editions (1995 and 2002 norming samples, respectively); the TerraNova Comprehensive Test of Basic Skills (1996 norming sample);

the TerraNova CAT (1999–2000 norming sample); the Gates-MacGinitie Reading Test (1998–1999 norming sample); and the Metropolitan Achievement Test (1999–2000 norming sample).

For each test, they looked at the differences in scores achieved by students from one year to the next and then divided by the pooled standard deviation. In other words, they calculated a standardized effect size for one year's regular instruction, with the end-of-year score as the experimental group mean and the beginning-of-year score as the control group mean. The results are shown in Figure 3.1 (Bloom et al., 2008).

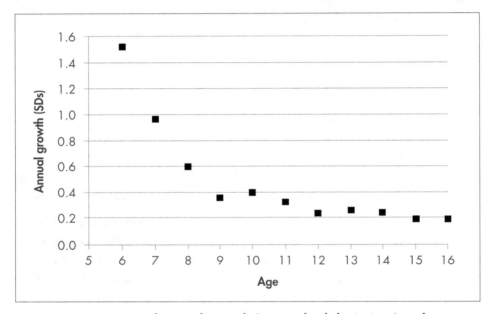

Figure 3.1. Variation of annual growth (in standard deviations) and age.

As can be seen, one year's growth is equivalent to an effect size of around 1.5 standard deviations for six-year-olds but around 0.2 standard deviations for twelve-year-olds. This is largely because, for older students, we are dividing the difference between what students knew at the beginning and the end of the year by a larger number, so we get a smaller result.

What this means is that an intervention that increased the rate of student learning by 50 percent would yield an effect size of around 0.75 for six-year-olds but an effect size of only 0.1 for twelve-year-olds. Now in response to this, advocates of meta-analysis have claimed that such differences average out across different experiments, but this argument is hard to sustain.

Some interventions are much more common with younger students, and others are more common with older students; therefore, when different kinds of interventions are ranked by their impact on learning, to produce a "league table" of educational interventions (as follows), the kinds of intervention that are more common with younger children are given greater emphasis than those that are more common with older children.

Now this is not a criticism of meta-analysis, as such, because it is relatively straight-forward to control for age effects in the way that the meta-analysis is conducted (Borenstein et al., 2011). However, the most commonly cited meta-analyses in education (e.g., Hattie, 2008; Marzano, 2003) have not even investigated, let alone controlled for, age in this way. As a result, the findings are difficult, if not impossible, to interpret.

It is also worth noting that the same problem affects experiments that are conducted on special populations, such as gifted students or students with special educational needs. When the group under study does not represent the full range of achievement of the population, then the denominator in the effect-size calculation (i.e., the standard deviation of the sample) is smaller, so the effect size is increased. This may partially explain why some educational interventions appear to be more effective for students with special educational needs.

The Sensitivity to Instruction of Outcome Measures Used

As noted earlier in this chapter, systematic reviews and the use of meta-analysis in particular have greatly improved the way in which research evidence is cumulated across different research sites. One reason that this has been so successful in medicine is that typically the outcome measure used is the same in the different studies. In the example of the use of antiarrhythmic drugs after heart attacks, the outcome measure was whether the patient died or not. Now of course, this is not always the case in medical research. If the outcome measure for an experiment with a less invasive form of surgery was time from treatment to discharge, different hospital policies might mean that this outcome measure had a slightly different meaning from one study to another. In an experiment on the use of a vaccine to treat influenza once symptoms had appeared, using time to recovery as an outcome measure would introduce a degree of subjectivity because understanding the results would require understanding what patients were told about what was meant by "recovery." Nevertheless, in medi-cine, the outcome measures used in different studies are relatively similar in different studies of the same intervention. This is not generally true in education.

For example, if we wanted to undertake a meta-analysis on the effects of cooper-ative learning in mathematics, even if we could agree on what counted as a study of cooperative learning in mathematics, comparing the results of different studies would be complicated by the fact that different studies use different outcome measures. One might use teacher-assigned grades, one might use state test scores, one might use a commercially produced standardized test, and another might use an assessment developed by the researchers themselves. To combine the results from different studies meaningfully, we need to assume that the intervention (e.g., cooperative learning) has the same impact on all of the different measures of mathematics achievement. The available evidence suggests that this is not a reasonable assumption.

For a start, the standard process of test construction tends to produce tests that do not measure what it is that students are learning. This sounds absurd, but it is quite true. To see why, imagine we are designing a mathematics test that is intended to be administered toward the end of seventh grade as a measure of how much students have learned during the year. Consider what would happen to an item that is answered incorrectly by all students at the beginning of seventh grade and is answered correctly by all students at the end of seventh grade. This item is clearly measuring something that students are learning in seventh grade, and yet it would not be included in a seventh-grade test. This is because test manufacturers want to maximize the reliability of their tests, and the reliability of a test is a kind of signal-to-noise ratio for a test (or more precisely, a signal-to-signal-plus-noise ratio). The reliability can therefore be increased by reducing the noise, *or by increasing the signal*. In other words, the more the test spreads out student scores, the more reliable the test will appear to be. Items that no students answer correctly or ones that all students answer correctly do not spread the students out, and so will not be included in the test, even though they are clearly measuring something that students are learning in seventh grade.

Perhaps even more strangely, replacing an item that all students get correct, or one that no students get correct, with one of average difficulty, even if it relates to something that is not in the seventh-grade standards, will increase the reliability of a seventh-grade test. For example, if we added to the test an item taken from an IQ test that was answered correctly, both at the beginning and at the end of seventh grade, by 50 percent of seventh-grade students, it would increase the reliability of the test because it would spread out the scores of the students to a greater extent than a question that nobody, or everybody, got correct.

The result is that many standardized tests are insensitive to instruction, in that they do not distinguish between students who have been well taught and those who have been poorly taught. The process of standardized test development leads to selecting items that maximize the differences between students, even if these differences are caused by socioeconomic status rather than differences in the knowledge that the tests are intended to assess (Popham, 2001).

In large part, this is why experiments in which student achievement is measured with teacher- or researcher-produced tests tend to show larger effect sizes than those that use standardized tests. It is not because teacher- and researcher-constructed measures are less valid. It is that they have not been through a process that reduces their sensitivity to what is being taught (Wiliam, 2008).

It is also important to realize that the impact of these issues on the effect sizes of studies included in meta-analyses is far from trivial. Benjamin Bloom and his colleagues (1984) argued that students learning from one-to-one tutorial instruction would make two standard deviations more progress than those learning from traditional group-based instruction. This claim might be credible for some kinds of assessments, but it is clearly ridiculous for others. For example, in the tests used for the National Assessment of Educational Progress (NAEP), one year's progress for an average fourth grader is equivalent to one-fourth of a standard deviation (National Assessment of Educational Progress, 2006). If one-to-one tutorial instruction is really two standard deviations more effective than group instruction, then students receiving one-to-one tutorial instruction would learn in one year what students receiving group instruction would take nine years to learn—clearly a nonsensical claim.

The important point here is that the outcome measures used in different studies differ significantly in their sensitivity to instruction. Ruiz-Primo, Shavelson, Hamilton, and Klein (2002) suggested a typology of assessments with five levels of distance from the actual curriculum students experienced:

1. *Immediate* (science journals, notebooks, and classroom tests)
2. *Close* (formal embedded assessments)
3. *Proximal* (a different assessment of the same concept, requiring some transfer)
4. *Distal* (large-scale assessment from state assessment framework)
5. *Remote* (standardized national achievement tests)

As would be expected, they found that the closer the measure was to the curriculum, the greater the sensitivity of the assessment was to the effects of instruction. What was surprising, however, was the magnitude of the variation. For example, one collection of interventions studied by Ruiz-Primo et al. (2002) showed an average effect size of 0.26 when measured with a proximal assessment, but an average effect size of 1.26 when outcomes were measured with close assessments. A meta-analysis of interventions that are evaluated with assessments that are close to the enactment of curriculum would, in this case, have produced effect sizes five times as great as a meta-analyses of interventions that are evaluated with assessments that are distal or remote from the curriculum.

Now of course, experts in meta-analysis will point out that this technique can handle all these problems, and this is perfectly correct. If all the studies in a meta-analysis were tagged as using either immediate, close, proximal, distal, or remote outcome measures, then the meta-analysis could identify whether the different kinds of measures did indeed produce different effect sizes (what is called looking for moderators of effect in meta-analysis). However, most of those who conduct meta-analyses are not aware of these issues and therefore have not thought to take the sensitivity of the measures to the effects of instruction into account. Moreover, even if researchers were aware of the importance of these issues, many of the studies identified for inclusion in meta-analyses are not reported in sufficient enough detail to allow the measures used in the study to be classified in terms of their sensitivity to instruction. The result is that the typical meta-analysis routinely includes studies with effect sizes that are not at all comparable, and what is worse, the researcher is not usually even aware that this is happening.

All these shortcomings would be bad enough, but there is a fifth problem with meta-analysis that renders the whole idea almost useless for education.

The Generalizability of the Studies

As has been mentioned several times already, the central idea of meta-analysis is that by systematically collecting together the research that has been done (and not just that which has been published), we get better estimates of the true impact of different interventions. This is better than just relying on published studies, but it is important to realize that the research that actually gets done is often a strange and quirky selection of the research that might get done. In particular, a significant proportion of published research on the efficacy of various approaches to teaching is conducted by psychology professors, on their own undergraduate students.

Li, Ruiz-Primo, Yin, Liaw, and Morozov (2013) conducted a review of over 9,000 published papers on the effectiveness of feedback in mathematics, science, and technology. After an initial review, a total of 238 studies were examined in detail, and of these, a total of 111 were identified as containing quantitative evidence of the impact of feedback on student achievement: sixty in mathematics, thirty-five in science, and sixteen in technology.

To avoid aggregating the results of theoretically incoherent studies (to avoid mixing up apples and oranges), Li et al. (2013) then analyzed the feedback studies in terms of nine main categories:

1. Who provided the feedback (teacher, peer, self, or technology)?
2. How was the feedback delivered (individual, small group, or whole class)?

3. What was the role of the student in the feedback (provider or receiver)?

4. What was the focus of the feedback (e.g., product, process, self-regulation for cognitive feedback or goal orientation, self-efficacy for affective feedback)?

5. On what was the feedback based (student product or process)?

6. What type of feedback was provided (evaluative, descriptive, or holistic)?

7. How was feedback provided or presented (in written, video, or oral form)?

8. What was the referent of feedback (self, others, or mastery criteria)?

9. How, and how often, was feedback given in the study (one time or multiple times; with or without pedagogical use)?

One surprising finding from this review was that in 80 percent of the studies retained (slightly more in mathematics, slightly fewer in science), feedback was a single event lasting just minutes, and fewer than one in six of the studies included multiple feedback episodes within a one-week instructional period.

Other surprising findings were that reliability estimates for the outcome measures were reported in fewer than half of the studies, and validity evidence was provided in only one-sixth of the studies. A summary of the main characteristics reviewed by Li et al. (2013) is shown in Table 3.2.

Table 3.2. Characteristics of Feedback in STEM Subjects

Study Characteristics	Mathematics	Science
Feedback treatment is a single event lasting minutes	85%	72%
Reliability of outcome measures	39%	63%
Validity of outcome measures	24%	3%
Dealing only or mainly with declarative knowledge	12%	36%
Schematic knowledge (e.g., knowing why)	9%	0%
Multiple feedback events in a week	14%	17%

Perhaps the most surprising feature was that in the vast majority of the studies, those given feedback were not told why they were being given feedback or given any time to use the feedback to improve their work. Here's what Li and colleagues said:

Another completely unexpected finding in our meta-analysis is that in most of the studies analyzed in science and mathematics we found no evidence of pedagogical advance or follow-up before or after the feedback episode. In these studies, the authors did not provide the receivers of the feedback with any background or introductions to orient them to the purpose of feedback, directions about how to interpret it, or descriptions about how the feedback information could be used to improve their performance. Similarly, in most studies, the teachers (or sometimes researchers) who implemented the feedback treatment—either in oral or written form—seldom took any instructional actions, such as allowing class time for students to read or respond to the feedback. The feedback treatment thus appeared as an add-on that did not fit into the flow of teaching and learning. This is completely in contrast to the assumption that a critical characteristic usually associated with feedback in formative assessment literature is the use of information for improvement in learning. Only four studies in science and none in mathematics were found with some type of subsequent instructional activity. (p. 218)

Now this is not intended to disparage the work being doing in researching the effects of feedback in STEM education. This kind of careful, laboratory-based research is essential in isolating variables in order to understand the underlying processes. However, it is far from obvious that the findings from the studies reviewed by Li et al. (2013) can be expected to generalize to K–12 classrooms, where students get feedback many times per week, where students are generally told why they are being given feedback, where students are given time to use the feedback to improve their work, and where teachers develop long-term relationships with their students.

From the foregoing arguments, it should be clear that meta-analysis has an important role to play in many fields, particularly medicine, in ensuring that research findings are synthesized as soon as possible. In time, as better theorizations of the work being done become available (as in the work of Ruiz-Primo et al. discussed previously), they may also be applied to education. However, right now, it is clear that in education, meta-analysis is simply incapable of yielding meaningful findings that leaders can use to direct the activities of the teachers they lead. They may identify some avenues as being more likely to be fruitful than others, but without the careful theoretical work, such as that being done by Li et al., the results of meta-analyses will be at best meaningless and at worst misleading.

Concrete evidence of this is easy to find. In his book *Visible Learning*, Hattie (2008) synthesized the results of over 800 meta-analyses. One aspect of the book that has attracted particular attention from teachers is a table of the impact of 138 different kinds of interventions, together with their effect sizes. The ten interventions with the largest effect sizes are shown in Table 3.3.

Table 3.3. Interventions Ranked by Impact

Rank	Influence	Effect Size
1	Self-report grades	1.44
2	Piagetian programs	1.28
3	Providing formative evaluation	0.90
4	Microteaching	0.88
5	Acceleration	0.88
6	Classroom behavioral	0.80
7	Comprehensive interventions for learning-disabled students	0.77
8	Teacher clarity	0.75
9	Reciprocal teaching	0.74
10	Feedback	0.73

From the foregoing analysis, it should be clear that what these results might mean in practice is far from clear. Recall that Figure 3.1 shows that for students between nine and eleven years of age, one year's learning is 0.4 standard deviations. The idea that in one year, students compiling self-report grades would make 4.6 years of progress ($1.44 \div 0.4 + 1$) is clearly absurd. Such an effect size might be more plausible in the context of children in kindergarten, but the idea that kindergarten students are able to do this in a meaningful way also strains the bounds of credulity.

To counter this, some have argued that even if the actual magnitudes of the effect sizes are not correct, then the rank order of interventions in Table 3.3 is probably correct. But for this to be the case, we would have to assume that for each of these interventions, the age of the students studied, the sensitivity of the outcome measures used to the effects of instruction, and indeed, the nature of the interventions themselves were similar across the different interventions or that the differences that do exist happen, by chance, to cancel each other out.

To conclude, right now, meta-analysis is simply not a suitable technique for summarizing the relative effectiveness of different approaches to improving student learning, and any leader who relies on meta-analysis to determine priorities for the development of the teachers they lead is likely to spend a great deal of time helping their teachers improve aspects of practice that do not benefit students. For the time being, and for the foreseeable future, leaders would be far better advised to look at best evidence reviews of research—reviews that take into account the quality of studies, the relevance of the findings to the particular age group being taught, and the contexts in which the teachers and students operate (Slavin, 1986).

Conclusion

This chapter has explored how we might use evidence from educational research to help focus the development of teachers on aspects of their practice that will have the greatest impact on their students. Research will never tell teachers what to do, but it can help them direct their efforts more effectively. Some popular ideas, such as Brain Gym, are unlikely ever to be useful to teachers. For others, such as learning styles, the evidence we have right now does not indicate that these will be useful, but it is always possible that new approaches will be more successful. Other approaches, such as lesson study, look promising, but there is little evidence that they are successful, and more important, we don't know which particular approaches will be most effective. Finally, there are those approaches, such as educational neuroscience, that will almost certainly be hugely important in the future, but currently, are simply not ready for prime time. Right now, for the sake of our students, we need to make the best use of what we already know.

In many fields, the best way to do this is through the use of systematic reviews and particularly through the use of meta-analysis. However, in this chapter, I have discussed five issues that make meta-analysis difficult, if not impossible, to use well in education. We need to control for the intensity and duration of the intervention, which is often hard to do because the research is not reported in sufficient detail, many studies produce insignificant effects and therefore remain in the researcher's file drawer, few meta-analyses take into account that the standardized effect size depends on the age of participants in studies and that the outcome measures differ in their sensitivity to instruction, and finally, studies conducted in laboratories may not generalize to classrooms. If we want to focus teacher improvement on the things that will have the greatest impact on our students' learning, we need to look at research in a more nuanced way. When we do that, we find that the research evidence suggests that the best way to improve student achievement is through greater use of classroom formative assessment, the focus of the next chapter.

[*Chapter 4*]

Formative Assessment

The relationship between instruction and what is learned as a result is complex. Even when instruction is well designed and students are motivated, increases in student capabilities are, in general, impossible to predict with any certainty. Moreover, this observation does not depend on any particular view of what happens when learning takes place.

For most of the last two thousand years, the dominant view about what happens when learning takes place was that associations were made between mental states. Learning was characterized by links between particular stimuli and particular responses. Because it is impossible to predict in advance how much practice will be required before the associations are established, determining what has been learned and then taking appropriate remedial action is essential. Within this view of learning, when students fail to learn, it indicates that the links between the stimuli and the desired responses are not strong enough, and they need to be reinforced through further practice.

While this view of learning is often disparaged as old-fashioned today, it does explain some aspects of learning, such as learning multiplication facts, quite well. That said, there are many aspects of learning that such a view cannot explain. In such an "associationist" view of learning, student errors are random. However, in the second half of the 20th century, there was increasing evidence that in many areas of learning, particularly in mathematics and science, student errors were far from random.

For example, when children between the ages of four and seven are asked, "What causes the wind?" a common response is, "Trees." Now, this is not the result of misremembering what they have been taught, nor is it the result of poor-quality elementary science instruction. It is the result of students constructing a model of how the world works on the basis of their experiences. This idea that learning is an active, constructive process is sometimes called "constructivism." The important thing about constructivism is that it is a view about what happens when learning takes place, rather than a specific approach to teaching. It means not assuming that a student is a blank slate but accepting that the student will already have ideas about things on which, as yet, he or she has had no formal instruction. In particular, it means finding out what students already know or believe about something before trying to teach them anything else that builds on that knowledge.

Other perspectives on learning focus on the fact that what gets learned is strongly tied to the context of the learning—that learning is situated. For many years, psychologists studied this as a problem (and specifically, a failure) of transfer—in other words, how much of the learning that happens in one context can transfer to another? However in recent years, situated approaches to studying learning have looked at the features that are present in the learning environment and to which the learner becomes accustomed, so that the learner is less likely to be able to demonstrate the same capabilities when those features are not present.

The important point here is that the idea that we need to review what our students have learned regularly and frequently is independent of any particular view of what happens when learning takes place. Whatever one's beliefs about what happens when learning takes place, the empirical evidence is that students do not necessarily—or even generally—learn exactly what they are taught and that, to be effective, teachers have to find out what their students did actually learn before moving on.

A second important point about the idea that what students learn is not generally predictable is that this does not depend on what it is that students are meant to be learning. For example, if being good at history is thought of as being more knowledgeable about facts and dates, then the teacher needs to establish which facts and dates have been learned and which have not. If, on the other hand, progress in history is defined as being able to construct historical arguments with an understanding of chronology, cause and effect, and the role of evidence, then different assessments would be used. Different views about the nature of a subject will result in different ways of finding out what students have learned, but the principle that we need to find out what students have learned before moving on is applicable to any learning.

Of course, the idea that effective instruction requires frequent checks for understanding has been around for a very long time, but about fifty years ago, a number of researchers and writers involved in education began to think of this process of checking for understanding explicitly as a form of assessment. This has a downside, in that whenever people hear the word *assessment*, they think of the formal mechanisms for determining what students know, such as quizzes, tests, and examinations, rather than more immediate but less easily interpreted sources of evidence, such as student facial expressions. However, it also represents an important advance because thinking about checking for understanding explicitly as an assessment process focuses on the quality of the evidence that teachers have for the instructional decisions they need to make.

Moreover, the practice of many, if not most, teachers is relatively underdeveloped in terms of eliciting and making use of evidence about student achievement. Teachers' instructional decisions are often based on evidence that is not representative of the learning needs of the group as a whole. In that sense, developing the ways that teachers check for understanding represents some of the lowest-hanging fruit in improving the quality of instruction. As David Ausubel (1968) remarked years ago:

> If I had to reduce all of educational psychology to just one principle, I would say this: The most important single factor influencing learning is what the learner already knows. Ascertain this and teach him accordingly. (p. vi)

The remainder of this chapter looks at the development of thinking about checking for understanding as a process of assessment. As is common in much of educational research, and as we saw in chapter 2, sometimes the same ideas are described with different terms, and sometimes the same term is used to describe very different ideas, so the assumptions underlying different approaches are examined and related to the evidence about the impact on student achievement. In the final part of the chapter, I show how formative assessment can be used as a unifying framework to draw together a number of other important current ideas in education, such as differentiated instruction and response to intervention. I will also show how classroom formative assessment can be used to highlight the particular aspects of generic teacher evaluation frameworks, such as Danielson's Framework for Teaching, that will have the greatest impact on student achievement.

The Origins of Formative Assessment

It appears to be widely accepted that Michael Scriven (1967) was the first to use the term *formative* to describe evaluation processes that "have a role in the on-going improvement of the curriculum" (p. 41). He also pointed out that evaluation "may serve to enable administrators to decide whether the entire finished curriculum, refined by use of the evaluation process in its first role, represents a sufficiently significant advance on the available alternatives to justify the expense of adoption by a school system" (pp. 41–42), suggesting "the terms 'formative' and 'summative' evaluation to qualify evaluation in these roles" (p. 43).

Two years later, Benjamin Bloom (1969) applied the same distinction to classroom tests:

> Quite in contrast is the use of "formative evaluation" to provide feedback and correctives at each stage in the teaching-learning process. By formative evaluation we mean evaluation by brief tests used by teachers and students as aids in the learning process. While such tests may be graded and used as part of the judging and classificatory function of evaluation, we see much more effective use of formative evaluation if it is separated from the grading process and used primarily as an aid to teaching. (p. 48)

Benjamin Bloom and his colleagues continued to use the term *formative evaluation* in subsequent work, and the term *formative assessment* was routinely used in higher education in the United Kingdom to describe what we might call "any assessment before the big one." The term did not feature much as a focus for research or practice in the 1970s and early 1980s, and where it did, the terms *formative assessment* and *formative evaluation* generally referred to the use of formal assessment procedures, such as tests, for informing future instruction (e.g., Fuchs & Fuchs, 1986).

In a seminal paper titled "Formative Assessment and the Design of Instructional Systems," Royce Sadler (1989) argued that the term *formative assessment* should be intrinsic to, and integrated with, effective instruction:

> Formative assessment is concerned with how judgments about the quality of student responses (performances, pieces, or works) can be used to shape and improve the student's competence by short-circuiting the randomness and inefficiency of trial-and-error learning. (p. 120)

He also pointed out that effective use of formative assessment could not be the sole responsibility of the teacher, but also required changes in the roles of learners:

> The indispensable conditions for improvement are that the student comes to hold a concept of quality roughly similar to that held by the teacher, is able to monitor continuously the quality of what is being produced during the act of production itself, and has a repertoire of alternative moves or strategies from which to draw at any given point. In other words, students have to be able to judge the quality of what they are producing and be able to regulate what they are doing during the doing of it. (p. 121)

The need to broaden the conceptualization of formative assessment beyond formal assessment procedures was also emphasized by Torrance (1993):

> Research on assessment is in need of fundamental review. I am suggesting that one aspect of such a review should focus on formative assessment, that

it should draw on a much wider tradition of classroom interaction studies than has hitherto been acknowledged as relevant, and that it should attempt to provide a much firmer basis of evidence about the relationship of assessment to learning which can inform policy and practice over the long term. (p. 341)

It seems clear, therefore, that while the origins of the term *formative assessment* may have been in behaviorism and mastery learning for at least two decades, there has been increasing acceptance that an understanding of formative assessment as a process has to involve consideration of the respective roles of teachers and learners.

The Definition of Formative Assessment

In 1998, Paul Black and I (1998a) published a review of the research on the effects of classroom formative assessment, which was intended to update the earlier reviews undertaken by Natriello (1987) and Crooks (1988), mentioned in the previous chapter. To make the ideas in their review more accessible, we produced a paper for teachers and policy makers that drew out the implications of their findings for policy and practice (Black & Wiliam, 1998b). In this paper, we defined formative assessment as follows:

> We use the general term assessment to refer to all those activities undertaken by teachers—and by their students in assessing themselves—that provide information to be used as feedback to modify teaching and learning activities. Such assessment becomes formative assessment when the evidence is actually used to adapt the teaching to meet student needs. (p. 140)

Some authors have sought to restrict the meaning of the term to situations where the changes to the instruction are relatively immediate:

- "The process used by teachers and students to recognise and respond to student learning in order to enhance that learning, during the learning" (Cowie & Bell, 1999, p. 32).

- "Assessment carried out during the instructional process for the purpose of improving teaching or learning" (Shepard et al., 2005, p. 275).

- "Formative assessment refers to frequent, interactive assessments of students' progress and understanding to identify learning needs and adjust teaching appropriately" (Looney, 2005, p. 21).

- "A formative assessment is a tool that teachers use to measure student grasp of specific topics and skills they are teaching. It's a 'midstream' tool to identify specific student misconceptions and mistakes while the material is being taught" (Kahl, 2005, p. 11).

The Assessment Reform Group—a group of scholars based in the United Kingdom and dedicated to ensuring that assessment policy and practice are informed by research evidence—acknowledged the power that assessment had to influence learning, both for good and for ill, and proposed seven precepts that summarized the characteristics of assessment that promotes learning (Broadfoot et al., 1999, p. 7):

1. It is embedded in a view of teaching and learning of which it is an essential part.

2. It involves sharing learning goals with pupils.

3. It aims to help pupils to know and to recognise the standards they are aiming for.

4. It involves pupils in self-assessment.

5. It provides feedback which leads to pupils recognising their next steps and how to take them.

6. It is underpinned by confidence that every student can improve.

7. It involves both teacher and pupils reviewing and reflecting on assessment data.

In looking for a term to describe such assessments, the group suggested that because of the variety of ways in which it was used, the term *formative assessment* was no longer helpful:

> The term "formative" itself is open to a variety of interpretations and often means no more than that assessment is carried out frequently and is planned at the same time as teaching. Such assessment does not necessarily have all the characteristics just identified as helping learning. It may be formative in helping the teacher to identify areas where more explanation or practice is needed. But for the pupils, the marks or remarks on their work may tell them about their success or failure but not about how to make progress towards further learning. (Broadfoot et al., 1999, p. 7)

Instead, they preferred the term *assessment for learning*, which they defined as "the process of seeking and interpreting evidence for use by learners and their teachers to decide where the learners are in their learning, where they need to go and how best to get there" (Broadfoot et al., 2002, pp. 2–3).

The earliest use of the term *assessment for learning* appears to be as the title of a chapter by Harry Black (1986). It was also the title of a paper given at AERA in 1992

(James, 1992), and three years later, was the title of a book by Ruth Sutton (1995). In the United States, the origin of the term is often mistakenly attributed to Rick Stiggins as a result of his popularization of the term (e.g., Stiggins, 2005), although Stiggins himself has always attributed the term to other authors.

Most recently, an international conference on assessment for learning in Dunedin, New Zealand, in 2009, building on work done at two earlier conferences in the United Kingdom (2001) and the United States (2005), adopted the following definition:

> Assessment for Learning is part of everyday practice by students, teachers and peers that seeks, reflects upon and responds to information from dialogue, demonstration and observation in ways that enhance ongoing learning. (Klenowski, 2009, p. 264)

The phrase *assessment for learning* has an undoubted appeal, especially when contrasted with assessment *of* learning, but as Bennett (2011) points out, replacing one term with another serves merely to move the definitional burden.

More important, as Paul Black and I and our colleagues have pointed out, the distinctions between assessment for learning and assessment of learning on the one hand, and between formative and summative assessment on the other, are different in kind. The former distinction relates to the purpose for which the assessment is carried out, while the second relates to the function it actually serves. We clarified the relationship between assessment for learning and formative assessment as follows:

> Assessment for learning is any assessment for which the first priority in its design and practice is to serve the purpose of promoting students' learning. It thus differs from assessment designed primarily to serve the purposes of accountability, or of ranking, or of certifying competence. An assessment activity can help learning if it provides information that teachers and their students can use as feedback in assessing themselves and one another and in modifying the teaching and learning activities in which they are engaged. Such assessment becomes "formative assessment" when the evidence is actually used to adapt the teaching work to meet learning needs. (Black, Harrison, Lee, Marshall, & Wiliam, 2004, p. 10)

Arguing about different definitions of formative assessment and assessment for learning may seem like the most self-indulgent of academic debates, but definitions are important. We cannot begin to assemble evidence about the impact of formative assessment on student achievement until we establish what, exactly, it is, and the range of practices that are described as formative assessment is indeed great. At one extreme, Leahy, Lyon, Thompson, and Wiliam (2005) emphasized formative assessment as an inherent part of effective instruction, with teachers using evidence from assessment to make instructional adjustments minute by minute and day by day. At the other extreme, many commercial test publishers have produced large collections of test items (often called "formative assessment item banks") that can be used to construct tests to gauge students' progress toward valued goals (Educational Testing Service, 2010). The idea is that these tests can be keyed to the curriculum pacing guide being used in a school district to help administrators determine whether students are on track to pass state-mandated tests. These assessments are often called "interim" tests, or "benchmark" tests, although there is no universally agreed-upon definition of these terms.

Shepard (2008) suggests that the term *formative assessment* should not be applied to the interim and benchmark assessments—not out of any desire to control the language used, but because "the official definition of formative assessment should be the one that best fits the research base from which its claims of effectiveness are derived" (p. 280). She points out that the research literature that is usually invoked to justify the use of benchmark and interim assessments actually does not support their use, because the theory of action for benchmark and interim assessments is quite different from the research evidence that does exist about the effectiveness of formative assessment that is more closely tied to the instruction.

While I can understand Shepard's view, my belief is that, not least because of the business interests at stake, it is unlikely that it will be possible to restrict the use of the term *formative assessment* to what the research evidence actually shows has an impact on learning. For this reason, I believe that it makes sense to define the term *formative assessment* broadly and then to examine which kinds of approaches to formative assessment are likely to have the greatest impact on student achievement.

The following definition, proposed by Paul Black and me, is intended to be consistent with the earlier definitions but also to be inclusive of the different approaches to formative assessment discussed so far.

> Practice in a classroom is formative to the extent that evidence about student achievement is elicited, interpreted, and used by teachers, learners, or their peers, to make decisions about the next steps in instruction that are likely to be better, or better founded, than the decisions they would have taken in the absence of the evidence that was elicited. (Black & Wiliam, 2009, p. 9)

There are several implications of this definition that may be helpful to draw out explicitly.

Formative assessment is not a thing. The distinction between summative and formative is grounded in the function that the evidence elicited by the assessment actually serves, and not on the kind of assessment that generates the evidence. From such a perspective, to describe a particular assessment as formative is to make what Ryle (1949) described as a category mistake—assigning something a property it cannot have.

As Cronbach (1971) observed, an assessment is really just a procedure for making inferences. We get students to engage in particular activities, and these generate evidence that we then interpret in order to draw conclusions. Where those conclusions are related to the student's current level of achievement, or to his or her future performance, then the assessment is serving a *summative* function. Where the conclusions are related to the kinds of instructional activities that are likely to maximize future learning, then the assessment is functioning *formatively*. The summative-formative distinction is therefore a distinction in the kinds of inferences that are supported by the evidence elicited by the assessment rather than the kinds of assessments themselves. Of course, the same assessment evidence may support both kinds of inferences, but in general, assessments that are designed to support summative inferences (i.e., inferences about current or future levels of achievement) are not particularly well suited to supporting formative inferences (i.e., inferences about instructional next steps). In other words, it is in general easier to say where a student is in his or her learning than what should be done next. It might be assumed that assessment designed primarily to serve a formative function would require, as a prerequisite, a detailed specification of the current level of achievement, but this does not necessarily hold. It is entirely possible that the assessment might identify a range of possible current states of achievement that nevertheless indicate a single course of future action—we might not know where the student is, but we know what he or she needs to do next.

Anyone—teacher, learner, or peer—can be the agent of formative assessment. While much of the early work in formative assessment focused on the way that teachers could collect evidence to inform their instructional decisions, it is clear that making full use of formative assessment requires changes in the roles of learners and of their peers. In particular, teachers who have developed their own practice of formative assessment routinely report that students have taken greater responsibility for their own learning (Black & Wiliam, 2012).

The focus of the definition is on decisions rather than data. Many of those who espouse the adoption of formative assessment talk about data-driven decision making. The idea that decisions should be driven by data rather than hunch, prejudice, or guesswork is, to be sure, very attractive. However, when the focus is on data, there is a tendency to collect data without any clear idea of how those data will be used. Howard Wainer (2011) points out that "data only become evidence when they are used to support a claim" (p. 148)—otherwise, they are just data. The danger with data-driven decision making, then, is that data are collected simply because they might be useful in the future. This is a particular issue with benchmark or interim assessments because often, by the time the results of such assessments arrive, the teacher has moved on to new material. In the definition proposed earlier, however, since the focus is on decisions, rather than data, then data should be collected only after it has been determined how and when the data will be used. A teacher might check ten minutes before the end of a lesson to see whether the class understands so she knows whether she should go on or review the material already covered. As another example, in Philadelphia, a benchmark assessment system was designed so that time to use the results from benchmark assessments to plan and implement instructional changes was built into the program (Bulkley, Christman, Goertz, & Lawrence, 2010). The important feature of both of these cases is that how to instructionally use the data was determined *before the data were collected*—not so much data-driven decision making as *decision-driven data collection*.

The definition does not require that the assessment is effective. Many definitions of formative assessment or assessment for learning require that to be formative, the assessment must improve the learning of students beyond what would have occurred without the assessment. However, this is a rather demanding standard to satisfy. Indeed, given the complexity of learning, it seems highly unlikely that *any* process could be guaranteed to improve the learning of all the students in a diverse group. For this reason, it is important that the definition is probabilistic rather than deterministic. All that is required for an assessment to function formatively is that the evidence elicited by the assessment is *likely* to improve the achievement of students.

The definition does not require that instruction is in fact changed. In *Embedded Formative Assessment* (Wiliam, 2011), I gave an example of a situation where a teacher asked a group of students in an Advanced Placement class to sketch the graph of $y = 1/(1+x^2)$ on dry-erase boards and then hold up their responses. The teacher could see that all the students had produced an appropriate sketch, and so she moved on. The important point here is that she did not change her instructional decision. Moving on is what she had planned to do, but now, because of the evidence she had collected, she knew that moving on was the right thing to do. So, the decision was not a better decision, because it was the decision she had planned to make. But it was a better *founded* decision because now the decision was based on evidence that moving on was indeed the right thing to do.

Another way of thinking about formative assessment that follows on from the preceding definition is that formative assessment is concerned with "the creation of, and capitalization upon, 'moments of contingency' in instruction for the purpose of the regulation of learning processes" (Black & Wiliam, 2009, p. 6).

Before discussing this idea in detail, it may be helpful to reflect on the word *regulation* used in the previous sentence. In English, the word *regulation* has two distinct senses: a rule that has to be followed and the idea of keeping a system performing in the way it should. It is the latter sense that is intended here. The main idea here is that instruction should be designed so that if the learning processes in which students are participating are not yielding the intended learning, then this becomes apparent, so that something can be done to put the learning back on track. One way in which this can be done is by designing moments of contingency, such as checks for understanding of instruction.

Of course, these moments of contingency do not occur in a vacuum. The way in which teachers, peers, and the learners themselves create and capitalize on these moments of contingency involves consideration of instructional design, curriculum, pedagogy, psychology, and epistemology. However, the focus on these moments of contingency in learning does restrict the focus to only those aspects of instruction that reasonably could be regarded as "assessment" and thus prevents the concept of formative assessment from expanding to subsume all of learning, thereby losing any useful focus.

Elsewhere (Wiliam, 2007), I have pointed out that moments of contingency can be synchronous or asynchronous. Synchronous moments include teachers' real-time adjustments during teaching or the way a teacher, after a class poll of student responses, suggests that students discuss their responses with a neighbor (Crouch & Mazur, 2001). Asynchronous examples include those situations where teachers get students to provide feedback for each other using a protocol such as "two stars and a wish" (Wiliam, 2011) or the use of evidence derived from student work (e.g., homework, student summaries made at the end of a lesson) to plan a subsequent lesson. Most commonly, the evidence would be used to modify the instruction of those from whom the evidence was collected. However, evidence about difficulties experienced by one group used to modify instruction for another group of students at some point in the future would also qualify, although there would, of course, be an inferential leap as to whether the difficulties experienced by one group would be relevant to a different group of students.

As Allal (1988) has pointed out, the regulation can be proactive, interactive, or retroactive. Proactive regulation of learning can be achieved, for example, through the establishment of didactical situations (Brousseau, 1997), where the teacher "does not intervene in person, but puts in place a 'metacognitive culture,' mutual forms of teaching and the organization of regulation of learning processes run by technologies or incorporated into classroom organization and management" (Perrenoud, 1998, p. 100). For example, if a mathematics teacher creates a culture in her classroom where students are routinely encouraged to reflect on the reasonableness of their answers, then the students may be able to detect errors themselves. Similarly, where students are encouraged to share their thinking with their peers, the chances that student learning proceeds effectively are increased.

Such didactical situations can also be planned by the teacher as specific points in time when she will evaluate the extent to which students have reached the intended understanding of the subject matter—for example, through the use of hinge-point questions (Wiliam, 2011) as specific parts of the lesson plan. While the planning of such questions takes place before the lesson, the teacher does not know how she will proceed in the lesson until she sees the responses made by students, so this would be an example of interactive regulation, in which teachers use formative assessment in real time to make adjustments to their instruction during the act of instruction. The preceding examples in which teachers reflect on instructional sequences after they have been completed, for the benefit of the particular students concerned or others, would be examples of retroactive regulation of learning.

Formative Assessment and Self-Regulated Learning

Many authors have focused on formative assessment largely as a process in which teachers administer assessments to students to ensure that the intended learning has taken place (e.g., Ainsworth & Viegut, 2006), but it is clear that for at least a quarter of a century, some authors have regarded the role of the learner as central. I have suggested (Wiliam, 1999a, 1999b, 2000) that formative assessment consisted of teacher questioning, feedback, and the learner's role (essentially, understanding criteria for success, peer assessment, and self-assessment), and a number of other authors have proposed similar ways of understanding formative assessment or assessment for learning. For example, Stiggins, Arter, Chappuis, and Chappuis (2004) proposed that assessment for learning consists of seven strategies:

1. Provide students with a clear and understandable vision of the learning target.

2. Use examples and models of strong and weak work.

3. Offer regular descriptive feedback.

4. Teach students to self-assess and set goals.

5. Design lessons to focus on one learning target or aspect of quality at a time.

6. Teach students focused revision.

7. Engage students in self-reflection and let them keep track of and share their learning.

While it could be argued that strategies 5 and 6 are not solely focused on assessment, it seems clear that a number of authors (e.g., Bailey & Heritage, 2008; Brookhart, 2007; Popham, 2008) writing about formative assessment have been addressing the same conceptual territory, although dividing it up in different ways.

Of course, where formative assessment is presented as a number of strategies, it is not clear whether the list is in any sense complete. To address this, Leahy et al. (2005) proposed that formative assessment could be conceptualized as five key strategies, resulting from crossing three processes (where the learner is going, where the learner is right now, and how to get there) with three kinds of agents in the classroom (teacher, peer, learner), as shown in Figure 4.1 (Leahy et al., 2005). This model could be criticized on the grounds that the strategies are not solely concerned with the assessment process. That said, provided that the two strategies that involve learners and peers (activating students as learning resources for one another and activating students as owners of their own learning) are interpreted as specifically focusing on moments of contingency in the regulation of learning processes, then the framework provided in Figure 4.1 does, I believe, provide a useful conceptual basis for formative assessment. More detailed explanations of the derivation of the model in Figure 4.1 can be found in Wiliam (2007) and Wiliam (2011).

	Where the learner is going	Where the learner is now	How to get there
Teacher	Clarifying, sharing, and understanding learning intentions and success criteria	Engineering effective discussions, tasks, and activities that elicit evidence of learning	Providing feedback that moves learning forward
Peer		Activating students as learning resources for one another	
Learner		Activating students as owners of their own learning	

Figure 4.1. Five key strategies of formative assessment.

The important point here is that within this view, self-regulated learning is an essential component of formative assessment.

The Evidence for Formative Assessment

At least in terms of the five strategies previously outlined, formative assessment is more of a framework for drawing together a number of related aspects of instruction than a single aspect of instruction. It is based on the idea that instruction presents teachers and learners with a constant stream of decisions, and the assumption being made is that these decisions will support learning more effectively if they are based on evidence.

The research evidence that formative assessment does have a significant impact on student achievement is reviewed in detail in my earlier book, *Embedded Formative Assessment* (Wiliam, 2011). For those interested in looking in detail at the academic research in this area, a summary of the main reviews of this research can be found in Wiliam and Leahy (2015). These reviews provide solid evidence that for learners of different ages, in different countries, and for different school subjects, attention to the five strategies of formative assessment has a substantial impact on student achievement. More important, as Paul Black and I noted in our 1998 review of the research:

> Furthermore, despite the existence of some marginal and even negative results, the range of conditions and contexts under which studies have shown that gains can be achieved must indicate that the principles that underlie achievement of substantial improvements in learning are robust. Significant gains can be achieved by many different routes, and initiatives here are not likely to fail through neglect of delicate and subtle features. (Black & Wiliam, 1998a, pp. 61–62)

In addition, it is worth noting that a best-evidence review of research on improving achievement in K–12 education identified the three most cost-effective strategies for improving learning in schools as feedback, peer tutoring, and metacognition and self-evaluation (Education Endowment Foundation, 2013). In other words, the three most cost-effective educational interventions were aspects of three of the five strategies of formative assessment identified previously.

Moreover, the other two strategies of formative assessment are necessary precursors to these three strategies. Feedback cannot be given unless evidence about what is going well and what is going not as well has been collected, so the second strategy—eliciting evidence—is a necessary precursor to effective feedback. And of course, without a clear idea about the intended learning, we do not know what evidence is worth collecting. The five strategies for formative assessment presented in Figure 4.1 do therefore appear to represent a minimum set of the most high-impact approaches to improving learning.

While the evidence in favor of formative assessment is strong, a number of critiques of the research on formative assessment have appeared in recent years. Perhaps the most important is that offered by Randy Bennett (2011), who identifies six issues with the research on formative assessment. Because Bennett's is the most comprehensive and rigorous of the critiques that have appeared, it seems worthwhile to discuss each of the issues in some detail.

The Definitional Issue

Bennett rightly shows that (as previously noted) there is no agreed-upon definition of what, exactly, is meant by formative assessment, which makes any discussion difficult (although he does acknowledge that the five strategies of formative assessment discussed above do represent an attempt to operationalize formative assessment in a way that could be implemented in practice). The advantage of a comprehensive definition of formative assessment, such as that previously presented, is that rather than debating which of the approaches to defining formative assessment is "correct," attention can be given to understanding the variables along which different approaches to formative assessment can be located.

Perhaps the most important variable is the theory of action implied in the approach to formative assessment. Put simply, what exactly is the formative assessment meant to *form*? Obviously, by definition, all approaches to formative assessment emphasize the role of assessment in forming student learning, but there are important differences in the mechanism by which this improvement takes place. As previously noted, for some, the defining feature of formative assessment is that it improves learning—a focus on outcomes. Others have emphasized improvements in the quality of instruction, specifically in terms of a match between the instruction and the specific learning needs of the students being taught. And, as already noted, the focus can be on improving the quality of decisions that are made during instruction.

The mechanism of improvement is also related to this decision making. Some approaches emphasize the instruments used, such as tests, quizzes, or probes, while others focus on the outcomes of those assessments, and still others emphasize the functions that evidence elicited by the assessments actually serve. I argued earlier that assuming any other than the last of these leads to contradiction, although in the future, it may be possible to show that other approaches to defining the formative-summative distinction could be coherent.

Another important difference in the various approaches to formative assessment is the role of the respective agents involved in the process, and specifically, whether students from whom evidence was elicited have to be beneficiaries of the process and whether they have to be involved. For example, if a seventh-grade math teacher learns something in teaching one section in period 1 and uses this to modify her instruction of the same material for the period 2 class, would this be an example of formative assessment? Furthermore, if the teacher changes her instruction based on the outcomes of a formative-assessment process, does not involve the students, and simply teaches the next lesson more effectively, would that be formative or not?

Finally, there is the length of the formative assessment cycle of evidence, inference, and action (Wiliam & Black, 1996). As noted above, some approaches to formative assessment involve cycles of several weeks, other approaches involve week-to-week cycles, while still others focus on minute-by-minute and day-by-day classroom interaction. To make clear that all of these are potentially formative, Wiliam and Thompson (2008) suggested using the terms *short-cycle*, *medium-cycle*, and *long-cycle formative assessment*, as shown in Table 4.1.

Table 4.1. Cycle Length, Focus, and Impact for Different Approaches to Formative Assessment

Type	Length	Focus	Impact
Long-cycle	Four weeks to one year	Across marking periods, quarters, semesters, years	Improved student monitoring and curriculum alignment
Medium-cycle	One to four weeks	Within and between teaching units	Improved student-involved assessment and teacher cognition about learning
Short-cycle	Minute to minute and day to day	Within and between lessons	Increased student engagement and improved teacher responsiveness

The Effectiveness Issue

The second issue identified by Bennett (2011) is with the evidence of effectiveness. In our review of the evidence published in 1998, Paul Black and I had explicitly rejected the idea of a meta-analysis, for reasons that should be clear after the discussion of meta-analysis in chapter 3. Here's what we wrote:

> It might be seen desirable, and indeed might be anticipated as conventional, for a review of this type to attempt a meta-analysis of the quantitative studies that have been reported. The fact that this hardly seems possible prompts a reflection on this field of research. Several studies which are based on meta-analyses have provided useful material for this review. However, these have been focussed on rather narrow aspects of formative work, for example the frequency of questioning. The value of their generalisations is also in question because key aspects of the various studies that they synthesise, for example the quality of the questions being provided at the different frequencies, is ignored because most of the researchers provide no evidence about these aspects.

> Individual quantitative studies which look at formative assessment as a whole do exist, and some have been discussed above, although the number with adequate and comparable quantitative rigour would be of the order of 20 at most. However, whilst these are rigorous within their own frameworks and purposes, and whilst they show some coherence and reinforcement in relation to the learning gains associated with classroom assessment initiatives, the underlying differences between the studies are such that any amalgamations of their results would have little meaning. (Black & Wiliam, 1998a, pp. 52–53)

However, we did indicate in a subsequent, less technical paper that the evidence we had reviewed indicated that formative assessment could be expected to have effect sizes in the range of 0.4 to 0.7. This was done to give policy makers and educators some indication of the kinds of increases in educational achievement that might be possible with formative assessment but in retrospect may have been a mistake, because, as Bennett (2011) points out, this claim has become "the educational equivalent of urban legend" (p. 12).

To be sure, the estimate of 0.4 to 0.7 is consistent with a range of other estimates available at the time and that have appeared subsequently. Meta-analyses of the effectiveness of feedback by Kluger and DeNisi (1996) and by Nyquist (2003) found that feedback improved achievement by around 0.4 standard deviations, and a more recent review of research on feedback by Shute (2008) found effect sizes of between 0.4 and 0.8. Hattie's estimate of the impact of feedback on student achievement is 0.73 (Hattie, 2008).

However, from the discussion of meta-analyses in chapter 3, it should be clear that effect sizes are likely to vary considerably in magnitude from one context to another, and it is this that many critics of the research on formative assessment appear not to appreciate. A study of twenty-four middle and high school math and science teachers developing their practice of formative assessment over the course of a year, with student achievement measured by externally scored standardized tests, found an increase in student achievement, compared with other teachers in the same schools, of 0.32 standard deviations (Wiliam, Lee, Harrison, & Black, 2004).

Some, following Cohen, have labeled this effect as "small." Hattie (2008) has pointed out that, as we saw in Figure 3.1, the average annual increase in achievement is around 0.2 to 0.4, so that effect sizes in this range should be regarded as average progress and that we would need an effect size larger than 0.4 to treat an intervention as promising. However, it is not clear whether Hattie regards the 0.4 as the annual gain we should expect or whether this is the *additional* gain, beyond the normal average annual progress, that we should want before regarding an intervention as worth recommending (support for both interpretations can be found in chapter 2 of *Visible Learning*). The effect size of 0.32 found by Wiliam et al. (2004) might indeed be regarded as modest if it was the total progress made by the students in the study. However, in this study, this was the *difference* in progress made by students taught by participating teachers and those taught by nonparticipating teachers over the course of a whole year. Moreover, given that the average age of the students participating in the study was 13.5 years, by reference to Figure 3.1, it can be seen that this is a rather substantial additional impact on learning. In fact, even taking into account that the tests used in the study were closely aligned to the curriculum, we estimated that the effect size of 0.32 we found would equate to an increase in the rate of learning of approximately 70 percent.

By any measure, this is a large impact on student achievement. A 70 percent increase in the rate of learning would, if replicated across an entire education system, result in students achieving the standards currently achieved by twelfth graders by the end of seventh grade. If the effect of formative assessment on student achievement is only 0.2, as estimated by Kingston and Nash (2011, 2015), then this would result in students reaching the achievement of current twelfth graders by the end of eighth grade. Even if 30 percent of the extra learning each year is forgotten by the beginning of the next year, an additional 0.2 standard deviations each year would result in US students scoring 112 points higher on PISA (eight years of education making an extra 0.14 standard deviations' progress each year is 1.12 standard deviations, or 112 points). This would take the average score of US fifteen-year-olds on PISA from 492 to 604, well ahead of students in Shanghai, who averaged 587 in 2012.

The dollar value of such increases in achievement would be extraordinary. Just in terms of the costs of education, an effect size of 0.2, if it were applied across K–12 education, would be worth $150 billion each year, and the cumulative impact on the US economy would be even larger. According to one estimate (Hanushek & Wößmann, 2010), over the next fifty years, a net increase of achievement of 0.14 standard deviations each year would have a current net value of $200 trillion.

The Domain Dependency Issue

In addressing the domain dependency issue, Bennett (2011) argues that "to be maximally effective, formative assessment requires the interaction of general principles, strategies, and techniques *with* reasonably deep cognitive-domain understanding" (p. 15). At one level, this is obvious. It is inconceivable that someone armed with a range of formative-assessment strategies and techniques could teach effectively a subject he or she knew nothing about. And, at the other extreme, it is well known that those who know the subject well, but have no idea about how to teach it, are not very effective (e.g., Baumert et al., 2009).

Moreover, it is now well established that the knowledge needed to teach effectively is not routinely acquired through advanced courses in the particular subject. Teachers need what has been called *pedagogical content knowledge* by Shulman (1986) and subject-specific *knowledge for teaching* by Hill, Rowan, and Ball (2005). This includes knowing what kinds of difficulties students are likely to encounter in learning a particular subject and the kinds of questions that are most likely to elicit relevant evidence. What makes a good question in mathematics tells us nothing about what makes a good question in social studies.

However, there is a much deeper point to be made here, and that is that particular pedagogical strategies and techniques are given more emphasis in some subjects than others. For example, redrafting a piece of work after having received feedback is a staple in English language arts but is less relevant in mathematics (at least the way mathematics is taught in most US schools). Furthermore, even when a technique is equally important in different domains, it may take a different form from one subject to another. This requires acknowledging that there are important differences between school subjects that mean that formative assessment will take different forms and will emphasize different aspects of practice in different school subjects.

This realization that to be maximally effective teacher professional development must address the particularities of the subject being taught has resulted, in many districts, in different programs of professional development for teachers in different subjects. English language arts teachers might be working on developing their use of the Protocol for Language Arts Teaching Observations (Grossman et al., 2009), while science teachers might be working on argumentation processes in science (Gabrielsen, 2014), and mathematics teachers might be developing their understanding of mathematical investigations (Boaler, 2009). While these approaches are effective within their respective subjects, they tend to lead to a balkanization of school improvement efforts, with little coherence to efforts across different subjects. It also suggests to students that there is little commonality to the process of learning in different subjects.

In order to counter this, to be most effective, approaches to school improvement need to identify as many commonalities as possible across different subject disciplines, while also paying attention to the particularities of each discipline.

In the earliest work that my colleagues and I conducted on formative assessment with mathematics and science (and later, English language arts) teachers, the professional development that we provided consisted of both generic and subject-specific components. Teachers met in generic groups, but during each one-day meeting, time was also reserved for teachers to meet in subject groups to explore aspects of formative assessment that were specific to their discipline (Black, Harrison, Lee, Marshall, & Wiliam, 2003). Subsequently, as well as producing generic books for teachers, we produced a series of subject-specific guides that explore how to maximize the impact of formative assessment in English language arts (Marshall & Wiliam, 2006), mathematics (Hodgen & Wiliam, 2006), science (Black & Harrison, 2002), and modern foreign languages (Jones & Wiliam, 2007).

The advantage of conceptualizing formative assessment as both domain specific *and* generic at the same time is that a school can ensure that practice is faithful to, and effective within, a particular discipline, while bringing greater coherence to the experiences of students. Learning intentions and success criteria may differ in character from subject to subject, but the idea of learning intentions and success criteria is equally relevant to all learning (although the learning intentions and success criteria may differ in their specificity). In some subjects, teachers will elicit evidence of achievement by questioning, while in others, they may do so by observing students engaged in complex tasks, but the important point is that there is always an intentional approach to eliciting evidence. As previously noted, feedback may prompt redrafting, extension, or a completely different activity, but again, the focus is on moving learning forward. And of course, efforts to activate students as learning resources for one another and as owners of their own learning will likewise take different forms in different subjects. However, by drawing attention to these processes as universally relevant to learning, students will be able to make connections across their different experiences. This will not, of course, suddenly result in students who are able to apply their knowledge in any domain, but it is likely to make the students more able to relate learning in one area to their experiences in another.

The Measurement Issue

One of the criticisms frequently made of the term *formative assessment* is that it is just good teaching, and using the assessment label is just confusing because, as noted above, when teachers hear the term *assessment*, they immediately think of the formal mechanisms of tests, quizzes, and examinations. However, as also previously noted, the important point about thinking of checking for understanding as an assessment process is that it focuses teachers on the quality of the evidence they have elicited and what conclusions can reasonably be drawn from that evidence. In his review, Bennett (2011) argues that formative assessment, as a process, gives too little attention "to the fundamental principles surrounding the connection of evidence—or what we observe—to the interpretations we make of it" (p. 16). This may, of course, be true for many approaches to formative assessment, but it is strange that he does not realize that two of the modules of the Keeping Learning on Track program developed by his own organization are specifically focused on generating items that allow teachers to draw appropriate inferences about student achievement. This idea of developing high-quality items is also given significant attention in *Embedded Formative*

Assessment and our more recent work (Wiliam & Leahy, 2015) and is also the focus of earlier theoretical work (Wylie & Wiliam, 2006, 2007).

The last two issues identified by Bennett are those of professional development and system-wide implementation, both of which are addressed in later chapters in this book.

To sum up, the critiques by Bennett and others raise important points about the gaps in our knowledge and, in particular, the complexity of integrating different aspects of expertise in real work contexts. Like researchers everywhere, Bennett (2011) and Kingston and Nash (2011) suggest that more research is needed. Of course, more research is *always* needed, and this is not just a self-serving plea by researchers for continued employment. Research, particularly in the social sciences, tends to reveal that the things we study are much more complex than we assumed them to be.

However, concluding that more research is needed is not an option for school leaders. For students, schooling is basically a one-shot deal, and leaders have to make decisions right now about where to invest their efforts in supporting the teachers they lead. More evidence about what works would be nice, but right now, it simply isn't there. As we saw in the previous chapter, systematic reviews of research are simply not capable, currently, of providing reliable guides to action, and so we have to go with the evidence we have. There are significant problems with the evidence about formative assessment, but right now, there appears to be nothing that leaders can prioritize that would have a greater impact on student achievement. This is important because it means that if the only priority of a district is raising scores on standardized tests, developing teachers' practice of formative assessment is likely to be the most effective strategy.

This is important also because many teachers say to me, "I'd love to teach for deep understanding, but I have to raise my students' test scores." What the research on formative assessment shows is that you don't have to choose. Developing the use of formative assessment is the best way to teach for deep understanding and, at the same time, the best way to improve test scores. The reason this matters is because there is a low road and a high road to test success. Taking the low road means drilling students to become better test takers. This can be effective for some students, such as those with good memories, but it is on average ineffective because such an approach de-skills students. When faced with a test item that they do not know how to answer, they tend to try to remember what they have been taught about such items, rather than thinking hard about the item that is in front of them. However, the real damage of taking the low road is that even for students who are successful, it is ineffective in the longer term. They can pass the test, but that's all they can do. Taking the high road means teaching for deep understanding so that the students can be successful on standardized tests *and* have capabilities on which they can build in the future.

Approaches to Formative Assessment

This chapter has adopted a deliberately broad approach to formative assessment to be inclusive and head off disputes about what is and is not formative assessment, because such disputes are unlikely to be productive. However, adopting a broad definition of formative assessment does not mean that all the different approaches that such a broad definition would include are likely to be equally effective in improving student achievement.

As Shepard (2010) points out, the research evidence reviewed in recent years very strongly indicates that the approaches to formative assessment that are likely to have the greatest impact on student achievement "typically involve much more immediate interactions between students and teachers during the course of a lesson or unit of study" (p. 247). This does not mean that other approaches to formative assessment cannot be effective. For example, when there is poor alignment between curriculum and instruction on the one hand and assessment on the other, then assessments that help teachers and administrators detect and address this can be helpful (Goe & Bridgeman, 2006).

Perhaps the most widespread approach to formative assessment currently in use in the United States, however, is focused on what might be called "instructional data teams" in which teachers meet regularly to review evidence on the progress of students, and where students are found not to be making adequate progress, appropriate interventions are made.

According to Richard DuFour (2004), three ideas are central to this approach. The first is that all students should be learning. While this is common as an aspiration, making it a reality involves substantial changes to the typical operating procedures of most schools. As DuFour himself says, "Don't tell me you believe all children can learn; tell me what you do when they don't" (Blackburn, 2014). It involves reengineering the school and its operating procedures to ensure that all students learn.

The second central idea is that teachers work collaboratively to solve problems. In many high-reliability organizations, significant advances have been made by treating failures as system failures rather than as failures of individuals (Roberts, 1990), and similar approaches appear to be highly effective in schools (Stringfield, 1995). In the same way that hospitals seek to improve the reliability of their processes, schools can do the same through collaboration:

> The powerful collaboration that characterizes professional learning communities is a systematic process in which teachers work together to analyze and improve their classroom practice. Teachers work in teams, engaging in an ongoing cycle of questions that promote deep team learning. This process, in turn, leads to higher levels of student achievement. (DuFour, 2004, p. 9)

The third central idea is that the work of professional learning communities must be focused on outcomes for students, assessed through common measures. This last point is essential. When teachers are free to determine their own learning outcomes for students, then the fact that some teachers' students do less well than other students does not, in itself, force those teachers to confront the issue. They can respond by saying that the results are lower than those of other teachers because other teachers have lower standards. However, when teachers collaboratively develop common assessments, which they agree encapsulate what they want their students to learn, then differences in student success generate much more focused discussions. In particular, when the results of the common assessments are broken down to identify different aspects of success, teachers can see which of their colleagues have been particularly successful in developing those particular aspects with their students and are thus likely to be ready to learn from their colleagues.

A study of schools receiving funds under Title 1 of the Elementary and Secondary Education Act in a large urban school district in Southern California compared student achievement in nine schools where teachers engaged in grade-based instructional data teams with that in six matched schools that did not (Saunders, Goldenberg, & Gallimore, 2009). In the first phase of the "Getting Results" (GR) project, which lasted two years, school principals met monthly with the regional superintendent for two hours, and in these meetings, principals were introduced to, and supported in, the role they were expected to play in leading change in their buildings. Specifically, principals were expected to establish an instructional leadership team (ILT) for the building, consisting of at least one representative from each grade level, the principal, and other relevant individuals at the school (administrators, coaches, coordinators, etc.), which would meet once each month for two hours.

The task of the ILT was to support the grade-level representatives in their work of leading weekly, grade-based teams that would examine student work to identify academic problems and indicators of progress. Unfortunately, over the first two years of the project, it quickly became clear that the project was not meeting its intended goals.

> However, despite continuing support by the regional superintendent and favorable principal responses to the GR intervention, the Phase 1 yielded limited implementation, minimal implementation or impact of any kind,

and no appreciable gains in student achievement. Competing demands for their time and attention were typically cited as reasons for the lack of progress in implementation. Principals expressed uncertainty about the content or structure of ILT meetings and how they should lead or guide ILT representatives, who were in turn expected to lead their colleagues at grade-level team meetings. It turned out to be very difficult for ILT representatives to function effectively as grade-level leaders for instructional improvement, and principals were challenged to provide them with the necessary guidance. It became clear that a "train the principal" approach yielded little implementation, ineffective teacher teams, or no gains in student achievement. (Saunders et al., 2009, p. 10)

In the second phase of the project, therefore, the amount of support was increased and focused more directly on supporting the work of the various teams. Principals continued to meet monthly with project advisors, but now project advisors also met individually with principals at their schools to discuss the progress of ILTs and grade-level teams. Project advisors also attended meetings of ILTs and, when requested, some grade-level team meetings.

Participating teachers also received training on analyzing standardized and periodic assessments, unit and instructional planning, and focusing on and addressing common student needs. A specific seven-step protocol for achieving this, developed by project staff, was given to all grade-level teams:

1. Identify and clarify specific and common student needs to work on together.
2. Formulate a clear objective for each common need and analyze related student work.
3. Identify and adopt a promising instructional focus to address each common need.
4. Plan and complete necessary preparation to try the instructional focus in the classroom.
5. Try the team's instructional focus in the classroom.
6. Analyze student work to see if the objective is being met and evaluate the instruction.
7. Reassess: Continue and repeat cycle or move on to another area of need. (Saunders et al., 2009, p. 11)

The results were dramatic. While there had been no improvement in the first phase of the project, during the three years of the second phase, compared with the matched schools who had chosen an alternative school-improvement plan, student achievement increased by approximately 0.2 standard deviations.

This study provides clear evidence that having teachers engaging in an inquiry cycle where students' needs are identified, and solutions are then proposed and developed, can be effective. However, the major strength of this model is also a weakness, and that is that it is focused on the progress of this year's students. Making sure that this year's students succeed is of course important. But if the only outcome of this process is higher achievement for this year's students, then the same problems are likely to arise in future years, because the teachers will not have improved. Now of course it could be that engaging teachers in problem solving to address the issue of students not making the progress that they need to make does result in increasing the quality of the teachers. However, if such improvements happen, they are a byproduct of the process rather than the main focus. So although time has to be found to ensure that all students are learning, time also has to be found for teachers to increase their classroom skills, so that next year, fewer students fail to progress, because the quality of instruction they have received is higher. And of course, given the research on formative assessment discussed earlier in this chapter, the most obvious focus for improving teacher quality is to focus on classroom formative assessment.

Investing in increases in teacher quality is particularly powerful as a mechanism for school improvement because once a teacher gets better, even if only slightly, the benefits of improved teacher quality are experienced by every student that teacher will ever teach. And if, the following year, the teacher gets better again, all the students that teacher will teach get the double benefit of the improvements that the teacher made in the first year and the benefits of the improvements that the teacher makes in the second year—rather like the effects of compound interest.

These two processes—making sure that this year's students are making appropriate progress and making sure that teachers have time to develop their classroom skills—are complementary. One way of thinking about the relationship between the two processes is in terms of the distinction between quality control and quality assurance.

Quality control is generally defined as a set of activities undertaken by manufacturers for ensuring that whatever they release is free from defects. As a process, quality control tends to focus on checking the quality of finished products at the end of the production process and before they are released. It is therefore mainly a reactive process.

Quality assurance is generally defined as a set of activities for ensuring that the processes used in manufacturing are designed so as to eliminate, or at least minimize, defects in the final product. As a process, quality assurance tends to focus on the design of production processes and is therefore primarily a proactive process.

In much of the management literature, it is common to find quality control being regarded as inferior to quality assurance. Quality assurance is sometimes described as designing quality into the production process, while quality control is described as inspecting quality in the final stage. Advocates of quality assurance often compare the traditions of automobile manufacturing in the United States and Japan in the 1960s. In the United States, the dominant approach was quality control; cars were manufactured and then inspected. Cars that failed the inspection were sent back to have the defects corrected. Beginning in the late 1950s, building on the work of Americans such as W. Edwards Deming, Japanese manufacturers—most notably the Toyota Motor Corporation—began to focus on quality assurance. The production process would be designed so that quality was engineered into each step of the production process. Every worker was given the right (and, indeed, the responsibility) to halt the production line if any issue that might affect the quality of the final product was seen.

Today, of course, all automobile manufacturers prioritize quality assurance as the central approach to ensuring quality, but it is important to realize that quality assurance cannot be the exclusive approach to quality, especially when what is being produced is highly complex. For example, many manufacturers of semiconductor chips have found that it is actually very difficult to design manufacturing processes so that every chip that is produced is guaranteed to work properly. Obviously they take care to design the manufacturing process so as to maximize the chances of success, but the optimum strategy consists of both quality assurance *and* quality control—making sure that the production process is well designed but also checking on the quality of the finished product.

Instructional data teams can be thought of as a process of quality control. The idea is that student achievement is assessed after a sequence of instruction has been completed, with a view to taking action if certain students are found not to have learned what they have been taught. In keeping with the definition of quality control mentioned previously, it is primarily a reactive process. In contrast, getting teachers to make greater use of classroom formative assessment can be thought of as a process of quality assurance. It is about designing instruction so that any failures of students to learn are identified and can be addressed while the instruction is still taking place. Both processes are necessary because, as Kirschner, Sweller, and Clark (2006) point out, "The aim of all instruction is to alter long-term memory. If nothing has changed in long-term memory, nothing has been learned" (p. 77). However, while we cannot be sure that students have learned something because they know it at the end of the lesson, if they do not know something by the end of the lesson, it is unlikely that they will know it weeks later. A summary of the main differences between these two approaches to formative assessment is shown in Table 4.2.

Table 4.2. Comparison of Two Main Approaches to Formative Assessment

Improving student achievement with instructional data teams	Building teacher quality through classroom formative assessment
Quality control	Quality assurance
Common assessments	Formative-assessment strategies and techniques
Improvement through better teamwork and systems	Improvement through increased teacher capability
Focus on individual outcomes for students	Focus on teachers' individual accountability for change
Regular meetings focused on data	Regular meetings focused on teacher improvement
Sixteen points on PISA (in two to three years)	Thirty points on PISA (in two to three years)

Given that leaders need to ensure that both of these processes are in place, the obvious question is how to divide time between the two approaches. The good news, as we shall see in chapter 6, is that there is not much point in having meetings focused on building teacher capability more frequently than once a month. Teachers' lives and working routines are so hectic and fragile that it takes most teachers a month to try out a new teaching technique. This suggests that if the school schedule allows time for teachers to work collaboratively once a week, then three meetings per month should be focused on instructional data, and one meeting a month should be focused on building teacher capability.

Furthermore, to make clear the difference between the two kinds of meetings, it is helpful if instructional data teams meet in *grade-based* teams, and meetings focused on building teacher capability involve *cross-grade* teams. Having teachers meet in cross-grade teams minimizes the likelihood that teachers spend time talking about curriculum or students, and as a result, they are more likely to spend time on the one thing that all teachers have in common—pedagogy. Detailed guidance about the structure and organization of meetings designed to support teachers in their use of classroom formative assessment is provided in chapter 6.

Relationships With Other Policy Priorities

So far in this chapter, I have argued that leaders who are serious about improving the outcomes for students in their schools have to develop the use of formative assessment, both retrospectively, as a way of ensuring that students do not fall behind, and also prospectively, as a way of increasing the pedagogical skills of teachers in the school. However, schools rarely have the luxury of focusing on a single priority. Particularly in recent years, states that have secured federal funds through the Race to the Top program have been required to implement rigorous teacher evaluation systems, which raises issues about the extent to which developing formative assessment is consistent with the common teacher evaluation systems being adopted by different states and districts.

Perhaps the most important point to remember in looking at teacher evaluation systems is that, by their very nature, they are designed to be comprehensive. They have to include all aspects of teacher practice that are likely to be relevant, no matter how important they are in contributing to student progress. We saw in chapter 2 (Sartain et al., 2011) that in Chicago Public Schools, there were significant correlations between the progress made by students and a teacher's rating on two of the four domains of Danielson's Framework for Teaching (Danielson, 1996): domain 2 (classroom environment) and domain 3 (instruction). However, no such correlation was found for domains 1 (planning and preparation) and 4 (professional responsibilities). As I said earlier, this does not mean that planning and preparation and professional responsibilities are unimportant aspects of teachers' performance. It could be that they are so important that all teachers take them equally seriously, so that teachers do not vary much in terms of these two domains, so the correlation is reduced. It could be that variations in terms of these two domains are important, but the definitions of the different levels of performance do not capture these differences. Finally, of course, it could be that the variations in student progress in these two domains are smaller than those produced by variations in classroom environment and instruction.

Whatever the reasons, a teacher evaluation system that did not cover planning and preparation and professional responsibilities would lack credibility, and so these dimensions of teacher performance have to be included. However, the empirical evidence is that these matter less than classroom environment and instruction. Put bluntly, it seems likely that if we want to improve a teacher's performance, attention to classroom environment and instruction will benefit students more than attention to planning and preparation and professional responsibilities.

The same argument can be made *within* each domain. While each domain is specified in terms of a number of subdomains, it is likely that certain subdomains will be more important than others (in the sense that improvement of that aspect of practice produces bigger improvements in student achievement than improvements in the other aspects of practice). Now of course, improving practice in some subdomains may be harder than others, so the fact that a particular aspect of practice has the highest correlation with student achievement should not necessarily lead us to focus on that aspect. We need instead to focus on aspects of practice that can be changed relatively easily and also, when changed, have a major impact on student achievement.

What this means is that it is highly unwise to use a teacher *evaluation* framework as a teacher *improvement* framework. Teacher evaluation frameworks have to be comprehensive, and specifically, they need to cover all aspects of teachers' work, so they include some aspects of practice that have a huge impact on student learning, and they also include aspects of practice that have small, or negligible, impacts on student learning. And yet, in almost all evaluation frameworks, all aspects of practice carry equal weight. What this means is that when teachers are under pressure to improve their ratings, the incentives to improve aspects of practice that have no impact on student achievement are the same as improving aspects of practice that really benefit their students. When evaluation frameworks are used as improvement frameworks, we create incentives for teachers to focus on the easiest things to improve, rather than what will benefit their students most. Put bluntly, *using evaluation frameworks as improvement frameworks makes it more likely that we improve teachers in ways that do not benefit their students.*

Fortunately, the research base on formative assessment provides a way of focusing teacher improvement so as to maximize the impact on student achievement. Figure 4.2 shows a crosswalk between the five strategies of classroom formative assessment presented in Figure 4.1 and the five subdomains of domain 3 in Danielson's Framework for Teaching.

To unpack the rather dense interconnections shown in Figure 4.2, the aspect of "communicating with students" within the Framework for Teaching that are given particular emphasis in formative assessment are the ideas of sharing learning intentions and success criteria with students and providing feedback that moves learning forward. What is called "using questioning and discussion techniques" in the Framework for Teaching maps in a fairly straightforward way to the strategy of "eliciting evidence" in classroom formative assessment. Aspects of what is called "engaging students in learning" in the Framework for Teaching that are a particular focus of classroom formative assessment are sharing learning intentions, activating students as learning resources for one another, and activating students as owners of their own learning. The last two subdomains of the Framework for Teaching, using assessment in instruction and demonstrating flexibility and responsiveness, of course map to all five of the strategies of classroom formative assessment. Indeed, it could be argued that the entire purpose of classroom formative assessment is to demonstrate flexibility and responsiveness, and it is only possible to demonstrate flexibility and responsiveness by using assessment as an integral part of instruction.

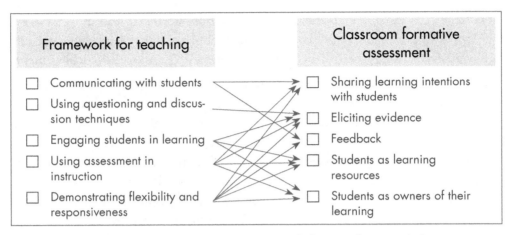

Figure 4.2. Connections between the Framework for Teaching and classroom formative assessment

In this way, classroom formative assessment can be thought of as placing a magnifying glass on the aspects of the Framework for Teaching that are likely to have the greatest impact on student achievement. To see why this really is a magnifying glass, refer back to where we saw earlier that improving a teacher from "below basic" to "distinguished" would equate to a 30 percent increase in the rate of learning, and such a process is likely to take several years at the very least (if it can be done). Getting teachers to develop their use of classroom formative assessment appears to result in a 50 percent increase in the rate of student learning within a year or two.

Other frameworks divide up the work of teachers differently, but the important point is that any comprehensive teacher evaluation framework will include all aspects of classroom formative assessment somewhere in the framework. This means that leaders can be confident that encouraging teachers to focus on classroom formative assessment will allow teachers to make progress with respect to the evaluation framework, which is obviously in the teachers' best interest. The leaders can also be confident that the aspects that are being developed are those that are most likely to benefit students, thus reducing the likelihood of improvements in teacher evaluations that are not associated with improvements in student achievement.

At this point, it is also worth noting that classroom formative assessment is an inherent element of two other important initiatives of recent years, differentiated instruction and response to intervention (and instruction). Each of these is discussed in turn.

Differentiated Instruction

Although the idea of differentiated instruction has received attention in the United States only in recent years, it is important to realize that there is nothing new in the idea. In several countries (e.g., Germany, Austria), the school performance of students is evaluated, and on the basis of that evaluation, students are directed to different kinds of educational institutions where they are expected to learn different things. In other words, different students are assigned different goals in education. In other jurisdictions, students might work toward the same goals but do so with different curriculum structures, different course content, different tasks, or different teaching approaches. Perhaps most common in the United States is the idea of differentiation in the pace of learning, with certain students being expected to cover course content more quickly than others, after which they might go on to work normally intended for older students (acceleration) or to undertake more in-depth study of the work already completed (enrichment). Finally, of course, particularly as a result of federally mandated testing of students, there are also differences in the way students are assessed, with some students receiving accommodations and adaptations of the assessment administered.

There does not appear to be any widely accepted definition of the term *differentiated instruction*. Carol Ann Tomlinson (2004)—who is the writer most closely associated with the idea of differentiated instruction in the United States—has suggested that

> While the concept of "differentiated instruction" can be defined in many ways, as good a definition as any is ensuring that what a student learns, how he/she learns it, and how the student demonstrates what he/she has learned is a match for that student's readiness level, interests, and preferred mode of learning. (p. 188)

Differentiated instruction has been widely adopted as a key element of instructional policy in many school districts in the United States, even though convincing evidence that it improves learning is rather difficult to locate (Schmoker, 2010). Partly, this is due to the lack of an agreed-upon definition, but even with such a definition, some aspects of differentiated instruction are simply unresearchable. For example, if students exercise choice in what they study, we cannot compare student achievements. In Robert Wood's memorable phrase, it makes no sense to say, "Your chemistry equals my French" (Wood, 1987). Similarly, if different students are assessed on different bases, meaningful comparisons are difficult, if not impossible.

When students are learning the same material and are assessed in the same way, then, as David Ausubel has pointed out in the quotation earlier in this chapter, it makes sense to start from where the learner is. Beginning instruction by assuming students know something they do not know is hardly likely to be a recipe for effective instruction. And even if students are at different starting points, what the teacher should do with that is determined by cultural as much as by scientific considerations. In the United States, it seems to be generally assumed that those who have learned something should move ahead of their peers, while in other cultures, students who have learned something are expected to help those in the class who haven't.

In a review of the research evidence about differentiated learning, Huebner (2010) states that "experts and practitioners acknowledge that the research on differentiated instruction as a specific practice is limited" (p. 79) but then goes on to suggest that there is research to support a number of practices that provide the foundation of differentiated instruction:

> using effective classroom management procedures; promoting student engagement and motivation; assessing student readiness; responding to learning styles; grouping students for instruction; and teaching to the student's zone of proximal development (the distance between what a learner can demonstrate without assistance and what the learner can do with assistance). (p. 79)

The problem with this claim is that the first three of these would probably be regarded as aspects of *all* effective instruction, and the last three are, at best, questionable. As we saw in chapter 3, there is no evidence that adapting instruction to mesh with students' preferred ways of learning has any impact on student achievement. Indeed, catering to students' preferred mode of learning may actually be suboptimal for student learning because of what Elizabeth and Robert Bjork (2009) have called "desirable difficulties" in learning. Within-class grouping of students for instruction can produce small improvements in student learning (Lou et al., 1996), but many studies have found that teachers end up spending up to half their time keeping groups engaged (e.g., Good, Grouws, Mason, Slavings, & Cramer, 1990). Finally, the characterization of Vygotsky's zone of proximal development does not reflect the careful distinction that Vygotsky drew between learning and development. Like Piaget, Vygotsky believed that children went through a series of stages of psychological development. For Vygotsky (1978), the purpose of teaching was to trigger a transition from one stage of development to the next, which is why he wrote, "Thus, the notion of a zone of proximal development enables us to propound a new formula, namely that the only 'good learning' is that which is in advance of development" (p. 34).

Therefore, while differentiated instruction has neither an agreed-upon definition nor a coherent research foundation, leaders are often required to ensure that the instruction in their buildings is differentiated. A way forward is suggested by the work of Hall, Strangman, and Meyer (2011) who define differentiated instruction in a similar way to Tomlinson:

> To differentiate instruction is to recognize students' varying background knowledge, readiness, language, preferences in learning and interests; and to react responsively. Differentiated instruction is a process to teaching and learning for students of differing abilities in the same class. (p. 3)

While this definition does not, in itself, add much to the earlier definition from Tomlinson, what is helpful in Hall et al.'s report (2011) is that they present a list of thirteen characteristics of differentiated instruction, and these are shown in Table 4.3. Also included in Table 4.3, in the final column, is an indication of whether each characteristic is also an aspect of classroom formative assessment. By encouraging teachers to develop their use of those characteristics of differentiated instruction that are also aspects of classroom formative assessment, leaders can maximize the chances that attention to differentiated instruction will also help learners.

Table 4.3. Aspects of Differentiated Instruction That Are Related to Classroom Formative Assessment

	Aspects of differentiated instruction	Formative assessment?
Content	Several elements and materials are used	
	Align tasks and objectives to learning goals	√
	Instruction is concept focused and principle driven	
Process	Flexible grouping is consistently used	
	Classroom management benefits students and teachers	
Products	Initial and ongoing assessment of student readiness and growth	√
	Students are active and responsible explorers	√
	Vary expectations and requirements for student responses	√
Miscellaneous	Clarify key concepts and generalizations	
	Use assessment as a teaching tool	√
	Emphasize critical and creative thinking as a goal in lesson design	
	Engaging all learners is essential	√
	Balance between teacher-assigned and student-selected tasks	

Response to Intervention (and Instruction)

The field of education is famous (or infamous) for its use of impenetrable jargon, but even so, the phrase *response to intervention* must be one of the most impenetrable and least intuitive descriptions to have appeared in recent years.

The origin of the phrase lies with the Individuals with Disabilities Education Improvement Act of 2004, which made a number of changes to methods for determining whether children had learning disabilities that had been implicit in the Individuals with Disabilities Education Act of 1990.

Traditionally, specific learning disabilities had been diagnosed by reference to differences in aspects of cognitive performance. For example, as Siegel (2006) notes:

> Until recently, the typical definition of dyslexia involved a discrepancy between an IQ score and a reading score. If the IQ score was found to be significantly higher than the reading score, then this discrepancy was used as an index of dyslexia. (p. 582)

However, this approach has been subject to a number of criticisms. It appears that the use of IQ testing is not particularly helpful in identifying specific learning disabilities, such as dyslexia (e.g., Siegel, 1989). Perhaps more important, given the association of IQ testing with the eugenics movement in the United States in the first half of the 20th century (Selden, 1999), it is not surprising that those tasked with updating the 1990 Individuals with Disabilities in Education Act sought to avoid the use of IQ testing in the diagnosis of learning disabilities. Whatever the reason, section 614 of the 2004 act states:

> When determining whether a child has a specific learning disability . . . a local educational agency shall not be required to take into consideration whether a child has a severe discrepancy between achievement and intellectual ability in oral expression, listening comprehension, written expression, basic reading skill, reading comprehension, mathematical calculation, or mathematical reasoning. (Title I/B/ § 614/b/6)

Instead, local education agencies are encouraged to adopt more direct ways of diagnosing learning disabilities, and the most obvious of all is that a student may have a learning disability if she or he fails to learn. The difficulty with such a definition is of course that a failure to learn may simply indicate ineffective instruction. That is why section 614 of the 2004 act also states:

> In determining whether a child has a specific learning disability, a local educational agency may use a process that determines if the child responds to

scientific, research-based intervention as a part of the evaluation procedures. (Title I/B/ § 614/b/6)

In other words, if a student does not *respond* to a research-based *intervention*, then the student may, indeed, have a learning disability.

Although the origins of the phrase *response to intervention* therefore lie in the desire to avoid requiring local education agencies to use IQ testing in the identification of learning disabilities, as it has become more widely used and applied, it is now being used much more generally as a protocol for preventing academic failure by monitoring progress and, when evidence reveals that students are not making progress, taking action—in essence, a way of implementing the quality control approach to formative assessment described previously. As defined by the National Center on Response to Intervention (2010):

> Response to intervention integrates assessment and intervention within a multi-level prevention system to maximize student achievement and reduce behavior problems. With RTI, schools identify students at risk for poor learning outcomes, monitor student progress, provide evidence-based interventions and adjust the intensity and nature of those interventions depending on a student's responsiveness, and identify students with learning disabilities.

The relationship with classroom formative assessment should now be clear. To maximize student achievement, the regular instruction provided to all students (often called "tier 1 instruction" within RTI approaches) must be as good as it can be, and this requires the use of regular classroom formative assessment. Formative assessment also involves assessing the progress made by learners, and where this is deemed inadequate, more intensive interventions (tier 2 and tier 3) are used. Moreover, because formative assessment, at least when it is done well, indicates not just that students are not learning but why and what can be done about it, then formative assessment actually increases the effectiveness of tier 2 interventions because they can be more effectively targeted to the specific difficulties the student is experiencing.

The purpose of these rather extended discussions into the Framework for Teaching, differentiated instruction, and response to intervention has been to show that classroom formative assessment is not just compatible with these initiatives. Rather, formative assessment becomes the vehicle for *delivering* them, and not just an addition to the load that teachers and leaders have to bear. By focusing on the aspects of the Framework for Teaching that have the greatest impacts on student achievement, classroom formative assessment aligns the attempts of teachers to improve their ratings with improved outcomes for their students, which might not otherwise happen.

By highlighting the aspects of differentiated instruction that are supported by evidence, leaders can ensure that compliance with district mandates that differentiated instruction should be in place will actually benefit learners. And finally, this chapter has shown that the whole idea of response to intervention is just one aspect of classroom formative assessment. The pieces really do fit together.

[*Chapter 5*]

Expertise, in Teaching and Elsewhere

Previous chapters reviewed why we need to increase student achievement, why this requires supporting the development of teachers already working in our schools, and why formative assessment appears to be the most powerful focus for that development. We also saw that there are two complementary aspects of formative assessment—using data to monitor student progress and improving the way that teachers use assessment during instruction. In the United States, most of the development efforts to date have focused on the first aspect of formative assessment—the use of data to monitor student progress—for perfectly understandable reasons. In particular, it generally appears to be much easier to change what teachers do when students are not present than to change what teachers do when students *are* present. Because of the emphasis this approach to formative assessment has received, there is now a significant amount of guidance available to teachers and leaders about how to generate common formative assessments and how to create professional learning communities that can examine the resulting evidence and take appropriate action. The work of Richard DuFour and his colleagues (e.g., DuFour, DuFour, Eaker, & Karhanek, 2004; DuFour, DuFour, Eaker, & Many, 2005; DuFour, Eaker, & DuFour, 2005) is particularly helpful in terms of advice for establishing and sustaining professional learning communities, and the publications of the Data Wise project at Harvard University provide comprehensive guidance on interpreting assessment data (e.g., Boudett, City, & Murnane, 2013).

However, the scale of improvements in educational achievement needed by young people today means that we cannot rely on instructional data teams as the sole mechanism for school improvement. We need to use instructional data teams, and we also need to support teachers in harnessing the power of classroom formative assessment to improve the quality of their instruction, for two reasons. First, as we saw in the previous chapter, improvements in the use of assessment during instruction appear to have a larger impact on student achievement than using assessment to monitor progress. Second, as we also saw in the previous chapter, improvements in teacher capability benefit all the students a teacher will teach in the future, and because subsequent improvements will build on previous improvements, investing in teacher capability is a compounding process. Even very modest improvements in a teacher's performance each year will therefore have a large impact on the achievement of future students over time.

Twenty years ago, the idea of changing teacher practice might have seemed impossible. Indeed, as noted in chapter 2, many economists of education focused on incentives for teachers precisely because they simply did not believe that teacher talent could be increased very much. But in recent years, a great deal of evidence has been accumulated about the role of practice in developing expertise in a wide range of fields, and this idea is the main focus of this chapter. Specifically, the arguments of this chapter are that

- Existing research on expertise indicates that expertise in teaching is similar to expertise in other areas.

- Expertise does not require much in the form of natural talent but rather requires ten years of deliberate practice to achieve.

- Existing research on teacher development indicates that most teachers improve little after their second or third year of practice.

- Many, if not most, of our existing teachers could be as good as the very best if they were supported to improve in the right way.

The first half of this chapter reviews the research on expertise across a range of human endeavors, and the second half explores the application of this research to expertise in teaching.

Research on Expertise

The differences between individuals in their ability to perform physical and mental tasks are extraordinary. Top tennis players will not drop a point, far less a game or a set, against good club players. The best chess players can play upward of twenty chess matches with others at the same time and win them all. Expert diagnosticians can immediately generate diagnoses that fully qualified, but less expert, doctors would take hours to identify, if they ever could.

For many years, these extraordinary differences have been attributed to differences in talent. While the debate continues about whether these differences are genetic in origin, are innate, or are the result of early childhood experiences, it is widely believed that, for whatever reason, some people are just more talented than others, that they have a gift for a particular sport or discipline, or that they just have what it takes to be extraordinary.

However, in recent years, it has become clear that, in the words of Geoff Colvin (2009), "talent is overrated." This is not to say that talent is irrelevant. In professional basketball, for example, despite the success of players such as Tyrone Curtis "Muggsy" Bogues (at 5'3" the shortest player ever to play in the National Basketball Association), height is clearly important. Approximately five out of every million American males aged between twenty and forty are in the NBA. For those over seven feet tall, it's around 17 percent (Epstein, 2013). Similarly, while hitters in major league baseball don't appear to have particularly fast reactions compared to the general population, they have *much* better eyesight. The average major league batter has 20/11 vision, which means that he can see at twenty feet what an average person can see only at eleven feet (Laby et al., 1996).

For many people, the idea that practice is more important than talent is associated with the work of Malcolm Gladwell (2008), who, in his book *Outliers*, suggested, "Ten thousand hours is the magic number of greatness" (p. 41). The figure of ten thousand hours is taken from a single study of just twenty outstanding violin players that found that they had accumulated an average of ten thousand hours of practice by the age of twenty (Ericsson, Krampe, & Tesch-Römer, 1993).

However, before placing too much emphasis on the figure of ten thousand hours, it is important to note that this figure is based on self-reports from the violinists about how much practicing they had done when they were younger (going back more than ten years), and perhaps more important, the figure is an average across the violinists in the study. While other studies have found that a similar amount of practice is common for outstanding young pianists (Sloboda, Davidson, Howe, & Moore, 1996), it appears that violinists and pianists practice more than those studying other instruments. For example, Jørgensen (1997) studied the amount of practice undertaken by 182 young musicians at the Norges musikkhøgskole (the Norwegian State Academy of Music). While the institution suggests that students should undertake about twenty-five hours of practice each week, pianists and violinists practiced, on average, over thirty hours each week, although the range was substantial, with violinists ranging from fewer than twenty hours to over forty-five hours per week, and pianists ranging from twenty-seven to forty-one hours per week. Specialists in other instruments practiced less. Other string specialists (e.g., violists, cellists, double bassists) practiced around twenty-six hours per week, but players of woodwind and brass instruments practiced only around eighteen hours per week.

Some years earlier, Chase and Simon (1973) had suggested that ten thousand hours was actually a *lower* limit for achieving grandmaster status in chess:

> There are no instant experts in chess—certainly no instant masters or grandmasters. There appears not to be on record any case (including Bobby Fischer) where a person reached grandmaster level with less than about a decade's intense preoccupation with the game. We would estimate, very roughly, that a master has spent perhaps 10,000 to 50,000 hours staring at chess positions. (p. 402)

However, more recently, Campitelli and Gobet (2011) have found that some players achieved master status with only 3,000 hours of practice, and some had not done so even after 50,000 hours.

So, it seems there is nothing special about the figure of ten thousand hours of practice. First, it depends on the definitions of *expertise*—for some the term means being one of a handful of the world's best, while for others, expertise means an outstanding level of performance, but one that is achieved by hundreds, or even thousands, of individuals. For example, at the end of 2014, the World Chess Federation's database listed 1,477 players as grandmasters and 6,728 players as masters (World Chess Federation, 2014).

Second, it depends on the kind of practice involved. For example, in chess, activities such as reading books and studying games online were associated with high-level performance, but playing games against computers was not (Campitelli & Gobet, 2008). Perhaps surprisingly, once the effects of solitary practice had been taken into account, there was little relationship with the number of tournament games played (Charness, Krampe, & Mayr, 1996; Charness, Tuffiash, Krampe, Reingold, & Vasyukova, 2005), and similar findings were obtained by Duffy, Baluch, and Ericsson (2004) for competitive darts.

Third, as already noted, the amount of time taken to achieve any particular level of expertise will be more for some people and less for others, and fourth, it will be more for some areas of expertise and less for others. However, buried in the previous quotation from Simon and Chase is a claim that actually has a far longer history, and far more supporting evidence, and that is that it takes *ten years* of practice to develop expertise in a given area.

A Very Brief History of Expertise Research

In the ancient Mesopotamian city of Uruk, writing first evolved by making marks on spherical and tetrahedral lumps of clay. Each mark on a piece of clay denoted one of the thousands of different syllables in the local language, but, presumably to keep things manageable, the writing system used only 500 different symbols, so that each symbol could stand for one of a number of syllables. This meant that the system required a great deal of time to learn—typically about ten years (Bernstein, 2013).

In the traditional guilds of medieval Europe, a fourteen-year-old boy (or much more rarely, a girl) would become apprenticed to a master, with whom he or she would learn a craft for a period of around seven years (Epstein, 1991). At the end of this period, apprentices were considered to have completed their basic training and were then permitted to work for other masters for pay, which often entailed traveling to other towns (which is why these people were often called *journeymen*). After a period as a journeyman, a craftsman might have saved enough money to purchase tools and a workshop and then would be able to apply for membership into a guild. Therefore, becoming a member of a guild took at least ten years, and often much longer.

A detailed study of telegraph operators at the end of the 19th century found that there were, over time, substantial improvements in the ability of the operators to receive and send messages, although improvements in the ability to send messages appear to be relatively smooth, while the ability to receive seems to have periods of rapid improvement, punctuated by periods where performance does not appear to improve much at all. However, the main conclusion was, "Our evidence is that it requires ten years to make a thoroughly seasoned press dispatcher" (Bryan & Harter, 1899, p. 381).

The idea that ten years of practice is needed for expert performance has, in recent years, been strongly supported by K. Anders Ericsson (2006)—one of the world's leading authorities on expertise—but he points out that mere practice is not enough. In the early stages of acquiring a skill, simple repetitive practice clearly does improve performance—Heathcote, Brown, and Mewhort (2000) suggest that the improvement in skill follows an exponential curve. However, beyond this basic level, while simply repeating activities does reduce the amount of effort required to undertake a task, it does not improve performance. After all, many of us have well over ten thousand hours of practice driving a car, and while this practice does make the task of driving a car less demanding on our mental faculties, it does not make the performance better.

In fact, across a large range of human experiences, there is now considerable evidence that just having more experience often does not improve performance, at least beyond the initial stages. Dawes (1994) found that more experienced psychotherapists were no more effective than their less experienced colleagues in treating patients. Rosson (1985) and Sonnentag (1998) found that those with more experience in software design did not perform consistently better on software-design tasks. In fact, in many areas, it has been found that performance declines with experience. For example, Bédard and Chi (1993) found that the more postqualification experience financial auditors had, the less effective they were, and Ericsson (2004) found that more experienced general practitioners were less effective at diagnosing heart sounds and reading X-ray films. At the same time, some studies have found that while those with more experience are often less effective, they can be overconfident (Glenberg & Epstein, 1987; Tetlock, 2005), although other studies have found no relationship between experience, confidence, and expertise (Jee, Wiley, & Griffin, 2006).

What is needed to reach expert levels of performance, Ericsson has argued, is ten years of what he calls *deliberate practice*. As defined by Ericsson and his colleagues (1993),

> Deliberate practice is a highly structured activity, the explicit goal of which is to improve performance. Specific tasks are invented to overcome weaknesses, and performance is carefully monitored to provide cues for ways to improve it further. We claim that deliberate practice requires effort and is not inherently enjoyable. Individuals are motivated to practice because practice improves performance. In addition, engaging in deliberate practice generates no immediate monetary rewards and generates costs associated with access to teachers and training environments. (p. 368)

This is not to say that talent is irrelevant. As Winner (1996) has pointed out, some children have a "rage to master." These are the children who have to be dragged away from their practicing—something rarely seen with young musicians. The point is that—as Ericsson indicates—practice is not inherently enjoyable, and therefore one needs some motivation to engage in it. For some, this may be the rage to master, while for others, it may be the desire to get good at something, and for others, it may be obligation.

While the kinds of activities listed above—chess, telegraphy, musicianship, medicine, accountancy, and so on—may seem to have little in common, in recent years, researchers have begun to investigate to what extent there are common features to expertise in different areas. While the field is still developing, and there are a number of unresolved issues that are being actively debated, there does seem to be reasonable consensus that expertise, in a very broad range of human activity, has a number of common features. The most important of these are discussed next.

Expertise Is Specific and Limited

In one of the most famous early studies on expertise in chess, Chase and Simon (1973) used a task that had been developed by Adriaan de Groot (1965/1978) in which three chess players were shown, for about five seconds, a chess board on which a number of chess pieces had been placed and then were asked to reproduce what they had seen. One of the players was a chess master, one was a class A player (one with a rating of between 1800 and 2000 on the rating system developed by Elo, 1978), and one was a beginner. Some of the trials involved a middle game situation, after about twenty moves by each player, with around twenty-five pieces on the board, and some of the trials were from end game situations, after about forty moves by each player, with twelve to fifteen pieces remaining on the board. In addition to these real-game situations, the participants were asked to reproduce chess boards with similar numbers of pieces, but where the pieces had been placed on the board at random (although each piece was placed entirely within a single square). Each player was asked to complete the task twenty times: ten positions from actual games and ten with the pieces placed at random. The average numbers of pieces placed correctly by the three players are shown in Table 5.1 (Chase & Simon, 1973).

Table 5.1. Number of Chess Pieces Correctly Remembered by Novice, Intermediate, and Expert Players From Random and Real-Game Situations

	Middle game		End game	
	Random	Actual game	Random	Actual game
Novice	2	5	1	4
Intermediate	3	9	2	7
Expert	3	16	3	8

Two features of this table are particularly noteworthy. The first is the extraordinary level of performance of the expert in the actual game situation, recalling the positions of about two-thirds of the pieces correctly. The second rather surprising fact is that where the pieces had been placed on the board at random, rather than from an actual game, the expert was no better than the other two players. The superior performance of the expert was limited to actual game situations.

The specificity of expertise has been demonstrated in a number of other experiments. Eisenstadt and Kareev (1979) applied a version of the de Groot task to two ancient Chinese board games, Go and Gomoku. Although the two games share many similarities and are played with the same pieces on the same board, expert players of

Go were rather poor at reproducing situations from a Gomoku game, and Gomoku players were rather poor at reproducing situations from a game of Go. This suggests that, as in chess, superior performance is based on recognition of meaningful configurations rather than superior short-term memory.

In a study in the field of political science, ten novices (students) and six experts were asked to produce plans for increasing crop production in the Soviet Union. As might be expected, the responses of novices were less developed and focused on features such as increasing the availability of fertilizer or tractors, while the plans produced by the experts focused more on the development of infrastructure. However, what is perhaps more surprising is that when the same tasks were given to chemistry professors, their responses were more similar to those of the students than the experts (Voss, Greene, Post, & Penner, 1983; Voss, Tyler, & Yengo, 1983).

In sports too, expertise appears to be limited to the specific activities at which the individual excels. Syed (2010)—himself a world-ranked table-tennis player—describes his inability to see, let alone return, a serve from Michael Stich, the tennis ace. Epstein (2013) documents the abject failure of major league hitters such as Mike Piazza, Albert Pujols, and Barry Bonds to make contact with a fast-pitch softball thrown by US Olympian Jennie Finch. Some have claimed that in sports, experts tend to have fewer eye fixations of longer duration (e.g., Abernethy, 1985), but this does not seem to apply to all sports. For example, expert defenders in soccer tend to have more eye fixations of shorter duration (Williams & Davids, 1998). In other words, whatever general features expertise may have, there will always be aspects of expertise that are highly specific to the particular activity.

A systematic review of research on novice-expert differences in physical sports by Thomas, Gallagher, and Lowry (2003) identified thirty-nine relevant studies and included data on 1,112 experts and 1,287 novices. The most important finding was that the greater the ecological validity of the tasks used in the studies (i.e., how close the tasks were to the area of expertise), the bigger the difference in performance between novices and experts. While this is not perhaps in itself that surprising, what is more interesting is that the effect was greater at higher levels of expertise, providing further evidence of the specificity of expertise.

Expertise Is Only Weakly Related to General Ability

In most professions, training people to undertake complex tasks is expensive and time consuming, so over the years, a great deal of effort has gone into trying to identify, ahead of the training, who are likely to be the best once training has been received. The general finding is that, just as we saw for teaching in chapter 2, things that might appear to be important do not seem to make that much of a difference.

For example, skill in surgery does not seem to correlate with medical school grades (Keck, Arnold, Willoughby, & Calkins, 1979; Papp, Polk, & Richardson, 1997) or even tests of manual dexterity (Schueneman, Pickleman, & Freeark, 1985; Squire, Giachino, Profitt, & Heaney, 1989). While visual-spatial ability has been found to correlate with skill as a surgeon, the influence declines, and ultimately disappears, as individuals get more practice (Wanzel, Hamstra, Anastakis, Matsumoto, & Cusimano, 2002; Wanzel et al., 2003).

This basic finding—that general ability predicts performance well to begin with, but prediction accuracy diminishes as individuals get more practice—has been confirmed in a range of diverse settings. This is not to say that general ability is irrelevant—indeed, almost all studies of expertise find that those with higher levels of general ability have higher levels of performance even after years of practice. However, it is clear that the correlation of measures of general ability with expert performance is rather modest. For example, Grabner, Stern, and Neubauer (2007) found that the most important predictor of a player's Elo rating was the age at which the player joined a chess club (i.e., the younger the player was when he or she joined a chess club, the higher his or her rating), followed by the number of tournament games he or she had played. Intelligence (and especially numerical intelligence), age, the ability to control emotions, and the motivation to play chess were also significantly associated with chess rankings, but on its own, intelligence only accounted for about 12 percent of the variation in chess player ratings.

Experts Perceive More Meaningful Patterns in What They Observe

One of the most interesting findings of the early work by Chase and Simon (1973) on expertise in chess described previously was that the superior expert performance was due largely to the fact that experts did not look at individual pieces on a chessboard, but instead looked at patterns of pieces. Native English speakers can see a phrase, such as *working inside the black box* and immediately reproduce it, but given the same phrase in Kazakh—ҚАРА ЖӘШІК ІШІНДЕГІ ЖҰМЫС—it would be unlikely they could do so unless they knew the Kazakh alphabet and also some Kazakh vocabulary. We do not see the phrase *working inside the black box* as a series of straight and curved strokes on a page, but instead as a series of chunks and chunks within chunks. We do not see the letter *w* as a series of four strokes, angled left and right, but as a whole, and this whole becomes part of a larger whole (the word *working*). Indeed, as Lesgold and Resnick (1982) showed, in a five-year longitudinal study of a group of children as they moved from kindergarten to fourth grade, if basic reading skills, such as decoding and encoding letters and words, do not become automatic, the ability to comprehend text does not develop. Moreover, because increases in the speed of word skills were associated with later increases in comprehension, whereas increases in comprehension were not associated with increases in word facility, it seems likely that the relationship is causal. Increases in word skill *cause* improvements in comprehension (see also Wolf, 2007).

In the same way, expert chess players see chess boards from real games as consisting of a number of (possibly overlapping) patterns, such as connected (i.e., mutually supporting) rooks, castled-king positions, and pawn chains (pawns placed on the same diagonal with no gaps). Chase and Simon (1973) estimated that master chess players have at least 50,000 such chunks, and that is why their performance on the memory task is so much better. They don't have better visual memories; what they see is much more familiar and makes sense as a result of their experience.

Sometimes, the starkest difference between experts and novices is not so much in the amount of knowledge but how it is organized. For example, in a study of physics problems (Chi, Feltovich, & Glaser, 1981), students were given a number of problems from an introductory physics textbook on index cards and were asked to sort them into groups that they would solve in a similar manner. Novices tended to group problems according to surface features, such as whether the problems involved springs or inclined planes, whereas experts grouped problems on the basis of major principles of physics, such as the conservation of energy or Newton's second law.

Similarly, Quilici and Mayer (1996) found that lower-achieving students were more likely to group statistical problems according to their cover story (e.g., whether the problem situation was about rainfall), whereas higher-achieving students were more likely to use the deep structure of the problem, such as the statistical method being used (e.g., *t*-test, correlation, chi-square).

Similar results have been observed in medicine. In one study, four expert radiologists (each with at least ten years' postresidency experience) and eight residents (in their first to fourth years of residency) were shown X-rays and asked to comment on what they saw and to provide a diagnosis. Not only did the experts—who would have seen on average 200,000 X-ray films—see more relevant features on the films they were shown, but they also saw relationships *between* different features on the films that helped them make more accurate diagnoses (Lesgold et al., 1988).

Another study (Alberdi et al., 2001) found little difference between junior and senior doctors in their ability to identify key events, such as a developing pneumothorax (collapsed lung) from a series of measurements of heart rate, transcutaneous oxygen, etc. However, the more experienced doctors were much better at spotting other relative but nonobvious events and were also better at detecting artifacts in the data, such as readings from faulty equipment.

This ability to see connections and inter-relations also helps experts remember details of related situations. For example, Spilich, Vesonder, Chiesi, and Voss (1979) investigated how well people recalled a description of half an inning of a fictitious baseball game. Those with deeper knowledge of baseball did no better than novices regarding details of the weather, the mood of the crowd, and so on, but did much better than novices on details of the action that were related to scoring (e.g., advancing runners). Similarly, Schneider and his colleagues (Schneider, 1996; Schneider, Körkel, & Weinert, 1989) found that elementary and middle schoolers who scored poorly on measures of general ability did just as well as high scorers in their ability to recall details of a soccer game if they knew a lot about soccer.

Even in playing sports, expertise seems to have a large component of knowledge. Williams and Davids (1995) found that expert soccer players exhibited greater recall, recognition, and anticipation than novices, but, echoing the findings of Chase and Simon discussed earlier, only for structured game-like situations. Of course, as might be expected, working memory does matter in recall of passages of play in sports (Hambrick & Engle, 2002), but its effect is dwarfed by the effect of knowledge about the subject matter being described.

This has led some researchers to conclude that expertise involves organizing information into larger and more integrated units. Indeed, some have claimed, "This is a classic and one of the best-established phenomenon in expertise" (Feltovich, Prietula, & Ericsson, 2006, p. 49). However, in some areas, experts organize information into *finer*, or *smaller*, units than novices.

For example, most humans are quicker with judgments made at the basic level ("Is this a dog?") than at the superordinate level ("Is this a mammal?") or the subordinate level ("Is this a bloodhound?"). However, dog experts recognized subordinate features of dogs, but not other animals, as fast as basic-level features (Tanaka, 2001; Tanaka & Taylor, 1991). Interestingly, the more expert someone was in recognizing cars, the greater the activity in the region of the brain that is primarily involved in recognizing faces (McGugin, Gatenby, Gore, & Gauthier, 2012).

As another example, a study of actors learning lines (Noice & Noice, 1993) found that they separate the text they need to learn into beats, which are segments of dialogue related to a single intention or idea, typically a goal-directed activity of the character being portrayed: "A beat begins under a given set of circumstances when an immediate objective sets in. It ends when that objective has succeeded or failed and new circumstances set in" (Hagen, 1973, p. 175).

The study found that the beats used by professional actors contained, on average, around five idea units. Novices tended to organize the text into larger units, containing, on average, around nine idea units, based on the topic of conversation and more akin to the chunks that experts use to organize their knowledge in other domains.

So expertise does not always consist of organizing knowledge into larger chunks. Sometimes they are smaller, but the important point is that experts organize knowledge and information into units that are the right size for the activity being undertaken, and the relationships between the units are meaningful. Moreover, the chunks tend to be more abstract, relating to deep features of the task at hand, rather than the surface features, and they help the expert reason about the situation at hand (Zeitz, 1997).

Expertise Involves Automation of Basic Routines

One of the most interesting findings of the telegraph operators mentioned earlier is that when receiving messages, novice telegraphers needed to write down each letter as it arrived. What Bryan and Harter (1899) called *fair operators* could work several words behind the instrument, but experts, they noted, actually *preferred* to work between six and twelve words behind the incoming signal. Because converting the incoming pattern of dots and dashes into letters was automatic, experts could focus on the meaning of the message.

This automation of basic routines, which enables experts to perform easily tasks that novices have to work hard to complete, is one of the hallmarks of expertise: "One becomes an expert by making routine what to the novice requires creative problem-solving ability" (Anderson, 1980, p. 292). The same insight was captured even more simply by Frederic Bartlett (1958), who noted that experts "have all the time in the world" (p. 15).

Moreover, this is not just a surface feature. As noted in chapter 3, while experts generally do things in the same parts of the brain as novices, they do so with far less effort, at least as indicated by fMRI studies (Hill & Schneider, 2006; Jansma, Ramsey, Slagter, & Kahn, 2001).

Studies of soccer players have found that expert defenders react significantly faster than novices in one-on-one, three-on-three, and full eleven-on-eleven situations (Williams & Davids, 1998; Williams, Davids, Burwitz, & Williams, 1993). However, as with the studies of tennis and table tennis mentioned earlier, this may not be due to faster reactions. For example, a longitudinal study of baseball players found that simple reaction time did not improve over a two-year period of training. What did improve was the go/no-go reaction time (Kida, Oda, & Matsumura, 2005). In other words, experts may not have faster simple reaction times than novices, but they are better at knowing how to react.

Because experts have automated basic routines, they tend to be less affected by stress. Baddeley (1972) reviewed research on the performance of individuals parachuting from aircraft and scuba divers in the open sea and found that those with more experience were better able to control their emotional reactions to stressful situations. As a result, they were less distracted by the most salient (as opposed to the most important) features of a dangerous situation. In a similar vein, Calderwood, Klein, and Crandall (1988) found that time pressure had a much greater negative impact on the performance of good (Class B) chess players than on outstanding ones.

One important question that has arisen in expertise research is whether the superior performance of experts is due solely to the faster cognitive processing. In other words, are they simply able to consider and evaluate a larger number of possible courses of action? Where this has been researched, the evidence suggests that experts tend to consider better, rather than just more, options. For example, while expert managers make decisions quicker (Eisenhardt, 1990), in stressful situations, experts are more likely to focus immediately on the best options, while novices tend to consider the ones that are not as good (Yates, Klatzky, & Young, 1995). Similarly, Klein, Wolf, Militello, and Zsambok (1995) found that when chess players were asked to generate a number of potential moves, the first moves generated by experts were much better than would be expected by chance, suggesting that human ability to play chess has more to do with generating a small number of good options rather than a large number of options and evaluating each, which is the approach used by most chess-playing computer programs. In other words, expertise consists of processing that is more automatic, faster, and better (Hancock, 1996).

Expertise Is Not Reducible to Propositional Knowledge

Wayne Gretzky is regarded as one of the greatest ice hockey players of all time. He won the Hart Memorial Trophy, given to the National Hockey League's most valuable player, nine times, eight times in consecutive years (1979–1980 through 1986–1987). He won the Art Ross Trophy for the most number of points scored in a season, ten times in all, and seven consecutive times (1980–1981 through 1986–1987). When he retired in 1999, he held or shared forty NHL regular-season records, fifteen playoff records, and six All-Star records.

Gretzky undoubtedly started out with some natural gifts. In his teens, he played box (indoor) lacrosse and baseball at a high level, and in 1980 was offered a contract with the Toronto Blue Jays Major League Baseball team. He also had physical stamina. Many of his goals were scored late in games, and this was, at least in part, due to his physiology. When his team's recuperation times were tested by a sports physiologist, the result for Gretzky was so extreme that the tester thought the machine was not functioning correctly (Gzowski, 1981). However, whatever natural gifts he had, it is clear that, as might be expected from the research on expertise discussed previously, talent was not enough.

For a start, he began skating at the age of two, in a rink his father constructed in the family's backyard. As he wrote in his autobiography:

> See, kids usually don't start playing hockey until they're six or seven. Ice isn't grass. It's a whole new surface and everybody starts from ground zero. . . . By the time I was ten, I had eight years on skates instead of four, and a few seasons' worth of ice time against ten-year-olds. So I had a long head start on everyone else. (Gretzky & Reilly, 1990, p. 19)

In addition, the time he spent practicing was rather extraordinary:

> All I wanted to do in the winters was be on the ice. I'd get up in the morning, skate from 7:00 to 8:30, go to school, come home at 3:30, stay on the ice until my mom insisted I come in for dinner, eat in my skates, then go back out until 9:00. On Saturdays and Sundays we'd have huge games, but nighttime became my time. It was a sort of unwritten rule around the neighbourhood that I was to be out there myself or with my dad. (Redmond, 1993, pp. 12–13).

As he said some years later, "From the age of 3 to the age of 12, I could easily be out there eight to 10 hours a day" (Duhatschek, 2014). Moreover, the practice that the young Gretzky engaged in with his father, Walter, was the kind of *deliberate practice* previously defined by Ericsson and his colleagues:

> Some say I have a "sixth sense" . . . Baloney. I've just learned to guess what's going to happen next. It's anticipation. It's not God-given, it's Wally-given. He used to stand on the blue line and say to me, "Watch, this is how everybody else does it." Then he'd shoot a puck along the boards and into the corner and then go chasing after it. Then he'd come back and say, "Now, this is how the smart player does it." He'd shoot it into the corner again, only this time he cut across to the other side and picked it up over there. Who says anticipation can't be taught? (Gretzky & Reilly, 1990, p. 87)

However, what most commentators single out as the most distinctive aspect of Gretzky's play is his ability to be in the right place at the right time, to skate not to where the puck was, but to where it was going to be:

> To most fans, and sometimes even to the players on the ice, hockey frequently looks like chaos: sticks flailing, bodies falling, the puck ricocheting just out of reach. But amid the mayhem, Gretzky can discern the game's underlying pattern and flow, and anticipate what's going to happen faster and in more detail than anyone else in the building.
>
> "To me, it's like everything is happening in slow motion," he once explained. Several times during a game you'll see him making what seem to be aimless

circles on the other side of the rink from the traffic, and then, as if answering a signal, he'll dart ahead to a spot where, an instant later, the puck turns up. (McGrath, 1997)

This, of course, picks up one of the strands of expertise mentioned previously—the ability to see meaningful patterns that are not apparent to novices—but there are two further important points here. The first is that this ability was not in any sense innate, but rather the result of extensive practice drills organized by his father, as the following extract from Gretzky's autobiography illustrates:

Him: "Where's the last place a guy looks before he passes it?"

Me: "The guy he's passing to."

Him: "Which means . . ."

Me: "Get over there and intercept it."

Him: "Where do you skate?"

Me: "To where the puck is going, not where it's been."

Him: "If you get cut off, what are you gonna do?"

Me: "Peel."

Him: "Which way?"

Me: "Away from the guy, not towards him." (Gretzky & Reilly, 1990, p. 88)

The second important point is that while being able to skate to where the puck is going to be, rather than where it is, was a key aim in the practice drills that Gretzky completed, telling a novice hockey player that he or she needs to skate toward where the puck is going to be, rather than where it is, is of no use at all without the ability to detect the meaningful patterns in the play. Expertise cannot be reduced to a set of instructions that can be given to someone to short-circuit the process of deliberate practice. Put bluntly, expertise cannot be put into words.

This was powerfully illustrated by a study of expertise in the performance of cardiopulmonary resuscitation (CPR) conducted by Helen and Gary Klein (1981). The researchers prepared six video clips of six different individuals performing CPR. Five of the videos featured students who were learning how to perform CPR, while one featured an expert paramedic who had been performing CPR for over twenty years. The six videos were then shown to participants, who were asked, "Which one of these six people would you want doing CPR on you if you needed it?" Approximately 90 percent of the experienced paramedics selected the expert from amongst the six videos, while only 50 percent of students—those learning to perform CPR—did so. However, what was most surprising was that only 30 percent of the instructors—people who teach others how to perform CPR—chose the expert paramedic from the six videos.

Klein and Klein (1981) suggested that the reason that instructors so rarely selected the expert paramedic was because the instructors were looking for CPR practitioners who enacted the "rules" of CPR that they taught. In particular, they were looking for the presence of step-by-step approaches that were often not apparent in the work of the expert paramedics. However, it is clear that while the expert paramedic may not have followed a predetermined set of rules, expert paramedics could identify another expert.

This suggests that even in something as simple as CPR, expertise cannot be reduced to a set of "rules" that can be communicated to others by telling them what to do. Much, and perhaps all, of the knowledge that experts possess is not in a form that can be put into words. It is *tacit* rather than *explicit* knowledge.

The idea that we can know things but not be able to express what we know in words is familiar to everyone. One can know how to ride a bicycle, but it seems rather unlikely that anyone could put what they were doing into words with sufficient clarity that someone who could not ride a bicycle would be able to pick up the instructions and use them to accelerate their own learning process. Indeed, how, exactly, a bicycle is able to stay upright is still not well understood (Kooijman, Meijaard, Papadopoulos, Ruina, & Schwab, 2011).

Michael Polanyi (1966/2009) summed this idea up neatly by saying, "We can know more than we can tell" (p. 4), and this dimension of tacit knowledge has been shown to be important in a number of areas of expertise. Donald Schön (1983) has shown that tacit knowledge is an important component of expertise in the professions, and, in more specific empirical studies, Wagner and Steinberg (1985) found that subject-specific tacit knowledge was important for job performance over and above measures of general intelligence for psychologists, managers, and bankers.

Some writers (e.g., Dreyfus, Dreyfus, & Anathanasiou, 1986) prefer the term *intuitive expertise* to the term *tacit knowledge*, but the problem with the idea of intuition is that, in popular language at least, it is akin to the sixth sense mentioned previously by Wayne Gretzky—something with which someone is born rather than the result of years of hard work. Others, such as Cianciolo, Matthew, Sternberg, and Wagner (2006), suggest that tacit knowledge is similar to what they term *practical intelligence*.

In addition, there are differences in views on how broadly the term *tacit knowledge* should be defined. Some writers use the term to describe only those kinds of knowledge that cannot be expressed in words, such as how to ride a bicycle. For others, tacit knowledge includes knowledge that might, in principle, be expressed in words, but where this has not yet been done (Hedesstrom & Whitley, 2000). For still others, tacit knowledge refers to knowledge that is "not directly taught or spoken about, in contrast to knowledge directly taught in classrooms" (Wagner & Steinberg, 1985, pp. 438–439), similar to what Elliot Eisner (1985) described as the *null curriculum*: "the options students are not afforded, the perspectives they may never know about, much less be able to use, the concepts and skills that are not part of their intellectual repertoire" (p. 107).

In considering the role of tacit knowledge in expertise, it is important to realize that under certain circumstances, the acquisition of expertise can be greatly accelerated. For example, determining whether day-old chicks are male or female (so that money is not spent on feeding chicks that will not lay eggs) was, for many years, believed to be a task that required years of practice (Lunn, 1946). However, Biederman and Shiffrar (1987) found that a training session lasting only a few minutes could increase the accuracy of novices almost to the level of experts. It is therefore certainly not correct to assume that expertise always requires ten years of deliberate practice. But in most areas that have been studied, it does appear that elite performance requires a considerable amount of deliberate practice.

The findings on expertise previously summarized suggest that while natural aptitude plays some role in expert performance, by far the most important determinant of the level of expertise is the amount of deliberate practice that the individual has undertaken. Ericsson et al. (1993) put it like this: "We view elite performance as the product of a decade or more of maximal efforts to improve performance in a domain through an optimal distribution of deliberate practice" (p. 400). As a result of this extensive practice, experts can interpret the situations with which they are faced in terms of a very large number of chunks, which allows them to process their sense data far more effectively and meaningfully than novices. In addition, such processing takes place extremely rapidly, partly because the routines have been practiced so much but also because experts tend to select the most appropriate options more quickly, at the outset, than novices.

All of this information suggests that high levels of performance are much more the result of disciplined development than talent. As has been stressed several times already, this does not mean, of course, that talent is irrelevant but rather that individuals are able to achieve high levels of performance if they are willing to invest the time in undertaking the necessary deliberate practice. So, given the theme of this book, the question that arises at this point is whether the nature of expertise in teaching is similar to the nature of expertise in the other domains that have been studied. In case the suspense is getting to you, the answer, as we shall see, is yes.

Expertise in Teaching

Over the course of a series of studies, David Berliner and his colleagues (1994) have shown that expertise in teaching does, indeed, share the characteristics of expertise identified in the earlier part of this chapter. First, expertise in teaching is specific and limited. A teacher might be very skilled at teaching seventh-grade math but much less effective at teaching math to seventh graders with special educational needs. For example, Gail Hanninen (1985) prepared a number of descriptions of gifted students and asked teachers to indicate how they would meet the needs of those students. One of the scenarios described an eight-year-old Asian boy with interests in mathematics, science, and information technology but who also had severe hearing deficits. Novice teachers, and experienced teachers with little experience teaching students with special needs, typically produced unsophisticated and bland responses, such as "Mark seems like a very talented individual with many diverse interests," "Mark should be encouraged by his teacher to continue his science experiments and work on the computer," and "He should be able to pursue his interests in greater depth" (Berliner, 1994, p. 175). In stark contrast, those with expertise in teaching students with special educational needs tended to adopt far more analytical and insightful responses such as, "Mark's needs can be broken into three broad areas: academic enrichment, emotional adjustment, and training to cope with his handicap" (Berliner, 1994, p. 175).

In another study undertaken by Berliner and his colleagues (1988), a number of teachers were asked to teach a thirty-minute lesson on probability to a group of high school students, for which they were given thirty minutes to plan. As might be expected, the lessons taught by more experienced teachers were judged better than those taught by novices. However, as Berliner et al. reported, "The task triggered a good deal of anger among this group of teachers. One of them quit the study, another broke down and cried in the middle of the study, and all were unhappy" (Berliner, 1994, p. 168). Novices and advanced beginners were happy with having just thirty minutes to plan the lesson, but the experts were unhappy that they did not know enough about the students they were about to teach. Of course, we do not know whether the more experienced teachers would in fact have been more effective if they had known the students better, but the fact that their reaction to such a task was so different from those of less experienced teachers suggests that the specific knowledge of the situation was important.

More recently, a study of teachers in New York reported by Jacob and Rockoff (2011) found that, as would be expected, the performance of teachers (as measured by the progress of their students) improved in their first few years of teaching, but the improvement was greater for those teachers who taught the same grade year after year. In a similar vein, a recent study of 30,000 elementary teachers in North Carolina found that a teacher who teaches the same grade year after year improves 50 percent faster than a teacher who changes grade assignment every year (Ost, 2014).

The second feature of expertise—that expertise is only weakly related to measures of general ability—has already been discussed at length. Clearly, teachers need to know the subject matter they are teaching, and a certain amount of intellectual ability is needed to be an effective teacher, but, beyond this threshold, those with a higher level of general ability do not seem to make better teachers. Also, in line with the research on expertise in general, initial levels of performance are not good predictors of future performance. A longitudinal study by Atteberry, Loeb, and Wyckoff (2013) examined the effectiveness of just over 800 elementary school teachers in New York over the first five years of their careers. Using data on state-wide standardized tests, a value-added score was generated for each teacher, for each of the first five years of their careers, and teachers were placed into five equally sized groups (i.e., quintiles) based on their effectiveness in teaching in their first year. The performance of the five groups of teachers for math over the first five years of their careers is shown in Figure 5.1 (Atteberry et al., 2013).

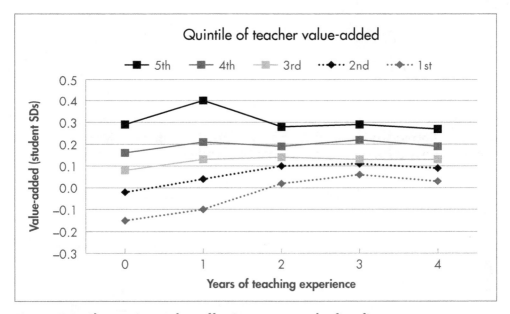

Figure 5.1. Change in teacher effectiveness over the first five years.

Perhaps the most interesting feature of Figure 5.1 is that while the least effective teachers (i.e., those in the first and second quintiles) improve rapidly, the teachers who are most effective at the start of their careers (i.e., the fourth and fifth quintiles) hardly improve at all. The result is that, as we saw with the training of surgeons earlier, the correlation of initial performance with current performance became weaker and weaker as time went on. To illustrate this, Figures 5.2 and 5.3 (Atteberry et al., 2013) show how well the teachers' effectiveness measured in a particular year predicts how good they will be in subsequent years, for the beginners discussed previously and their more experienced colleagues. For example, in math (Figure 5.2), the correlation between the teachers' value-added in their first year and their second year of teaching (base+1) is around 0.37. However, the correlation between the performance in the first year and the sixth year of teaching (base+5) is only around 0.18. In other words, how good teachers are in their first year of teaching does not tell us much about how good they will be in five years' time.

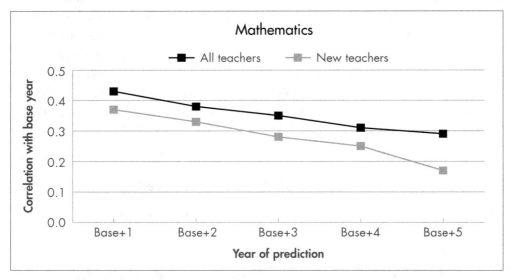

Figure 5.2. Correlation of initial estimates of effectiveness in teaching math with those in subsequent years, for novices and all teachers.

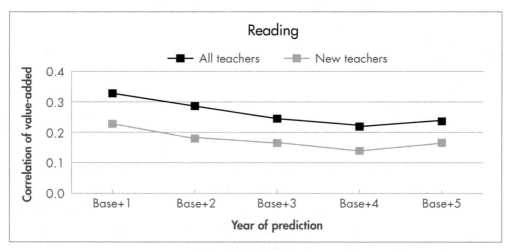

Figure 5.3. Correlation of initial estimates of effectiveness in teaching reading with those in subsequent years, for novices and all teachers.

Third, as is the case for expertise in general, expert teachers perceive more meaningful patterns in what they observe. For example, in what they called the "Look

Again" task, Berliner and his colleagues showed a slide to novice and expert teachers and asked them to describe what they saw. They were then shown the slide a second time and asked to describe what they saw. Then, they were shown the slide for a third and final time and again asked to describe what they saw.

One slide, of students in a science laboratory, elicited the following response from an expert teacher:

> "It's not necessarily a lab class. There just seemed to be more writing activity. There were people filling out forms. It could have been the end of a lab class after they started putting the equipment away . . ." After the third viewing of the slide, the expert said, "Yeah—there was . . . very little equipment out and it almost appeared to be towards the end of the hour. The books appeared to be closed. Almost looked like it was a clean-up type of situation." (Berliner, 1986, p. 11)

In contrast, Berliner (1986) notes, "Novices did not usually perceive the same cues in the classroom and could not, therefore, make the inferences that guided the expert's understanding of the classroom" (p. 11).

A math teacher, participating in a different Look Again task, described what he had seen as follows:

> "The first time I saw a student raising his hand in the classroom and I sub-consciously, apparently, was looking for the teacher and I did not notice the teacher in the classroom the first time. The second time I was curious. I was still looking for the teacher and didn't see the teacher. The third time I saw some students that were apparently seated in such a way that they were facing another direction of the classroom. It was an unusual seating arrange-ment. My impression was that part of the class was facing one direction and another part of the class was facing another direction." (Berliner, 1986, p. 11)

Berliner comments, "Very few of our novices . . . seemed to have this kind of sen-sitivity to perceptual information" (p. 11).

In another series of studies, novices, advanced beginners, and expert high school science teachers were shown a video recording of a science lesson that was displayed on three monitors so as to capture simultaneity, multidimensionality, and immediacy of teaching in as natural a way as possible (Sabers, Cushing, & Berliner, 1991). After watching the video, participants were asked to describe what they had seen, specif-ically focusing on the instructional and management strategies they had observed, and then they were asked a specific series of questions about what they had observed, such as those shown in Table 5.2.

Table 5.2. Follow-Up Questions Asked of Teachers Participating in an Observation Task

On the left monitor did you see:	On the middle monitor did you see:	On the right monitor did you see:
Four girls at a table?	A boy with a paper airplane?	A girl folding a note?
A girl turned sideways?	A boy pretending to play a piano?	A girl watering plants at the sink?
A girl reading a magazine?	A boy listening to the alarm on his watch?	A girl sitting on top of a desk?

Reminiscent of Chase and Simon's (1973) early studies of chess, there was little difference between novices, advanced beginners, and experts in their memory of specific details of what had happened in the lessons. The average percentages of correct answers for the questions for the different kinds of participants are shown in Table 5.3 (Sabers et al., 1991).

Table 5.3. Responses to a Video Observation Task

	Participant group		
	Novice	Advanced beginner	Expert
Left monitor	77	68	78
Middle monitor	72	66	73
Right monitor	83	83	84

However, while experts differed little from novices in their memory for specific details about the lesson, there were considerable differences in what they had observed in terms of the structure and design of the lesson. The written observations made by the participants were coded as either descriptions, interpretations, evaluations, conclusions, or suggestions. The breakdowns for novices, advanced beginners, and experts are summarized in Table 5.4 (Sabers et al., 1991). In particular, novices and advanced beginners gave far more straightforward descriptions of what they had seen, such as, "The kids walk in. She doesn't say hello to any of them. They're sort of wandering in" (advanced beginner, p. 73). In contrast, the experts made far more evaluative statements, such as, "On the left monitor, the students' note taking indicates that they have seen sheets like this and have had presentations like this before;

it's fairly efficient at this point because they're used to the format they are using" (expert, p. 72). Also, while the experts did not make more interpretive statements, the statements they did make tended to reveal deeper insights into the situation observed: "Left monitor again, I haven't heard a bell, but the students are already at their desks and seem to be doing purposeful activity, and this is about the time that I decided they must be an accelerated group because they came into the room and started something rather than just sitting down or socializing" (expert, pp. 72–73).

Table 5.4. Responses to a Video Observation Task

	Participant group		
	Novice	Advanced beginner	Expert
Descriptions	45	37	24
Interpretations	29	27	21
Evaluations	9	16	29
Conclusions	16	18	21
Suggestions	2	3	5
Totals	100	100	100

These differences are similar to those found in other comparisons of experts and novices (Borko & Livingston, 1989; Livingston & Borko, 1990).

Fourth, expert teachers develop automaticity for the repetitive operations that are needed to accomplish their goals. In my work with teachers on pre-service teacher education programs, I have found that novice teachers typically take around four hours to prepare one hour of instruction, while expert teachers plan lessons of higher quality in five minutes or less. In other words, planning a lesson is something an expert does as much as fifty times faster than a novice. The more often we do things, the better and faster we get at them.

Leinhardt and Greeno (1986) compared the performance of expert and novice elementary school mathematics teachers, using one task that would be familiar to most teachers: checking on homework. They described how an expert teacher used a number of routines to check on attendance, verifying who had and had not done the homework and establishing which of the students were likely to need individual help during the lesson. This was in marked contrast to a novice teacher undertaking a similar task, who was not able to establish which students had and had not done the homework, had difficulty in taking attendance, and did not learn which students were likely to have difficulty later in the lesson. Moreover, this phase of the lesson took three times longer for the novice than it did for the expert.

In a similar vein, Sharpe and Hawkins (1993) compared the performance of expert and novice teachers of physical education. They found no predictable patterns in the actions of the novice teacher, but the expert teacher used repetitive, but conditional, chains of behavior far more. For example, if behavior 12 was followed by behavior 18, then routine A was usually used, but if it was followed by behavior 16, routine B was usually used. The speed at which these behaviors took place suggests that they really were automated routines.

Finally, as the work of Christopher Day (1999) has shown, expert performance in teaching relies on a substantial amount of tacit knowledge in teaching. This has also been found to be true for teachers in higher education (Shim & Roth, 2008).

The argument of this chapter so far is that the nature of expertise in teaching is reasonably similar to the nature of expertise in the other areas in which expertise has been studied. Some might object to this conclusion by pointing out that most of the studies of expertise in teaching, and particularly those involving expert-novice comparisons, were conducted over twenty years ago. This is true, but this is largely because researchers don't generally bother researching things that are already well known. Indeed, even to be called "research," inquiries must be directed at generating new knowledge. More important, for the research on expertise in general not to be applicable to expertise in teaching, it would have to be the case that all the areas that have been studied in recent years are, in some way, similar to each other and different from teaching in important respects. This does not seem likely. The simplest interpretation of the available evidence is that expertise in teaching is similar to expertise in other areas.

If expertise in teaching really is like expertise in other areas, then it seems likely that, as is the case for other areas, expertise in teaching would require at least ten years of deliberate practice—ten years of "maximal efforts to improve performance" as Ericsson and his colleagues (1993) put it (p. 400). The question that arises at this point is, "Do teachers improve for at least ten years?"

Returns to Teaching Experience

The impact of teaching experience on student achievement has been extensively researched in the United States, not least because in most school districts, teaching experience is a major determinant of teacher compensation. The main finding of this large body of research is that in their first year or two, most teachers improve rapidly. In other words, students make less progress if they are taught by novice teachers. However, what is less clear is what happens subsequently. Many studies have found that the rate of improvement in teachers slows rapidly, and many studies have failed to find any improvement in teacher performance after three years of practice. Indeed, some studies have found that after a decade or two, teacher performance actually declines, although because most such studies are cross-sectional rather than longitudinal, it could be that this effect is caused by the most effective teachers becoming administrators and no longer teaching.

For example, Rivkin, Hanushek, and Kain (2005) analyzed the progress of 200,000 students in 3,000 schools in Texas from third or fourth grade through to seventh grade. As well as annual test scores for the students, the database included a range of demographic data, including ethnicity, eligibility for free or reduced-price lunch, and the size of the class in which each student was taught. The way the database was constructed also allowed students to be tracked even if they moved to other schools or districts in the state. Rivkin et al. (2005) explored four different ways of modeling the relationship between the progress made by students and their teacher's experience (for those who are interested, they used models with no fixed effects, with fixed student and school effects, with fixed effects for student and school-by-year, and finally a model that added school-by-grade effects). The results of the four models, for mathematics and reading, are shown in the two panels of Figure 5.4 (Rivkin et al., 2005).

To make the graphs in Figure 5.4 easier to interpret, I have rescaled the data from Rivkin et al. (2005) so that the zero represents the average for all teachers, and the impact of teacher experience on student achievement is shown in additional months of extra progress (based on the assumption that one year's progress for the students in the Texas sample is 0.4 standard deviations).

As can be seen, for both reading and mathematics, teachers improve in their first two years, but after that, improvement slows. More important, the graphs show that once teachers have three to five years' experience, they are close to the average for all teachers.

Other studies have found the same basic pattern—rapid early increase, with smaller improvements thereafter—but have found that increases in teacher quality were still detectable after fifteen to twenty years (Leigh, 2010; Papay & Kraft, 2015). More interesting, some recent studies have found the improvements in teacher quality over at least the first ten years of a career to be almost linear (Ladd & Sorensen, 2015).

Now if teachers are improving for at least ten years, this might indicate that all teachers are about as good as they could be, but in fact, the variation in teacher quality for experienced teachers is only slightly less than that for novice teachers. This suggests that even if teachers improve for ten (or fifteen or twenty) years, because most of them are still not as good as the best, they could be even better if we create a climate in which all teachers work hard on improvement, not because they are not

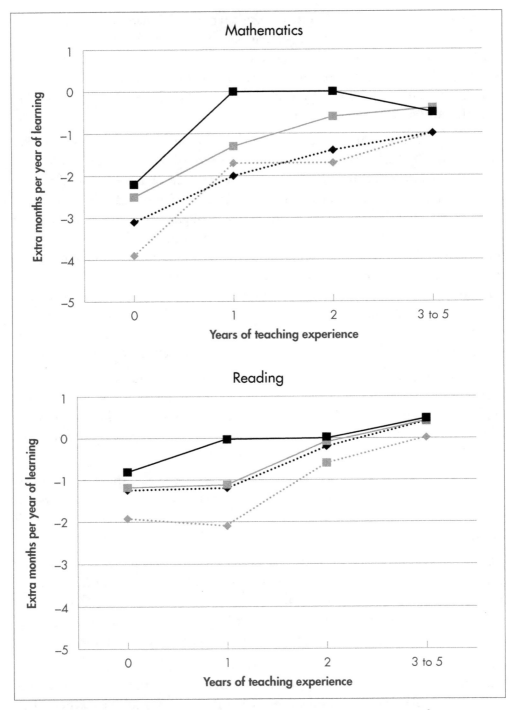

Figure 5.4. Impact of teacher experience on student progress in mathematics and reading.

good enough, but because they could be even better. And if we are serious about maximizing outcomes for young people, then the focus of teacher improvement needs to be on classroom formative assessment.

Conclusion

This chapter, with its discussion of expertise in sports and chess, may seem to have taken us a long way from the idea of "leadership for teacher learning." However, the main idea of this chapter, as stated in the introduction, is that while some degree of talent is useful in most human pursuits, high-level performance is almost always the result of a great deal of hard work focused specifically on the area of expertise, which means that expertise is specific and limited. As individuals undertake more and more deliberate practice, the initial level of job performance becomes less and less important as a predictor of how good someone can be, with general measures of ability accounting for between 5 and 10 percent of the variation in performance. Experts don't always have more knowledge than novices, but their knowledge is organized in richer and more complex ways, and the patterns they see in what they observe are much more meaningful for the task at hand. In addition, because experts tend to rely on automated routines, they are less affected by stress and appear to have more time for strategic thinking. Finally, expertise is not, in general, reducible to a set of rules that can be communicated from one person to another. It is a commitment to sustained, deliberate practice that is the most important element in producing expert performance.

While the research is never as clear-cut as one would like, there is reasonably compelling evidence that expertise in teaching shares many, if not most, and possibly all, of the characteristics of expertise in other areas. This means that while there will always be natural teachers, who are extraordinarily gifted practitioners from their first day, the current variation in teacher quality that we saw in chapter 2, and the fact that this variation is still present many years later, means that many teachers are not achieving the level of performance of which they are capable. Put simply, it seems that most teachers could be as good as our best if they committed to at least ten years of consistently pushing themselves to be better than they are right now and if they get the support of their leaders in making these improvements.

The research on expertise also shows that not all kinds of practice activity are equally effective at improving performance. The evidence suggests that classroom formative assessment is probably the most important component of teacher expertise, so the quest for higher student achievement comes down to what kinds of activities we should organize for teachers to maximize the impact on student achievement. That is the subject of the next chapter.

[*Chapter 6*]

Teacher Learning

In previous chapters, we have seen that our best hope of improving learning outcomes for young people is to invest in the professional development of teachers already working in our schools, and this investment should be focused on supporting teachers in their development of classroom formative assessment. We have also seen that expertise in teaching is similar to expertise in other areas, which suggests that the amount and nature of practice is at least as important as any natural talent in determining how good a teacher can be. In this chapter, we focus on what kinds of learning activities are likely to be the most effective in helping teachers improve their practice of classroom formative assessment.

Perhaps the most important idea in designing learning for teachers is that the means should be determined by the ends. In other words, we should decide how to do something only once we are clear about what we are trying to do. This is important because too often a particular process for organizing teacher learning—such as teacher coaching triads or professional learning communities—is proposed as a solution before the goal has been decided. As Abraham Maslow (1966) once remarked, "I suppose it is tempting, if the only tool you have is a hammer, to treat everything as if it were a nail" (p. 15). For example, if the goal was to increase teacher subject knowledge, then some form of direct instruction would be far more likely to be effective than teacher coaching triads or professional learning communities (Stockard, 2014). Since developing classroom formative assessment involves changes in what teachers do in their day-to-day teaching, the kinds of structures that are likely to be useful will be very different from those that will best support instructional data teams (e.g., Boudett, City, & Murnane, 2013). In particular, since changing what teachers do in their classrooms involves changing highly automated routines, changing practice is essentially a process of habit change.

Content, *Then* Process

In 1991, Michael Fullan wrote, "Nothing has promised so much and has been so frustratingly wasteful as the thousands of workshops and conferences that led to no significant change in practice when teachers returned to their classrooms" (Fullan & Stiegelbauer, 1991, p. 315). A significant cause of the failure of professional development to impact classroom practice has been a failure to understand the importance of attending to both *process* and *content* in teacher professional development (Reeves, McCall, & MacGilchrist, 2001). In particular there has been a tendency for professional development to focus more on how it is that teachers are learning, rather than on what they are learning, and that the sessions must not be too challenging for participants (Wilson & Berne, 1999). In some ways, this is perfectly understandable. In much professional development, teachers are volunteers, and if the experiences are too uncomfortable, they can withdraw and seek other forms of professional development that are less challenging.

As an example of this, Suzanne Wilson describes a course she ran for history teachers in which they read extracts from Simon Schama's account of the French revolution, *Citizens* (Schama, 1989). While the group examined the rhetorical devices used by Schama, the conversations were animated and lively. Then Wilson asked the group to undertake something familiar to any student or teacher of history—the construction of a timeline—and immediately the engagement evaporated. Participants felt that they were being tested. One participant said, "I feel like I'm 16 years old back in school, worried about a test, scared of what I don't know" (Wilson & Berne, 1999, p. 201).

As previously noted, the argument being made here is that the design of professional development for teachers should begin by determining the content of teacher professional development—what teachers are expected to get better at—and that this should be primarily driven by the needs of students and not the wishes of teachers. Once the "what" of teacher professional development is clear, then the focus should turn to the "how" of professional development, and in particular, the process of teacher learning should be tailored to the focus of teacher learning that has been identified as a priority.

This may not seem particularly radical, but in fact, this has not been the focus of research into teacher professional development over recent years. There is now a reasonable degree of consensus that the predominant forms of professional development offered to teachers—such as one-day workshops or summer institutes—are rather ineffective (TNTP, 2015). However, most of the research into making teacher professional development more effective has sought to determine the characteristics of effective professional development by looking at what kinds of existing professional development have the biggest impact on student achievement (e.g., Cordingley et al., 2015). Because, as noted in chapter 3, research can only tell us what was, rather than what might be, using existing research into teacher professional development is unlikely to identify the most effective ways of improving outcomes for students. That is why the idea of "content, then process" is so radical. Rather than trying to work out which kinds of processes are likely to be most effective, we focus first on what kinds of changes in teacher practice will have the biggest impact on student achievement, and then look only at the processes that will best support those particular changes in practice.

As my colleagues and I have worked with teachers over the last ten years to support them in their development of the practice of classroom formative assessment, and as we have explored a number of different models, five principles of teacher learning have appeared to be especially important: choice, flexibility, small steps, accountability, and support (Wiliam, 2007).

Before discussing each of these process elements in turn, it is important to be clear about three things. First, we cannot prove that the five principles we have identified are the most important for improving teachers' formative assessment practice. Much of our work with teachers has proceeded by a process of trial and error, and it may be that other principles of which we are not aware might improve the effectiveness of this work. Second, I am certainly not claiming that if one of these features is missing, then any attempt to improve teaching is bound to fail. What I am saying is that our experience has been that if one of these elements is missing, the chances of success do appear to be lower. Third, and perhaps most important, as far as we know, what follows applies *only* to attempts to help teachers improve their practice of classroom formative assessment, because this is what I and my various colleagues have spent most of our time trying to achieve over the last fifteen years. It may be that some of these ideas apply to other kinds of teacher learning, but because we have not applied these ideas in other contexts, we just don't know.

Choice

In the late 1960s, Meredith Belbin, a researcher at the University of Cambridge's Industrial Training Research Unit, began studying individuals participating in training programs at the Administrative Staff College at Henley-on-Thames in England (which later became Henley Management College). One set of studies involved analyzing the way that people interacted while engaged in workplace simulations where they worked in groups to solve business problems. One of the things that was most surprising was that there was little relationship between a team's chances of success and the abilities of the individual team members, or even their personalities. In a book based on these experiences titled *Management Teams: Why They Succeed or Fail,*

Belbin (1981) proposed that the roles played by individuals in work teams were more important than their individual abilities or their personalities. Based on his observations, he suggested that there were eight team roles that needed to be contributed by individuals in the group if the group was to have a reasonable chance of success (later he added a ninth role: specialist). The eight team roles he proposed were:

1. Company worker
2. Chairman
3. Shaper
4. Plant
5. Resource investigator
6. Monitor-evaluator
7. Team worker
8. Completer-finisher

Belbin observed that individuals had strong preferences for the roles they played in groups. While individuals might have two or three roles they were happy to play, when the team needed individuals to play other roles, individuals were rarely able to sustain focus in these nonpreferred roles for long. Especially when the team was under pressure, individuals tended to revert to the team roles with which they felt most comfortable. The most effective teams were therefore those where the preferences of the members covered the eight team roles.

The other important point that Belbin made was that each role had key strengths and *allowable* weaknesses. In other words, when an individual had strengths, he or she would also have weaknesses that were, in effect, the other side of the same coin. Someone who has lots of imaginative ideas may not be very good at thinking through the practical implications of the ideas, and someone who is very detail oriented may have a tendency to worry about small, and possibly irrelevant, details. A summary of strengths and weaknesses of the eight roles is shown in Table 6.1 (Belbin, 1981).

Criticisms of this work have pointed out that the questionnaires used to establish which team roles an individual favors are not particularly reliable, and some of the roles are more clearly distinguishable from others (e.g., Furnham, Steele, & Pendleton, 1993). However, a review of forty-three empirical studies of the Belbin questionnaire concluded that there was reasonable evidence in support of the model: "Through its coverage of important areas of teamworking, the paper contributes to the practitioner and research communities by providing fresh insights into aspects of teamworking" (Aritzeta, Swailes, & Senior, 2007, p. 96).

Table 6.1. Principal Strengths and Allowable Weaknesses of Belbin's Eight Team Roles

	Principal strengths	Allowable weaknesses
Company worker	Disciplined, hardworking	Lack of flexibility
Chairman	Valuing contributions	Not particularly creative
Shaper	Drive	Impatience
Plant	Thinking outside the box	Impractical
Resource investigator	Openness to new ideas	Short attention span
Monitor-evaluator	Hardheaded	Poor motivator
Team worker	Responsive to others	Not good in crises
Completer-finisher	Detail oriented	Obsessive

Perhaps the most important feature of Belbin's framework is the obvious yet profound idea that different people bring different things to teamworking. It is profound because many attempts at improving employee performance begin with an analysis of the employee's relative strengths and weaknesses and then formulate a professional development plan to address the weaknesses. In fact, this approach is so ingrained that it is common in many organizations not to refer to "weaknesses" at all, but instead to talk about "areas for development."

To see why this can be a really bad idea, consider the kind of person that Belbin describes as a completer-finisher. These are the people who actually like dotting i's and crossing t's. They are often, quite simply, worth their weight in gold. Many studies of creative teams have found that they never get anything done, because the members of the team are too busy having ideas to follow through with any of them. So what sort of professional development would be best for a completer-finisher? A needs analysis might show that the individual was not particularly creative, which would suggest that perhaps sending him or her to a course on how to be more creative might be useful. But in the commercial world, they have realized that the organization is likely to benefit far more by having the completer-finisher develop his or her project management skills, while perhaps also giving some attention to the allowable weaknesses, such as countering the tendency to be obsessive. Indeed, there is now considerable evidence that there can be many benefits to organizations when employees focus on developing their strengths rather than their weaknesses (Buckingham, 2007).

Belbin's work focused on the work of teams, rather than individuals, and in teams, it is easy to see how one member's weaknesses can be balanced by another member's strengths. In teaching, however, this balancing needs to be done carefully. I am certainly not suggesting that one teacher can ignore some of the standards he or she should be teaching because the teacher who will teach the class next year has a better grasp of how to teach those standards. If we are talking about content standards, the teacher needs to be an expert on all the aspects of the subject he or she is teaching. But in terms of pedagogy, it seems to me that *a weakness is not necessarily an area for development.* In general, talent development involves attending to both strengths and weaknesses, and the balance between these two will be different for different teachers. In particular, for novice teachers, it may well be that attention to their weaknesses is likely to bring the greatest benefits to their students. But for experienced teachers, it could well be that their students will benefit more by having their teachers become outstanding at the things they are already good at, rather than worrying too much about weaknesses. The aim of professional development is not to make every teacher into a clone of every other teacher, but rather to support each teacher in becoming the best teacher he or she can be. Teachers are often at their best when they are their quirky, idiosyncratic selves, and that is why choice is so important. Each teacher will find different ways of incorporating classroom formative assessment into his or her practice.

In my experience, the idea that teachers should choose for themselves what to develop is one of the most challenging for leaders to accept. How do we know they will work on the right things? We don't. But what we have learned is that when we start out by assuming the best of people, rather than the worst, then, in general, good things happen.

This idea has been around for over half a century. In *The Human Side of Enterprise,* Douglas McGregor (1960) suggested that there are two main theories of management, which he called *Theory X* and *Theory Y.* Theory X is that people can't be trusted, and they need to be managed constantly to check that they are doing what they should be doing. In contrast, Theory Y holds that people want to do a good job and that the job of the manager is to create the conditions in which people can get on with doing just that. Now it is important to note that Theory X isn't always wrong, and Theory Y isn't always right, but Theory Y is in general a more productive initial assumption.

An important benefit of giving more experienced teachers choice over which aspect of their practice to develop is that it is much less likely to be seen as a bureaucratic imposition. The choice does need to be constrained in some way to maximize the likelihood that students will indeed benefit—we do not want teachers choosing to work on Brain Gym or learning styles, for example. But when teachers are given choice over which aspects of their practice of formative assessment they will develop, this is far more likely to be seen as serving the agenda of the teacher, rather than the agenda of administrators. Many teachers regard collecting building-level data on the achievement of their students as serving the needs of bureaucrats and administrators. Every teacher, in my experience, accepts that it is part of his or her job to find out what his or her students have learned. That is why classroom formative assessment is just a smart place to start the conversation.

Flexibility

As well as choosing which aspects to work on, teachers need flexibility to adapt and modify classroom formative assessment techniques to make them work for them. In *Embedded Formative Assessment* (Wiliam, 2011), I described how a history teacher had asked students to use "traffic lights" (red, yellow, or green circles) to indicate their confidence that they had achieved the objective for a lesson. A mathematics teacher, hearing about this, decided that waiting until the end of the lesson was probably too late, so she gave students large colored disks, red on one side and green on the other, so that they could indicate whether they felt they were keeping up with the lesson or not. A third teacher tried this out and found that it was difficult for her to see the color of the disks being displayed by the students because of the fluorescent lights in the classroom. So she gave students three colored paper cups: green to indicate that they were keeping up with the lesson, yellow to indicate they were struggling to keep up, and red to indicate that they wanted to ask a question (the stinger is that when a student shows a red cup, the teacher chooses, at random, one of the students showing green, to answer the question).

In the same book, I also mentioned Charlotte Kerrigan, an English language arts teacher, who had been convinced of the benefits of providing feedback in the form of comments rather than scores or grades for many years but was still unhappy with the amount of attention the students were giving to her comments. To address this, when one of her classes had written responses to an excerpt from a Shakespeare play, instead of writing her comments on the students' work, she wrote them on strips of paper. Each group of four students was given their four pieces of writing and the four comments, and the students were asked to match the comments to the writing.

Both of these accounts illustrate how the ability of teachers to modify the techniques to make them work in their own classrooms is an important feature of any effective model of teacher development.

Sometimes, the modifications can be very small and yet have a profound effect. In one project, I persuaded a group of seventh-grade teachers to explore how they might incorporate more classroom formative assessment into their teaching and had a TV crew follow the teachers and the students around for a total of twenty weeks.

The resulting two-hour show, *The Classroom Experiment*, was shown on prime-time network TV in the United Kingdom on consecutive evenings in September 2010 (Barry & Wiliam, 2010; Thomas & Wiliam, 2010). At one point, the mathematics teacher, Miss Obi, was trying to pick students to answer her questions at random by using ice-pop sticks on which the names of the students in the class had been written. However, many of the students believed that she was somehow able to choose particular students, and their complaints about the perceived unfairness made it very difficult to keep the focus on the mathematics. Her solution was simply to give the cup of sticks to a student, so that after the students had been asked the question and been given time to think and discuss their responses with a peer, Miss Obi would ask the student who had been assigned the responsibility of looking after the sticks for a name. Just having a student, rather than the teacher, select the stick seems like a trivial change, and yet it was the difference between failure and success in this case.

There is a second reason to give teachers not only the right, but also the responsibility, to modify the techniques they are using, and that is that once teachers have modified techniques to make them work in their own classrooms, they are much more likely to persist with the techniques. Many people involved with supporting teachers have had the experience of suggesting an idea to a teacher, only to have the teacher come back within a week or two and say something along the lines of, "I tried what you told me to do, and it didn't work." No one can make anything work in someone else's classroom. To make things work in their classrooms, teachers have to make the ideas their own. Otherwise, we are, in Lawrence Stenhouse's (1980) memorable phrase, treating the teacher like "a kind of intellectual navvy" (p. 139) who is told where to dig a trench but not why.

This represents a radically different model of the dissemination of educational research. In the standard model, researchers research, find out things, and then tell teachers what to do. In other words, the researchers gain insights into classrooms and learning and attempt to communicate their insights to teachers as knowledge. According to the traditional model of dissemination (e.g., English, Jones, Lesh, Tirosh, & Bussi, 2002), all we need to do then is to tell teachers to, say, give more task-involving feedback and less ego-involving feedback (Kluger & DeNisi, 1996). Of course, it's not as simple as that because whether feedback is ego involving or task involving depends on the context in which it is given, the attitudes of the recipient, and the relationship between the donor and the recipient of the feedback (for more on this, see chapter 3 of Wiliam & Leahy, 2015).

One of the main reasons that educational research has had so little impact on educational practice is because the very hardest task of all—working out how to implement research findings in real contexts—has been left almost entirely to teachers, and this is both unfair and foolish. The idea running through our work on classroom formative assessment is that by starting with the research literature, it is possible to build up a theory of formative assessment that can then be manifested in a set of classroom techniques, such as ice-pop sticks or colored cups. Because they are derived from research evidence, these techniques form a set of validated practices that may not work in every setting, but *are* likely to be effective in *most* contexts because of the framing provided by the five strategies of formative assessment discussed in chapter 4 and the research evidence on which they are based. Teachers then take these techniques and, through regular use, incorporate them into their own theories of classroom practice and thus change their own ideas about practice.

The difference between the model being described here and traditional models of dissemination has been neatly encapsulated by the idea that "we are all much more likely to act our way into a new way of thinking than to think our way into a new way of acting" (Pascale, Millemann, & Gioja, 1998, p. 179). In the traditional model, researchers generate insights into certain phenomena and then communicate them to practitioners, who are meant to incorporate the insights into their practice. Such models can work reasonably well where the knowledge that needs to be communicated is explicit knowledge, but, as we saw in the previous chapter, much of the knowledge that experts possess cannot be reduced to words. Any dissemination model that deals only with the kind of knowledge that can be reduced to words will clearly be of limited relevance when tacit knowledge is an important element of capability.

The importance of both explicit and tacit (or implicit) forms of knowledge is emphasized by Nonaka and Takeuchi (1995) in their discussion of "the knowledge creating company." They point out that much of the knowledge in an organization is not explicit but tacit knowledge, which they define as "personal knowledge embedded in individual experience and involves intangible factors such as personal belief, perspective and value system" (p. vii). Indeed, many organizations are unaware of how much tacit knowledge exists in the organization until the people possessing it leave!

The existence of two types of knowledge—explicit and tacit—results in four different modes of knowledge conversion, as shown in Figure 6.1 (Nonaka & Takeuchi, 1995). (The distinction between explicit and tacit is in reality, of course, a continuum, but for clarity, it is presented as a dichotomy in the figure.)

When one person's explicit knowledge gets passed on to another as explicit knowledge—for example, as occurs when a new teacher is told that morning recess ends at 10:25—Nonaka and Takeuchi (1995) describe this as a process of *combination*. However, although this might be the official end of recess, it could be that, in practice, 10:25 just marks the point at which teachers and students think about moving to their classrooms, so that lessons rarely, in practice, begin before 10:30. Over time, the new teacher begins to understand this. Nothing is said, but the teacher comes to share the tacit knowledge of those already in the organization through a process of *socialization*. When one person's tacit knowledge is communicated to another by being made explicit, this is a process of *externalization*. For example, many teachers report that being asked to take responsibility for a student teacher forces them to put into words aspects of their practice that they had previously undertaken intuitively, thus deepening their own understanding of their practice. The complementary process, which Nonaka and Takeuchi call *internalization*, is when someone receives something initially as explicit knowledge but makes it their own when they understand what it means to do it in practice.

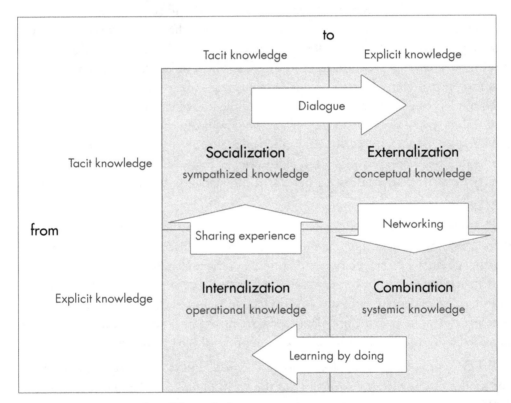

Figure 6.1. Four modes of knowledge conversion

Nonaka and Takeuchi (1995) propose that these four processes typically occur in what they call a "knowledge-creating spiral" in the following sequence:

> First, the socialization mode usually starts with building a "field" of interaction. This field facilitates the sharing of members' experiences and mental models. Second, the externalization mode is triggered by meaningful "dialogue or collective reflection," in which using appropriate metaphor or

analogy helps team members to articulate hidden tacit knowledge that is otherwise hard to communicate. Third, the combination mode is triggered by "networking" newly created knowledge and existing knowledge from other sections of the organization, thereby crystallizing them into a new product, service, or managerial system. Finally, "learning by doing" triggers internalization. (pp. 70–71)

It is in the process of internalization that flexibility is so important. By giving teachers not just permission, but active encouragement, not only to choose, but also to modify, the techniques they try out—in other words to adopt and adapt—teachers make the techniques more appropriate for their classroom and, at the same time, are more likely to make the techniques work because of the sense of ownership generated by the modification process.

The danger in all this, of course, is that teachers make such radical modifications to the techniques to which they are introduced that the techniques are no longer effective—they suffer what Ed Haertel once called "lethal mutations" (Brown & Campione, 1996, p. 291). This is why the framing provided by the five strategies of formative assessment is so important. Because of the research basis that underpins each of the five strategies, as long as teachers are choosing techniques that are linked to the strategies, their implementation is likely to be relatively faithful to the underlying principles; therefore, the changes are likely to improve student achievement.

Small Steps

In April 1997, Tiger Woods won the US Masters golf tournament. His margin of victory (twelve strokes) and his total score for the four rounds (270 strokes, 18 under par) are still unsurpassed. And then, he decided to change his swing. Four years later, he described why:

> One night, a week or so later, after the elation had started to die down, I decided to sit down and watch a tape of the entire tournament. I was by myself, so I was really able to concentrate on critiquing my full swing to see if there was some flaw I might be able to work on.
>
> I didn't see one flaw. I saw about 10.
>
> I had struck the ball great that week, but by my standard I felt I had gotten away with murder. My clubshaft was across the line at the top of the backswing and my clubface was closed. My swing plane was too upright. I liked my ball flight, but I was hitting the ball farther with my irons than I should have been because I was delofting the clubface through impact. I didn't like the look of those things, and the more I thought about it, the more I realized

> I didn't like how my swing felt, either. From a ball-striking standpoint, I was playing better than I knew how.
>
> Even before the tape ended, I committed myself to making some big changes in my swing. Butch had pointed out some of these swing flaws before, and we had been working on them slowly, but I decided right then and there to pick up the pace. I got on the phone and called Butch and let him know what I was thinking. He was all for the swing overhaul I had in mind. (Woods, 2001)

Over the next year, he worked with his coach, Butch Harmon, to develop his swing, but during this period, his performance deteriorated. He entered only two of the first seven PGA tour competitions of the year, and in the twenty tournaments he entered over the year, he won only one—the BellSouth Classic—and his average position in the nineteen competitions he finished was 11th. As Woods himself noted:

> That overhaul took more than a year before the changes really began to kick in. First, my full swing started to look better. Then, the ball started to behave better. Finally, my swing started to feel right, and that's when I knew I had it. I had a very good year in 1999, and in 2000 I played by far the best golf of my life. (Woods, 2001)

In fact, in 2000, he achieved six consecutive wins, taking him to nine wins in the twenty PGA tour events he entered, and he broke the record for the best average score in PGA tour history.

Perhaps the most remarkable thing about this story is that after winning the US Masters by a record margin, Woods decided that he could be even better and worked on getting better even though this caused his performance to deteriorate in the short term. Moreover, he was able to take time away from competition to work on his swing.

No teacher gets to do this. Teachers are never given a couple of months with only minimal teaching commitments so that they can practice new techniques in front of a mirror. Teachers have to improve their teaching while teaching—what one teacher called "engine repair, in flight."

This is why teachers have to make small, incremental, evolutionary changes to their practice. Teachers have to improve their practice while keeping all the other routines functioning normally. For this reason, we recommend that teachers change only a small number—ideally one or two, and certainly no more than three—aspects of their practice at any one time. And, more important, they should continue to focus on the aspects they have chosen until these new aspects of practice are second nature. This often means working on a single idea, such as "no hands up, except to ask a question" (Wiliam & Leahy, 2015) for several months. I have lost track of the number of times I have described a formative assessment technique to a group of teachers, and someone has said to me, "Oh, yes. I used to do that. It was good!" The teacher used to do it, but because it had not become second nature, a new idea displaced the previous idea, rather than building on it. Perhaps the most important reason for asking teachers to take small steps is that only when something has been repeated and rehearsed to the point of being completely integrated into a teacher's practice is the teacher ready to move on and take on something else.

Accountability

The idea that teachers should be accountable to those with a stake in education seems difficult to argue against. Public school teachers are paid from money raised from taxes, so it seems unexceptionable that districts, schools, and teachers should be required to give an account of the way that public funds have been spent.

However, as Smith and Fey (2000) point out:

> To call for accountability is to assert a political right—to demand that a particular individual or institution assume some responsibility and demonstrate it in a certain form. Although there are many varieties of accountability in education (moral, professional, fiscal, market, bureaucratic, and legal), the term has come to mean the responsibility of a school (district, teacher, or student) to parents, taxpayers, or government (federal, state, city, or district) to produce high achievement test scores. (p. 335)

While the use of standardized testing can improve student achievement (Wiliam, 2010), the way that high-stakes accountability testing is carried out in the United States presents a number of problems for holding districts, schools, and teachers accountable.

The major problem is that students' scores on high-stakes tests are affected by a number of factors over which districts, schools, and teachers have little control. For a start, the stakes attached to the results of the tests are high for districts, schools, and teachers but usually not for students. In other words, districts, schools, and teachers are held accountable for results of tests taken by students who have little or no incentive to do well. If students regularly undertake homework, their achievement will be higher, and while teachers do have some influence over the extent to which students do homework regularly, the student's home circumstances are at least as important. In this context, it is worth noting that few people believe that doctors should be held accountable if their patients fail to take the medications they have been prescribed. And yet, if students fail to undertake homework as directed by their teachers, and this impacts their test scores, this is somehow the fault of the district, school, or teachers.

In fact, the available evidence shows that in most countries, the particular school a student attends has only a small effect on student achievement. For example, only about 8 percent of the variation in the achievement of US fifteen-year-olds in the triennial PISA tests administered by the OECD are attributable to the school the student attends (Organisation for Economic Co-operation Development, 2007). The other 92 percent is due to factors outside the school's control. Of course, as shown in chapter 2, the teacher effect can be much larger than the school effect—perhaps as much as five times as great—but even so, the factors outside the school's and the teacher's control are more significant influences.

What every teacher does control, however, is whether he or she improves. It therefore seems to me that every teacher can discharge her or his responsibilities to be accountable to key stakeholders in education by committing to improve his or her practice. We could waste a huge amount of time trying to determine whether individual districts, schools, or teachers are providing value for money or not, but, as we saw in chapter 2, the best we can do is to distinguish between the very best and the very worst teachers. The time spent trying to evaluate teachers would be far more effectively spent supporting teacher improvement.

This is why my colleagues and I have become convinced that all teachers should have a written action plan that specifies the focus of their development priorities. Writing something down makes the ideas concrete and creates a record. It also helps the teacher focus on a small number of priorities for change. Perhaps more important, when shared with colleagues, a written action plan can produce a highly productive form of accountability—accountability to one's professional peers.

Time and time again, teachers have told us that it was the promise they had made to a group of their colleagues that they were going to try something out that made them prioritize that over all the other tasks that they were required to complete in a given month. The following quotation, from a high school mathematics teacher, is typical. After a year working on developing his practice of formative assessment, during which time he had made substantial improvements in his teaching, he was asked which aspects of the process had been most significant in helping him improve.

> I think specifically what was helpful was the ridiculous NCR [no carbon required] forms. I thought that was the dumbest thing, *but* I'm sitting with my friends and on the NCR form I write down what I am going to do next month. Well, it turns out to be a sort of "I'm telling my friends I'm going to do this" and I really actually did it and it was because of that. It was because I wrote it down and I had it in my little packet and that idea of making improvements and sort of informally, which is much more powerful than formally, committing to doing it. I was surprised at how strong an incentive

that was to actually do something different, so I was happy with that, that idea of writing down what you are going to do and then because when they come by the next month you better take out that piece of paper and say "did I do that" and even if you didn't do it, you *knew* that you made a commitment to do and that's a—you weren't going to write me up, nobody was going to do anything terrible to me—but just the idea of sitting in a group, working out something, and making a commitment, even something as informal, I was impressed about how that actually made me do stuff. (Lyon, Wylie, & Goe, 2006, p. 18)

A similar reaction was reported by Barr (2014) in a year-long study of the implementation of teacher learning communities (TLCs) in a secondary school:

What made the TLC work for me? By having to commit to trying something out, and being asked to reflect on it and feed back to others. With other CPD sessions that are stand-alone, I tend to be inspired and end up trying something once or maybe twice, but I end up being too busy to put the effort into embedding it into my regular practice. This negative cycle does not happen with TLCs, as you need to feedback on it within a few weeks, so you keep the momentum up. (p. 67)

Support

The last design principle—support—is really just the other side of the coin from accountability, and for that reason, we often combine the two principles into the idea of "supportive accountability" (Thompson & Wiliam, 2008, p. 18). The idea is that the structures that hold teachers accountable for making improvements in their practice also provide support for the changes needed. From teachers, just two things are needed. First, all teachers agree that they need to improve their practice, not because they're not good enough, but because they can be even better. Second, teachers agree to focus on things that are likely to have benefits for their students, so no more time on Brain Gym, learning styles, lesson study, or neuroscience because it's frankly self-indulgent to spend time on things that may or may not help students when there is solid evidence about what does help students. Teachers may, of course, choose to engage in research on lesson study, or educational neuroscience, or even learning styles, if they wish to do that, but that should be outside their contract. In contractually committed time, teachers should prioritize what makes the most difference to students.

This last point is important, because, as pointed out in chapter 3, if there were no evidence about what we could be doing to improve learning outcomes for young people, then it might, perhaps, be justifiable to explore things that as yet have no evidence in their support. Since there is clear evidence that formative assessment will improve student achievement, however, then until the potential gains from formative assessment have been exhausted, it should certainly be the main—and perhaps the exclusive—focus for teacher improvement. After all, as long as teachers are reflecting on the relationship between what they did as teachers and what their students learned as a result—the idea of assessment as the bridge between teaching and learning—then they will continue to improve.

For leaders, there are four aspects to the creation of supportive accountability:

1. Creating expectations for continually improving practice

2. Keeping the focus on the things that make a difference to students

3. Providing the time, space, dispensation, and support for innovation

4. Supporting risk-taking

Each of these is discussed in turn.

Creating Expectations for Continually Improving Practice

The idea of creating an environment in which all teachers improve sounds easy, but it is not. Every leader I have ever met espouses a philosophy of continuous improvement, but too often, this involves a kind of triage process for teachers—get rid of the very weakest, leave the best alone, and provide support for those who are struggling. The problem with such an approach is that the kinds of improvements in student achievement that can be secured by helping only the weakest teachers improve will, as pointed out in chapter 1, never be enough to help young people meet the challenges of the 21st century. And as we saw in chapter 2, identifying these teachers in the first place is far from straightforward. Even for the very best teachers in a district, the needs of their students creates a moral imperative to get even better, and every teacher, no matter how bad or good, *can* get better.

Keeping the Focus on the Things That Make a Difference to Students

The second aspect of supportive accountability for leaders is that of keeping the focus on the things that make a difference to students. This, too, sounds as if it ought to be simple and straightforward but again turns out to be surprisingly difficult. Part of the problem is that, as discussed in chapter 3, many teachers are excited by new developments, such as educational neuroscience and lesson study, and so there is always a pressure, after some time has been spent on formative assessment, to move on to the next big thing. It turns out that keeping the focus on the small number of things that really matter is extraordinarily difficult, in any organization.

Take, for example, McDonald's. The first McDonald's restaurant was opened by Maurice and Richard McDonald in 1940, and their Speedee Service System was piloted in San Bernardino, California, in 1948. In 1954, Ray Kroc, a milkshake-mixer salesman, was impressed by the operation and persuaded the McDonald brothers to give him the franchise for the Midwest, and the following year, he opened a restaurant in Des Plaines, Illinois. Six years later, Kroc bought out the McDonald brothers for $2.7 million. While the success of McDonald's has been due to a number of factors, one of the most important was Kroc's emphasis on keeping McDonald's restaurants clean, as exemplified by Kroc's mantra, "If you've got time to lean, you've got time to clean" (Love, 1995, p. 143).

As Tom Peters and Robert Waterman (1982) point out in their book *In Search of Excellence*, keeping restaurants clean might not sound too impressive, but McDonald's rivals found it impossible to manage. In fact, Peters and Waterman argue that a relentless focus on a small number of priorities is the most important characteristic of successful organizations. While many have criticized the central argument of *In Search of Excellence*, the companies selected by Peters and Waterman subsequently did very well (unlike those selected by Collins and Porras in *Built to Last* [1994]). In fact, over the twenty years after the publication of *In Search of Excellence*, the thirty-two publicly quoted companies selected by Peters and Waterman outperformed the Dow Jones Industrial Average by 2.8 percent annually, resulting in 73 percent higher total earnings (Ackman, 2002).

Shell, the oil company, provides another example of an obsessive focus on a small number of factors. A few years ago, I did some consultancy work with some members of their exploration team in Aberdeen, Scotland. Before I was given a visitor's pass, I had to sign a document detailing the conditions of being allowed to enter a Shell facility. Among the dozen or so things I had to agree to were "I will not read while walking along a corridor" and "When going up or down stairs, I will have a hand on a handrail at all times." Quite simply, it is impossible to visit a Shell facility without being aware of the organization's obsession with safety.

The important point here is that, as has been stressed several times already, there will always be pressure to find the next big thing. However, as long as things that are known to improve student achievement are not being used to the fullest extent possible, the focus needs to be relentlessly on those things. Anything else is a disservice to students.

Just to be clear, I am not saying that teachers should be treated like drones and told to implement some policy mindlessly. Figuring out which aspects of classroom formative assessment will work best with which students, and with which subjects, is a significant intellectual task. It is also one that requires substantial creativity. However, leaders need to be aware that keeping the focus on a small number of priorities for improving student learning takes a huge amount of energy. It doesn't seem difficult, but the fact that very few schools have managed to do it would suggest that, like keeping restaurants clean, simple things are rather hard to do.

Finally, as somewhat of an aside, I personally would find it refreshing to find on a school sign, instead of "Home of the Hurricanes" or some other sports team, something like, "Home of the best learners in the state." That would speak very powerfully about a school's priorities.

Providing the Time, Space, Dispensation, and Support for Innovation

The third aspect of supportive accountability for leaders is the idea that teachers should be given time, space, support, and dispensation to improve. As noted in the previous section on accountability, each teacher's action plan requires the teacher to focus on a small number of changes. In addition, the action plan must require that teachers identify what they will do less of or give up doing entirely to make room from improvement. This point is especially important because most teachers are working as hard as they can right now. This means their plates are full, and they cannot possibly take on anything new until they take something off their plate.

Unfortunately, when teachers are asked to identify something that they will stop doing or do less of to create time and space for them to explore improvements to their teaching, they fail miserably. They go through the list of their current tasks and duties and conclude that there is nothing they can stop doing or do less of, because everything that they are doing contributes to student learning. This is why improvement in education is so much more difficult than improving in the world of business.

In the business world, improving performance is most often done by cutting costs and, specifically, by eliminating unproductive activities. If teachers are doing things that are completely unproductive, then it would, of course, be a good idea to stop them from undertaking such activities. However, in my experience, it is hardly ever the case that teachers are doing things that are unproductive. This is why leadership in education is so challenging. The essence of effective leadership is stopping people from doing good things to give them time to do even better things. Stephen Covey (1989) described a man trying to cut through a big log of wood with a blunt saw. When someone suggests to him that he might make faster progress by sharpening the saw, the man replies, "I haven't got time." This is the problem that most schools face. Teachers are so busy doing what they are doing that they don't have time for anything else. And all the things they are doing are contributing to student learning. But if you want to saw through the log, while sawing is good, stopping sawing to sharpen the saw is better.

The problem is exacerbated in education because teachers are professionally invested in what they do. For example, when I suggest to teachers that they may be spending too much time grading, they ask, "Are you saying what I'm doing is no good?" Providing feedback to students is good. The important question is whether the hour spent grading a set of notebooks could have been spent in a different way that would have resulted in even more learning.

Supporting Risk-Taking

The fourth and final aspect of the leader's role in creating supportive accountability is to support teachers in taking risks. Whether teachers are more risk averse than other professions is a matter of debate, although some recent research has indicated that they may indeed be (Bowen, Buck, Deck, Mills, & Shuls, 2014). However, whatever the natural risk preferences of those entering the profession, it seems likely that pressure to improve test scores makes it more difficult to try anything other than business as usual but with greater ardor.

As noted in chapter 4, time and time again, teachers have told me that they would like to make greater use of formative assessment in their practice, but they feel they cannot do so because of the pressure to increase test scores. This is, of course, rather ironic because the research evidence suggests that there is nothing that will have a greater impact on test scores than formative assessment.

Whatever the cause, teachers do appear to need support in trying out new ideas, and in particular, they need to be supported in taking a few risks. By risk-taking, I do not mean doing something crazy, but rather taking a chance on doing something where success is not guaranteed and, indeed, something that might not work.

To that end, I looked for an example of risk-taking where the stakes were higher than are typically found in teaching. I found one in research done at the United Kingdom's leading specialist hospital for children—the Great Ormond Street Hospital in London (Bull, Yates, Sarkar, Deanfield, & de Leval, 2000).

Around 1 in every 4,000 babies is born with a condition called "transposition of the great arteries," or TGA. The aorta should emerge from the left ventricle of the heart, but in these babies, it emerges from the right ventricle, and so receives oxygen-depleted blood, which is then transported around the body. The pulmonary artery, which should emerge from the right ventricle, in fact emerges from the left ventricle, and so carries oxygen-rich blood back to the lungs. From the mid-1960s to the mid-1980s, the standard treatment for this condition was to create a tunnel between the two sides of the heart and to insert a baffle to direct some of the oxygen-rich blood from the left ventricle to the right ventricle, so that it could then be transported via the aorta to the body. The procedure was first carried out by Ake Senning in Sweden in 1957, and a similar procedure was performed by William Mustard in Canada in 1963. The main difference between the two procedures is that in the Senning procedure, the patient's own tissue is used to create the baffle, while in the Mustard procedure, synthetic materials are used.

At Great Ormond Street Hospital, the Mustard and Senning procedures were the most common approach to the treatment of TGA until 1992. The early death rate for this procedure, defined as the proportion of babies receiving the procedure who died in the first thirty days of life, was 12 percent, so that seven out of every eight babies were surviving, but life expectancy for those born with this condition was only around forty-seven years. For this reason, in 1992, a decision was made to recommend to parents a different procedure—the switch procedure—which involved reconnecting the aorta and the pulmonary artery to the appropriate ventricle and separately transferring the coronary arteries to the *new* aorta.

The switch procedure had been used since 1979 for patients with additional complications that prevented the Senning or Mustard procedures from being used. However, in January 1986, the procedure was first used, on an elective basis, for babies who could also have received the Mustard or Senning procedure.

Figure 6.2 (Bull et al., 2000) shows the outcomes for 325 consecutive patients treated at Great Ormond Street Hospital between August 1978 and February 1998 who could have been treated with either the Mustard/Senning procedure or the switch procedure. Patients treated up to the end of 1985 would have received the Mustard/Senning procedure, and from 1992 on, would have received the switch procedure. From January 1986 to 1992, the procedure used depended on the choices made by parents. In the graph, each step horizontally represents an infant receiving either the Mustard/Senning or the switch procedure, and each step vertically represents an early death.

The most important feature of Figure 6.2 is the rise in the early death rate at the beginning of the transitional period between the Mustard/Senning and the switch eras. Had the doctors at Great Ormond Street Hospital played safe and continued to use the Mustard/Senning procedure, the early death rate would have been around 12 percent. During the transitional era, the early death rate rose to 25 percent. However, by the end of the transitional period (1992), the early death rate was below 10 percent, and from 1995 on, a total of fifty-five switch procedures were carried out without a single early death. The life expectancy for those receiving the switch procedure is sixty-three years, and, because of the improved blood flow to their bodies, they are able to lead fully active lives. The price that was paid for this substantial increase in both longevity and quality of life is that fifteen infants died during the transitional period between the Mustard/Senning era and the switch era—infants who would have survived if the team at Great Ormond Street Hospital had played safe. So when

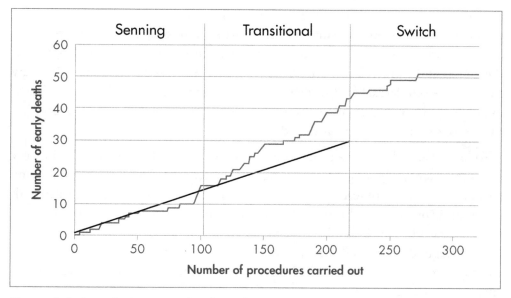

Figure 6.2. Cumulative mortality for infants receiving Mustard/Senning and switch procedures at Great Ormond Street Hospital, 1978–1998.

teachers tell me that changing their practice is frightening, I suggest they consider the risks taken by the medical team at Great Ormond Street Hospital.

Now of course this does not mean that teachers should take foolish risks. One of the most interesting features of the study of the treatment of infants with TGA is that before deciding to move toward the switch procedure, the team developed a sophisticated actuarial model of the relative risks of Mustard/Senning and switch procedures (McCartney, Spiegelhalter, & Rigby, 1987). Specifically, the model allowed the team to understand better the trade-off between short-term versus long-term risks and benefits for the different procedures.

What I think it does mean is that leaders need to understand that teachers need support in taking risks, and there are a number of strategies that leaders can use to achieve this.

Perhaps the most straightforward approach is to lower the stakes. For example, where teachers teach a number of classes, some of which have students taking high-stakes tests or examinations and some of which do not, it makes sense to encourage the teachers to try out innovative practices with those classes where the stakes are lowest and where there is more time to recover if things go awry. It is worth noting, however, that this was precisely the advice we gave to teachers in the King's-Medway-Oxfordshire Formative Assessment Project (Black, Harrison, Lee, Marshall, & Wiliam, 2003), and the teachers completely ignored us. While they did start out by trying the techniques with nonexamination classes, they found the impact on the students' learning so powerful that they immediately applied the same ideas to their examination classes. As a variant on this, teachers can be encouraged to try the ideas out on standards that are important but not too consequential (e.g., understanding the phases of the moon is important, can be fun to teach, and is mentioned in many state science standards, but if students do not master the content, little future learning is affected). Another way to lower the stakes is for teachers to team-teach so that the responsibility for failures is shared.

To lower the stakes, it is also important that key stakeholders are involved in any changes. Parents rely on grading as a signal that the school is doing its job, so any changes in the kinds of feedback their children receive are likely to be regarded with some suspicion and even hostility. Teachers need to know that if parents raise issues about changes in the kinds of feedback their children are receiving, then administrators will support them. And administrators, in turn, need to know that school boards will support the measures they, the leaders, are taking to create a supportive learning environment for teachers.

However, in the longer term, the more powerful strategy is to normalize risk-taking—in other words, to make risk-taking normal rather than unusual in the school. Some schools have built risk-taking into their teacher evaluation systems. Half of the formally scheduled teacher evaluations use standard teaching-quality frameworks, such as those discussed in chapter 2. For the other half, the evaluations are based on what the teacher *learned* in teaching the lesson. This creates an incentive for teachers to innovate and experiment because if the lesson goes completely as planned, there is little opportunity for the teacher to learn. Learning is much easier when things go wrong than when things go right.

In this respect, the work of Michael Mauboussin mentioned in chapter 1 is particularly important. The empirical work on teacher quality discussed in chapter 2 shows that the quality of teaching seen in an individual lesson is not a particularly good guide for the quality of that teacher or for the amount of student learning. When success is influenced by a number of random factors, the right thing to do does not always result in success, and strategies that lead to success are not always the right thing to do. For example, in the card game blackjack, twisting on 18 is an unwise decision even if, on a particular occasion, it results in success. More extreme, the fact that you survive one round of Russian roulette does not make it a safe game. Leaders therefore need to be careful to praise teachers only for the things that they want to encourage. Many schools share good practice by having regular whole-staff briefings in which aspects of good practice that they have observed in their learning walks or walk-throughs are shared with staff. It is important that in doing this, where success is unpredictable, it is the process that is praised, not the outcome. Otherwise, leaders risk appearing to praise teachers for being lucky—reputedly, the method that Napoleon used to choose his generals, and look where that got him.

Finally, it is worth considering the role that more experienced teachers play in normalizing risk-taking. For younger teachers, it can seem as if they are the only ones who are struggling. When more experienced teachers, especially those who are seen as being more successful, talk about the mistakes they have made, it seems to make it easier for less experienced teachers to take risks. As Mario Andretti, the race car driver, once said, "If everything seems under control, you're not going fast enough."

The five design elements of effective teacher learning discussed previously—choice, flexibility, small steps, accountability, and support—underpin effective teacher development where pedagogy is the focus of improvement. However, while these five elements do provide a set of general principles that can be used to evaluate whether a given set of ideas for organizing teacher learning is likely to be effective or not, they are not specific enough to tell us how to go about designing such learning. For that, we need to look in much more detail at the kinds of changes that are required when teachers develop their practice of classroom formative assessment. Specifically, we need to understand that this is a process of habit change.

Changing Teacher Habits

Some years ago, I was working with a group of teachers in New Jersey who were developing their use of classroom formative assessment. One fifth-grade teacher had decided to focus her efforts on selecting students at random to respond to her questions—the technique sometimes called "No hands up, except to ask a question" mentioned earlier. At one of our regular meetings, we were discussing how things were going, and she said, "Every time I ask a question, I always say, 'Does anyone . . .?' or 'Has anyone . . .?'" Even though she wanted students not to raise their hands, she was asking questions in a way that encouraged them to do so. With tears welling up in her eyes, she asked, "Why am I finding it so hard to change the way I ask questions?" I asked her how long she had been teaching, and she replied, "Twenty-two years." I pointed out that teachers typically ask well over 200 questions per day (Levin & Long, 1981), so in her career, she had probably asked well over half a million questions. When you've done something one way half a million times, you'll be pretty good at it, but doing it a different way is going to be difficult.

This is why developing classroom formative assessment is so different from participating in instructional data teams. Developing one's practice of classroom formative assessment entails changing habits, ingrained, for many teachers, over years and sometimes decades. Moreover, our understanding of classrooms comes not just from our experience as teachers, but also from our experiences as students. All teachers have spent thousands of hours in classrooms as students, where they internalize the scripts of how classrooms operate. That is why even novice teachers have just as much trouble with implementing innovative practices. They have had little time to develop habits as teachers, but where innovative practices are inconsistent with their experiences as students, they are still engaged in a process of habit change.

As Chip and Dan Heath (2010) point out in *Switch: How to Change Things When Change Is Hard*, change is difficult even when people know what they should be doing. Perhaps one of the clearest indications of this is the issue of hand hygiene in hospitals.

In the 19th century, many women died shortly after childbirth. The disease was named "puerperal fever," which was more of a label than a diagnosis, since literally it just means a fever of a woman in childbirth (the disease was also sometimes called "childbed fever"). Ignaz Semmelweis, a doctor at Vienna General Hospital, noticed that the prevalence of this disease had increased sharply in 1823, after the introduction of pathological anatomy, in which doctors, while waiting for women in labor to give birth, carried out postmortem examinations in a nearby anatomy laboratory (Semmelweis, 1861). However, no such increase had been seen where the mothers were attended by midwives (who were of course not involved in postmortems). The mortality rates for the Vienna General Hospital, and for comparison purposes, at The National Maternity Hospital, in Dublin, are shown in Figure 6.3.

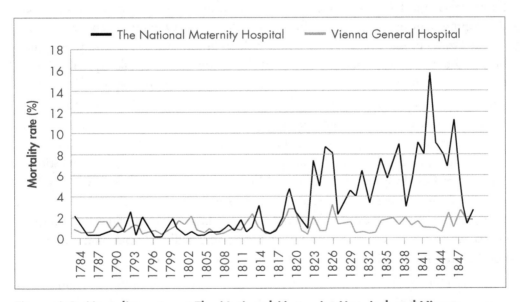

Figure 6.3. Mortality rates at The National Maternity Hospital and Vienna General Hospital: 1783 to 1849.

Although the germ theory of disease had not yet been developed, Semmelweis believed that childbed fever must be caused by doctors transferring cadaverous particles from the anatomy laboratory on their hands and suggested that doctors wash their hands in a weak solution of calcium hypochlorite (common household bleach). The suggestion was widely reviled at the time, although the introduction of the procedure, in May 1847, can clearly be seen to reduce the incidence of puerperal fever at Vienna General Hospital from an average of around 15 percent to less than 5 percent. A century and a half on, it is now accepted that good hand hygiene is essential to avoiding cross-infection in hospitals. Except, a century and a half later, we don't seem to have made much progress.

The surgeon Atul Gawande (2007) has pointed out that we have made far greater progress in advanced techniques of surgery than in apparently easier areas, such as basic hygiene. He quotes the example of washing hands after contact with patients, where the compliance rate in many hospitals is around 50 percent even though it is widely accepted that much higher rates are required to control the spread of resistant forms of *Staphylococcus aureus*, such as vancomycin-resistant *Staphylococcus aureus* (VRSA) and methicillin-resistant *Staphylococcus aureus* (MRSA). Quite apart from the impact on patient health, the cost of dealing with MRSA and VRSA for hospitals is significant. Just the MRSA and VRSA infections caused by hand hygiene noncompliance typically cost around $1.75 million annually for a 200-bed hospital (Cummings, Anderson, & Kaye, 2010), and just increasing hand hygiene compliance by 1 percent would be worth $40,000 a year to the hospital.

However, a review of hand-hygiene studies by Pittet (2001) found that compliance rates were often well below 50 percent, as can be seen in Table 6.2.

The problem is not ignorance, nor willful disobedience. In most hospitals, a strict procedure is specified for hand washing, but as Gawande (2007) points out:

> Almost no one adheres to this procedure. It seems impossible. On morning rounds, our residents check in on twenty patients in an hour. The nurses in our intensive care units typically have a similar number of contacts with patients requiring hand washing in between. Even if you get the whole cleansing process down to a minute per patient, that's still a third of staff time spent just washing hands. Such frequent hand washing can also irritate the skin, which can produce dermatitis, which itself increases bacterial counts. (p. 18)

Fortunately, in recent years, a considerable amount has been learned about how to get people to change their behavior, and the book by the Heath brothers mentioned previously provides a highly readable account of the key messages from the research on behavior change.

Table 6.2. Compliance With Hand-Hygiene Policies

Study	Focus	Compliance rate
Preston, Larson, & Stamm (1981)	Open ward	16%
Preston, Larson, & Stamm (1981)	ICU	30%
Albert & Condie (1981)	ICU	28% to 41%
Larson (1983)	All wards	45%
Donowitz (1987)	Pediatric ICU	30%
Graham (1990)	ICU	32%
Dubbert (1990)	ICU	81%
Pettinger & Nettleman (1991)	Surgical ICU	51%
Larson et al. (1992)	Neonatal ICU	29%
Doebbeling et al. (1992)	ICU	40%
Zimakoff et al. (1992)	ICU	40%
Meengs et al. (1994)	ER (casualty)	32%
Pittet, Mourouga, & Perneger (1999)	All wards	48%
Pittet, Mourouga, & Perneger (1999)	ICU	36%

To organize the presentation of their ideas, they begin by adapting an analogy from a book titled *The Happiness Hypothesis* (Haidt, 2005). In this book, Jonathan Haidt draws on the work of ancient philosophers to cast light on current issues, and one of the issues he focuses on is the tension between our emotional and rational selves. In his dialogue *Phaedrus*, Plato described this in terms of a charioteer and a pair of horses, one of which represents intellect and reason, while the other represents irrational passions and desires (sections 246a to 254e of *Phaedrus*). The task of the charioteer is to prevent the two horses from pulling in different directions. Haidt describes this same tension by means of a slightly different analogy—that of an elephant and *mahout* (i.e., rider). Sitting on the back of the elephant's neck, the rider holds the reins, and seems to be in charge, but of course this is only because most of the time, the elephant is happy to go along with what the rider wants. However, if the rider and the elephant disagree, there is not much a 200-pound man can do to force a 12,000-pound elephant into submission. The rider is rational, focused on the longer term, and good at complex planning, but is easily distracted, gets bogged down in detail, and tires easily. In contrast, the elephant is instinctive, compassion-ate, protective, and powerful but is emotional, can be skittish, and tends to focus on the short term.

To this analogy of the rider and the elephant, the Heath brothers add a third element, the path. The idea is that we imagine the rider and the elephant in a city landscape. For all its strength, the elephant is not powerful enough to walk through buildings, so the path directs and constrains both the rider and the elephant. Heath and Heath (2010) suggest that effective habit change comes about when we *direct* the rider, *motivate* the elephant, and *shape* the path. For each of the three approaches to habit change, they propose three strategies, each of which they illustrate with a number of case studies. For those who do not wish or have time to read the book, I discuss each of the nine strategies in turn, illustrated with some of the examples given by Heath and Heath.

Direct the Rider

Find the Bright Spots

As one illustration of the power of finding the bright spots, the Heath brothers describe the work of Jerry and Monique Sternin in Vietnam. In 1991, Jerry Sternin had been asked by Save the Children to establish an office in Vietnam, specifically to address the problem of malnutrition in children. Realizing that most of the conven-tional approaches to malnutrition required changes over which he had little influ-ence (poverty, sanitation, clean water, education), he and his family instead traveled to rural villages and looked for bright spots—families where children seemed to be thriving without any obvious explanation (such as a rich relative who sent money regularly). What the Sternins found was that the mothers whose children were thriv-ing were supplementing their children's diet with sweet-potato greens (considered a low-class food) and small fresh-water shrimps and crabs from the rice paddies (con-sidered inappropriate for young children). They also fed their children four times a day (rather than the usual two) and made sure they ate when they had diarrhea, whereas conventional wisdom was that children should not eat when suffering from diarrhea (Dorsey, 2000). The Sternins arranged for health volunteers then to meet daily with eight to ten mothers at a time, who were asked to bring shrimps, crabs, and sweet-potato greens as the price of admission to the meetings. Over the next two weeks, participants learned to cook meals for the group using the new ingredients, the idea being that once they were used to collecting shrimp, crab, and sweet-potato greens, they would continue to do so after the formal training sessions had ended.

An evaluation of the work conducted in December 1999 and January 2000 found that children who had not even been born when the Save the Children workers left the villages for the last time were as healthy as those who had been directly helped by the interventions years earlier (Mackintosh, Marsh, & Schroeder, 2002) because the practices introduced earlier had stuck. Focusing on the bright spots enabled local, feasible, sustainable solutions to be identified, shared, and adopted. It is hard to imagine that any solution developed from outside these villages and suggested by foreign aid workers would have been nearly as successful.

Script the Critical Moves

Although the evidence linking the amount of saturated fat that people consume to coronary heart disease is far from clear cut (Harcombe et al., 2015), in 1977, the US government recommended reducing dietary fat intake to no more than 30 percent of total energy intake and that the amount of saturated fat in the diet should be below 10 percent (Select Committee on Nutrition and Human Needs, 1977).

Getting people to reduce their intake of dietary fat is notoriously difficult. Even when people are aware of how much fat might be in the food they eat, they are not very good at keeping track of what they have eaten. For this reason, attempts to get people to eat healthier have had little success. Two professors at West Virginia University, Bill Reger and Steve Booth-Butterfield, had been discussing how they might help people reduce their intake of dietary fat, and they realized that, for most people, the greatest source of fat in the diet of most Americans at the time was milk. Moreover, if Americans switched from whole milk to 1 percent milk, most would achieve the USDA dietary guidelines straightaway.

Reger and Booth-Butterfield realized that the key to getting people to drink 1 percent milk was getting them to buy 1 percent milk—people drink what's in their refrigerators—so they began a campaign in two cities in West Virginia, Clarksburg and Bridgeport, selected partly because the mortality rates from heart disease there were 13 percent higher than the national average and partly because these two cities had their own media market, so that advertisements could be targeted in a cost-effective way. Moreover, because the media market was so localized, they could use the town of Wheeling, seventy-five miles away and similar in terms of unemployment rate, age, and per capita income, as a comparison community.

The intervention consisted of two thirty-second television commercials that were broadcast a total of 366 times during the first two weeks and the last two weeks of a seven-week campaign, together with two sixty-second radio advertisements that were aired a total of 244 times in the middle of the seven-week campaign. In addition, a number of press conferences and related activities generated coverage of the campaign in news broadcasts. The message was also spread through community and school programs.

The results were striking. Before the campaign, sales of low-fat milk (defined as skim milk, ½ percent, and 1 percent milk) totaled 18 percent of all milk sales in Clarksburg and Bridgeport. At the end of the campaign, the total reached 41 percent and was 35 percent six months later. In Wheeling, the comparison city, low-fat milk sales changed little: 28 percent before the campaign, 33 percent at the end of the campaign, and 32 percent at the six-month follow-up (Reger, Wootan, Booth-Butterfield, & Smith, 1998).

The important point here is that Reger and Booth-Butterfield did not ask people to "eat more healthily." Such advice would cause the rider to endlessly agonize over whether to eat more or fewer carbohydrates, whether it was better to reduce the intake of saturated fats by eating more unsaturated fats. Instead, they gave people clear instructions. As Heath and Heath (2010) point out, "What looks like resistance is often lack of clarity" (p. 16). Because the rider gets tired easily, attempts to change habits are much more successful when clear advice is given. Of course, there are times when decisions cannot be planned in advance and have to be made on the spot, but, wherever possible, it is better to script the critical moves.

Point to the Destination

In the 1980s, British Petroleum's (BP's) success rate in drilling for oil was around 20 percent. However, this average concealed some rather interesting biases. For example, when explorers estimated that the chance of success was between 20 percent and 70 percent, the actual chances of hitting oil were close to the estimate. But when the estimates were at least 75 percent, they almost always hit oil, and when the estimates were 10 percent, the actual success rates were much lower—typically only around 1 percent. Part of the problem was that exploration teams justified their decisions to drill on the *expected value* of the find (the actual value of the well multiplied by the probability of the strike). Even if drilling in a particular spot had a very low probability of success, by increasing the inevitably subjective determination of the value of the find, the cost of drilling would appear to be justified.

Ian Vann, who was at the time BP's head of exploration, wanted to reduce drilling costs from $5 per barrel to $1 per barrel and realized that asking explorers to increase expected value or strike rate by some percentage would be unlikely to produce the required change. That's why, in 1991, he announced that from that point on, the goal for BP's exploration team would be "no dry holes."

Predictably, the explorers thought the idea was ridiculous. Achieving the goal would require reducing dry holes from 80 percent of attempts to zero. Part of the reason that the goal was so intimidating is that it was an all-or-nothing goal. In the past, if an explorer had predicted the chances of success as one in five, then a failure just proved the explorer right. A failure was, after all, more likely than success. Now, there was no margin for error. Every dry hole would be a failure.

Over the next few years, the clarity of focus produced by the goal of no dry holes changed the internal culture of the organization. In particular, as Heath and Heath (2010) point out, the all-or-nothing nature of the goal was helpful in removing two common rationalizations for holes that really should not have been drilled. One was that the exploration team would learn something from drilling. As Ian Vann said, "I can give you a hundred examples where people made a mistake because they didn't use knowledge they already had, for every one example where we learn something that is valuable for next time" (Heath & Heath, 2010, p. 91). The other common rationalization was that drilling a particular hole had strategic value (e.g., to placate a business partner or a government). The all-or-nothing nature of no dry holes meant that a dry hole was a failure no matter how strategic the decision to drill had been. In turn, this empowered less senior employees to resist pressure from their supervisors to drill when the odds of success were not good.

By 2000, BP's success rate was over three times its success rate a decade earlier when the goal of no dry holes was adopted; over two-thirds of the holes they drilled struck oil. BP had not achieved its goal of no dry holes, but it seems unlikely that they could have made the progress they made if the organization had concentrated on gradual, incremental improvement. Sometimes, the clarity of an ambitious and all-or-nothing goal is necessary to galvanize the organization to reconsider the way it does things.

Motivate the Elephant

One aspect of decision making that is not widely appreciated is that decisions that appear to be entirely rational often have a strong underlying emotional basis. Indeed, in his book *Descartes' Error*, Antonio Damasio (1994) points out that emotions are inseparable from rationality. Any approach to habit change, therefore, needs to address the emotional side of decision making.

Find the Feeling

In *The Heart of Change*, John Kotter and Dan Cohen (2002) recount a story from Jon Stegner, who was responsible for procurement for Delphi Automotive—a large organization with a number of manufacturing plants. He had a suspicion that purchasing costs could be reduced substantially, but to get a sense of the scale of the problem, he asked a summer intern to do a small study of how many different kinds of protective gloves were purchased across the organization and how much was paid for each pair. The answer was that the organization was purchasing 424 different kinds of gloves, from different suppliers, and the same pair of gloves could cost $5 at one factory and $17 at another.

Stegner knew that just telling the division presidents about the problem would be unlikely to lead to effective action. The severity of the problem would be acknowledged, and all would agree that "something must be done," but nothing would happen. Instead, he asked the intern to tag each pair of gloves with its price and the factory in which it had been purchased. Then Stegner and the intern piled all 424 pairs of gloves on the boardroom table and invited all the division presidents to meet in the boardroom. Stegner describes what happened next:

> What they saw was a large expensive table, normally clean or with a few papers, now stacked high with gloves. Each of our executives stared at this display for a minute. Then each said something like, "We buy all these different kinds of gloves?" Well, as a matter of fact, yes we do. "Really?" Yes, really. Then they walked around the table. Most, I think, were looking for the gloves that their factories were using. They could see the prices. They looked at two gloves that seemed exactly alike, yet one was marked $3.22 and the other $10.55.
>
> It's a rare event when these people don't have anything to say. But that day, they just stood with their mouths gaping. (Kotter & Cohen, 2002, p. 30)

Very soon after this, the company changed its purchasing policy, thus saving a great deal of money. But it wasn't the rational appeal to good sense that caused people to take action. It was the emotional impact of seeing 424 pairs of gloves piled on a boardroom table.

Shrink the Change

In September 2010, I left my job as a university provost to spend more time on writing, researching, and working with teachers. During my thirty-five years as an academic, I had accumulated a large number of papers—photocopies of journal articles and technical reports—that were stored in a number of filing cabinets; three, thirty-six-inch, four-drawer lateral filing cabinets to be exact. Because I now travel so much, I need to be able to access these documents wherever I am, so I realized that I would have to scan them all. I had a highly efficient document scanner that could scan up to fifty double-sided pages at a time and convert the documents into searchable pdf files, but the task was still daunting. In total, the filing cabinets contained around 10,000 documents, which, taken out of the cabinets and piled up, would make a stack of paper over thirty feet high. The task of scanning 10,000 documents seemed overwhelming, impossible even.

So instead, I gave myself a different task. I wasn't going to scan a thirty-foot pile of paper. I was going to scan half an inch of paper each day. That was it. Each day I was at home, I gave myself the task of scanning just a half-inch pile of paper, and when I had done that, I was done for the day. The next day, of course, there would be another half-inch of paper to scan, but that was tomorrow. As long as I scanned and catalogued half an inch of paper that day, I had done my job.

In February 2014, the task was finished. It had taken me three and a half years, and probably over two hundred hours in total, but the important point is that I would not have been able to contemplate beginning the task of scanning 10,000 documents; it was just too enormous. But the task seemed manageable when broken down into manageable pieces.

The same insight underpins the Chinese proverb that "the longest journey begins with a single step" and Alcoholics Anonymous's suggestion that alcoholics stay sober for just one day at a time. It is also at work in Marla Cilley's five-minute room rescue (Cilley, 2014). Rather than having to clean a room until it is spotless, you set a kitchen timer for five minutes and pick up or clean the room until the timer rings. Of course, five minutes of tidying up isn't going to have a big impact in itself, but it does overcome the paralysis produced by a perception of the task as so big that it seems impossible. As Karl Weick (1984) points out, small wins make us believe that we can be successful, so shrinking the change so that it feels manageable can help us embark on changes that we would not have the courage to attempt.

This advice may seem to contradict the idea of ambitious goals mentioned in connection with "point to the destination" (discussed later), but there is no real paradox here. When belief in one's ability to carry through with one's plans—what psychologists call "self-efficacy"—is low, small steps are better. When self-belief is high, then what Jim Collins and Jerry Porras (1994) call a "big, hairy audacious goal" is likely to be more appropriate (Bandura & Schunk, 1981).

Grow Your People

In a research program stretching back over four decades, Carol Dweck and her colleagues have explored the way that people make sense of successes and failures in classrooms, and in particular, the beliefs about the nature of ability that underpin these attributions (Dweck, 2006). For example, many people believe that ability in, for example, mathematics is something that one has or does not have—what Dweck calls a "fixed" mindset. The reason this is so important is that when individuals with a fixed mindset are given a task, the first thing they do is decide whether they can succeed at the task. If they believe they can succeed at the task, without too much effort, then they engage in the task in order to have their view of themselves as smart confirmed, provided that not too much effort is needed (if you have to work hard at a task, this might suggest that you are not that smart). If they believe that they may fail at the task, they make a second calculation, which is about the chances of others' success on the task. The logic here is that if everyone fails at the task, then failure is acceptable, and success on a task at which everyone else fails is even more gratifying. However, if individuals with a fixed mindset are given a task at which they think they might fail, and at which others might succeed, then the natural reaction is to disengage—after all, it is better to be thought lazy than stupid.

Others have what Dweck calls a "growth" mindset—a belief neatly encapsulated by Jeffrey Howard (1991) with the saying, "Smart is not something that you just are, smart is something that you can get" (p. 7). For those with a growth mindset, a challenging task provides a chance to improve one's ability, and whether you succeed or not, you will improve your ability by engaging in the task. What is most interesting is that the same learners can see ability in some fields as fixed, while having a growth mindset about other fields. For example, many individuals see ability in mathematics as fixed, while having a growth mindset about ability in athletics. They believe that training at, say, triple jump, improves their ability at triple jump, but they do not believe that training in algebra improves their ability in algebra.

It is not particularly surprising that those with growth mindsets tend to do better than those with fixed mindsets, but what is, perhaps, more surprising, is that mindset can be changed very quickly. In one study, Dweck and her colleagues divided ninety-one seventh graders into two groups. For twenty-five minutes a week, for eight weeks, forty-three of the students received training on study skills, while the other forty-eight received presentations on the malleability of intelligence, including ideas that the brain is like a muscle and gets stronger as it is exercised. For students receiving the study-skills training, their mathematics grades declined over the course of the experiment, as is typical in seventh grade (Gutman & Midgley, 2000). However, for the students receiving the growth mindset intervention, there was no drop in grades (Blackwell, Dweck, & Trzesniewski, 2007).

More recently, Dweck (2012) has applied these ideas to adults and found that when people have growth mindsets, and, just as important, when they believe that others can have growth mindsets, then long-standing conflicts are easier to resolve. Most important for the idea of habit change, those with a fixed mindset are more likely to find that willpower is depleted by undertaking a strenuous task, while those with a growth mindset show no such depletion. Having a growth mindset means the rider does not get as tired.

Shape the Path

The way we behave is not just the result of the conflict between the rider and the elephant. The environment makes a difference too. In their book *Nudge*, Thaler and

Sunstein (2009) discuss how the way that default options are framed can often have a large effect on the decisions that people make. For example, if people have to make a decision to opt out, rather than to opt in, to employment-based pension schemes, enrollment is higher. The goal of such framing of the environment is not to manipulate people into making choices that they would not normally make—it is essential that people are free to make their own choices. The aim is rather that where individuals have no clear preference for which course of action to take, the default option is selected to be the one that is most socially desirable—what Thaler and Sunstein call "liberty-preserving paternalism." In other words, habit change requires thinking about the environment in which choices are made and thinking about how changes in that environment can help people do what they want to do. As with directing the rider and motivating the elephant, the Heath brothers identify three main strategies to shape the path.

Tweak the Environment

In April 1998, Wansink and Park (2001) conducted a research study in a suburban Chicago movie theater. A total of 161 people attending a matinee were handed a soft drink and, at random, either a medium (four-ounce) or a large (eight-ounce) bucket of popcorn (the time had been selected so that most of those attending would have just eaten lunch and would therefore not be particularly hungry). The popcorn and the drink were free, but in return, recipients were asked to stick around at the end of the movie (*Payback*, in case you're interested) to answer some questions. The cover story was that the theater was conducting an evaluation of the concession stands, but in fact, it was a study of eating habits.

Unknown to the moviegoers and to the graduate students assisting in carrying out the research, the popcorn had, in fact, been prepared five days earlier and stored in sterile conditions until it was so stale that it actually squeaked when eaten (one participant later said it was like eating Styrofoam packing peanuts). At the end of the movie, participants were asked to bring their buckets of popcorn with them and complete a questionnaire that asked them to rate a number of statements, such as "I ate too much popcorn," on a scale of 1 (strongly disagree) to 9 (strongly agree). While the participants completed the questionnaire, the researchers weighed the popcorn remaining in each bucket.

What Wansink and Park (2001) found was that none of the people given popcorn had eaten it all—the popcorn was just too stale and most had just eaten lunch—but while those who had been given the four-ounce buckets had on average eaten 2.2 ounces of popcorn, those given eight-ounce buckets ate 3.3 ounces—50 percent more. Just being given more popcorn made people eat more. Even more interestingly, those who had eaten more were convinced that the size of container they had been given had not affected how much of the popcorn they ate. The main takeaway message here is that small changes in the environment can have a big change in what people do.

Build Habits

In my role as a university provost, one of my responsibilities was to advise young academics about career development, and, of course, in the modern university, career advancement is largely about publications, especially articles in peer-reviewed journals. The aspiring academic sends an article to the editor of an academic journal who will seek reviews from authorities in the field, and, when the reports from the referees have been received, the editor will write to the author with a decision about whether the paper will be accepted for publication or rejected. As might be imagined, rejection is painful, as noted by Benton Underwood (1957):

> The rejection of my own manuscripts has a sordid aftermath: a) one day of depression; (b) one day of utter contempt for the editor and his accomplices; (c) one day of decrying the conspiracy against letting Truth be published; (d) one day of fretful ideas about changing my profession; (e) one day of re-evaluating the manuscript in view of the editor's comments followed by the conclusion that I was lucky it wasn't accepted! (p. 87)

Although rejection is painful, sometimes, as Underwood notes, it can protect academics from making fools of themselves in public. More important, the rejection letter is accompanied by reviews from the referees about how the article could be improved, but such advice is hard to take when it comes with a rejection.

This is why I advise all young academics to decide, before they send their article off to a journal editor, what they will do if the paper is rejected. In other words, they should determine plan B at the same time as plan A. The reason this is so powerful is that plan B is devised without the emotions that accompany rejection, so if the article is rejected, then the plan of action is clear.

The general idea here is that action triggers—deciding in advance what actions will follow a particular event—can help overcome the emotions of the elephant and the tiredness of the rider. Peter Gollwitzer (1999), one of the leading researchers in this area, suggests that when people decide in advance what do to—what he calls "implementation intentions"—they "pass the control of their behavior on to the environment" (p. 495). A particularly interesting use of implementation intentions occurred in the 2008 US presidential election. Voters were contacted by phone to encourage voting. At random, some were just reminded of the importance of voting, some were asked whether they were likely to vote, and some were asked three additional questions if they said they were likely to vote: what time they would vote, where they would be coming from, and what they would be doing beforehand. Those who received the three additional questions were 10 percentage points more likely to vote than the other two groups, but only if they were the only voter in the household (Nickerson & Rogers, 2010).

A recent meta-analysis of eighty-five studies found that people who set action triggers did better than 74 percent of people on the same task who didn't set one, equivalent to an effect size of around 0.63 standard deviations (Sheeran, Milne, Webb, & Gollwitzer, 2005). Action triggers are particularly useful in difficult situations because they protect goals from tempting distractions, bad habits, or competing goals. In one study, action triggers produced only modest increases in success for easy goals (78 percent to 84 percent success rate), but with more challenging goals, the success rate rose from 22 percent to 62 percent (Gollwitzer & Brandstätter, 1997).

Rally the Herd

According to the Institute of Medicine, medication errors injure 1.5 million Americans each year, with an annual cost of $3.5 billion from lost productivity, lost wages, and increased medical costs (Aspden, Wolcott, Boorman, & Cronenwett, 2007). Mistakes can occur in prescribing, transcribing, dispensing, and in administering the drugs, and also in monitoring the patient receiving drugs. However, the administration phase is particularly important since nurses intercept six out of every seven errors made by physicians, pharmacists, and others in the earlier phases (Leape et al., 1995) and because there are few safeguards against administration errors since they occur at the end of the process.

There is some debate over how to define medication-administration errors. At one extreme, administering a drug at the wrong time or failing to ensure that all windows were closed in the area where the medications are being dispensed could count as a medication error even if there are no adverse consequences for the patient. At the other extreme are errors, such as administering the wrong dose or the wrong drug, that can be fatal.

Investigation of medication errors at Kaiser South San Francisco Hospital revealed that nurses were generally very accurate in administering drugs—one nontrivial error for every 1,000 medications administered—but due to the number of medications administered, that led to around 250 nontrivial errors each year. Becky Richards, director of Adult Clinical Services at Kaiser South, realized that the source of many of the errors was likely to be the interruptions that nurses experienced while preparing medications. As Heath and Heath point out, this isn't a rider problem (the critical moves are clear) nor is it an elephant problem (the nurses were generally irritated by the interruptions and wished there were fewer of them). The problem was the cultural norms of the hospital; it was regarded as acceptable to interrupt nurses administering drugs.

To change the norms, Richards decided that when administering drugs, nurses would don medication vests—high-visibility orange vests bearing the text "Medication round: Please do not disturb." The idea was that this would send a clear message to all that the nurse was engaged in something important and should not be interrupted. Two units at Kaiser South were selected for a six-month pilot study, which began in July 2006 (Richards, 2008).

The problem was, everybody hated the vests. The nurses didn't like the color, they didn't know how to keep the vests clean, and, perhaps most important, they thought that the vests were demeaning, implying that the nurses were not capable of administering drugs without being isolated. Physicians also disliked the vests because they could not talk to their nurses as they passed them. In fact, the opposition to the vests was so strong that at one point, serious consideration was given to abandoning the pilot.

But then, the data came in. In one of the units, the number of medication errors dropped from 2.9 to 1.1 errors per month, and in the other, errors declined from 3.9 to 2.8 errors per month. Errors dropped by 47 percent overall (Pape & Richards, 2010).

Because of the success of the pilot, in April 2007, the medication vests were rolled out across the hospital, although in a concession to the nurses, a more muted color was used. Within a month, medication errors dropped by 20 percent across the hospital, and by January 2008, errors were down by 60 percent across the hospital compared with January 2007. There was one unit where medication errors actually rose—from 1.5 to 2.8 errors per month. This was a unit that had decided that the vests were unnecessary.

Later in 2008, the medication vests were introduced in all twenty-two Kaiser hospitals in Northern California, one in Southern California, one in Oregon, and one in Hawaii (Becky Richards, personal communication, March 1, 2015). As the scheme is being rolled out elsewhere, refinements continue to be made (Craig, Clanton, & Demeter, 2014). Nurses now have the option of wearing a sash rather than a vest, which is easier to put on and take off. In addition, a safety zone has been created in the rooms where medications are prepared. This is a region marked out with red floor tape or red tiles where nurses prepare medication and where no one else is allowed to cross into the space or talk to a nurse who is in the zone.

A number of factors have contributed to the success of the medication vest scheme. The environment has been tweaked. Without the vests or sashes, someone might interrupt a nurse administering medications inadvertently. However, because of the vests or sashes, no one could claim not to know that the nurse was administering medications. Nurses also built habits; after a while, putting on the vests came to seem natural. But perhaps the most important change was the creation of a new set of social norms. Staff at the Kaiser hospitals accept that administering medication is important work, and nurses need to be given time to do it without interruption. This idea of rallying the herd—creating a group ethos around particular practices—completes the nine strategies of habit change identified by Heath and Heath (2010) and provides a strong foundation for supporting change in schools.

Switch and Classroom Practice

Switch was published in 2010, six years after we began to explore the use of TLCs to support teachers in their development of formative assessment. Had the book been published earlier, we could have saved ourselves a lot of blind alleys and false starts. However, what is perhaps most interesting is that the model we developed is entirely consistent with the nine change strategies identified by Heath and Heath, as is shown in the final section of this chapter.

Follow the Bright Spots: Start With Volunteers Rather Than Conscripts

One of the first issues we explored as we worked with schools and districts was whether it was better to begin with volunteers or conscripts, and we have concluded that in general it is better to start with volunteers. Conscripts will always find reasons why a particular strategy or technique will not work, but it is much more difficult for them to argue this when it is working in the classroom next door. Starting with volunteers does create some particular issues, however. When the work involves only volunteers, it is treated as additional rather than core, and, in particular, finding the time for the volunteers is difficult. If this is regarded as part of the volunteers' work, then it is not clear what the nonvolunteers should be doing at the same time. If it is additional, then finding time is difficult, as discussed earlier. Indeed, as we shall see in the next chapter, finding time for teachers to meet does seem to be very difficult in most schools.

Script the Critical Moves: Highly Structured Meetings

Many approaches to teacher professional development leave the structure of teacher meetings up to the participants. This can be highly effective, allowing teachers to explore in greater depth the issues that are most significant for them. However, as I and my colleagues have worked with teachers, schools, and districts, we have found that more often, the lack of structure led to less productive meetings.

We also found that when we provided a structure, if the structure varied from meeting to meeting, teachers spent a considerable amount of time trying to figure out what they were meant to be doing, so we realized that it would be helpful if every meeting had the same structure.

This decision was, in part, influenced by Lee Shulman's (2005) work on the signature pedagogies of the professions—approaches to professional learning in law, medicine, and the clergy, which are not perfect but are good enough. The important point about such approaches to professional learning is that if participants arrive at the learning session understanding the structure of the session and understanding their own roles, then the structure of the meeting fades into the background, and the professional learning comes into the foreground.

After a few years of experimentation, we adopted a model in which each meeting of teachers had six items on the agenda. Further details of the meeting protocols can be found in Wiliam and Leahy (2015), and complete agendas for eighteen monthly meetings, together with a number of other resources, are available in Wiliam and Leahy (2014). In outline, the structure is as follows:

1. Introduction and learning intentions for the meeting (5 minutes)
2. Warm-up activity (5 minutes)
3. Feedback session (25–50 minutes)
4. New learning about formative assessment (20–40 minutes)
5. Personal action planning (15 minutes)
6. Review of the meeting (5 minutes)

The active ingredient of the meeting is the third item, feedback, during which each participant reports back to the group about the progress he or she has made with his or her chosen priority since the previous meeting. However, we also found that attendance was much better when there was something novel in each meeting, hence the activity on "New learning about formative assessment." Activity 5 provides fifteen minutes of quiet time for teachers to sharpen the saw—time to reflect on how they plan to be a better teacher next month than they were this month.

Point to the Destination: All Students Proficient

When I first heard about the No Child Left Behind Act in 2001, I thought that was a really unfortunate title for a piece of legislation. In particular, I wondered about the pressure there would be on the very last child—the one who was holding things up and preventing this extraordinary goal from being reached. Now, however, it seems to me that no child left behind is best thought of as a big, hairy, audacious goal—a goal that, even if not reached, galvanizes people into action. Too often we think of schools as talent refineries where we provide the same experiences to all students, and some thrive, while others do not. I note that in most schools, sports teams do not seem to function on the same basis. I have never heard a football coach say, "We only have five good players this year so we're not going to bother playing football." Instead, the best coaches treat their programs as talent factories, building talent rather than just allowing it to emerge. So, just like Ian Vann's goal of no dry holes, a goal such as "all students proficient" can create a reappraisal of long-entrenched practices. People will tell you, as they did Ian Vann, that the goal is impossible, but what is important is the changes in thinking that occur when a goal is stated in such clear terms. What would have to change about how the school does its work for such a goal to be possible?

Of course, it is also necessary to provide a degree of challenge for those for whom proficiency is an easily achievable goal, so as well as "all students proficient," it should also be the case that many students reach standards of excellence, and the opportunity to reach these standards of excellence should not depend on gender, race, ethnicity, or socioeconomic status. The goal is therefore: "all students proficient, many excellent, with all student subgroups proportionately represented in the excellent."

Framing a goal in this way would also have the advantage of avoiding the problem with so-called achievement gaps, which is that the gap can be reduced either by helping those with lower achievement or by doing less for those with higher achievement. Reducing funding for special programs for gifted and talented youth may well reduce the achievement gap, but that doesn't mean it's a good idea.

Find the Feeling: The Moral Imperative

As my various colleagues and I have worked with teachers all over the world, we have come across a few teachers who clearly feel that they have no need to change because they are already getting great results. However, we come across far more people who say that they agree that all teachers need to improve, but that their school is full of such people who do not feel the same. The fact that teachers tell me that there are many experienced teachers in their schools who feel there is no need to improve, combined with the fact that I meet few such teachers, makes me think that this is not as great a problem as is often claimed.

Nevertheless, there is often a need, particularly in schools that attract high-achieving students, to get teachers to reach for even higher achievement, and that is why the kinds of ideas presented in chapter 1 can be helpful. No matter how good a teacher is, if he or she improves, his or her students will be healthier, live longer, and contribute more to society. Reconnecting teachers with this moral imperative can reduce resistance, especially when combined with the ideas of choice, flexibility, and small steps discussed earlier in this chapter.

Shrink the Change: Small Steps

Teachers in the United States and elsewhere are regularly told that they should be teaching like teachers in another country. In the 1980s, we were told that we should copy Hungary; in the 1990s, it was Japan; in the 2000s, it was Finland, and now it's Shanghai. Even when the suggestions are grounded in research evidence, as discussed earlier in this chapter, teachers are not going to be given sabbaticals so that they can spend a few months making wholesale changes in their teaching approaches before actually using them with their students. Making change seem both manageable and sustainable is therefore very important in getting teachers to embrace change. Many teachers believe they can recall a bygone era of stability in education when teachers were left alone to do their jobs. I have no idea whether such a period existed, but given the moral imperative discussed previously, even if it did, our students would be ill-served by a return to such an environment. Continuous change is the new normal.

Grow Your People: All Teachers Can Improve

Carol Dweck's ideas about mindset, discussed earlier in this book, have captured the imagination of many educators in recent years, but one aspect of this work that has not, in my view, gained sufficient attention is that the idea of mindsets is at least as important for teachers as it is for students. That is why it can be sometimes more effective to start by asking teachers not, "Do you need to improve?" but "Could you be even better than you are now?" In my experience, teachers are unwilling to answer that question in the negative—it seems highly unlikely that any teacher would feel able to claim that he or she is perfect in every conceivable respect.

Tweak the Environment: Create Time for Teacher Learning

The central argument of this book is that teacher learning should be the main priority for every school leader. Many leaders embrace this idea and encourage teachers to improve their practice, but too often, teacher learning happens around the margins of the other activities of the school. In the next chapter, I describe a project where a number of school leaders identified formative assessment as a policy priority but found it hard to provide teachers with the time to work on improving their practice. One of the participating schools (given the pseudonym "Willow" in the next chapter) realized that their first attempts at developing formative assessment had been rather unsuccessful, but they had noticed that where teachers had been able to find time to meet, the impact on their practice and on student achievement was profound. The following year, they decided that time for teacher learning should be the first thing written into the school schedule, before any student classes were scheduled. Of course, many districts in the United States provide late starts or early dismissals to create time for teacher learning, but even where this is done, leaders need to be vigilant in ensuring that a significant proportion of the time is spent on teacher learning, rather than other aspects of the school's work.

Build Habits: Create Routines and Structures

As we explored different models of teacher meetings, one of the variables we investigated was the frequency of meetings. We started with meetings every two weeks, but what we found was that many of the participating teachers had not been able to try out the ideas they had committed to trying out two weeks earlier. People who have never been teachers find this surprising. Two weeks to try out one new technique seems like plenty of time, but that is because, as noted earlier, people who have not been teachers do not understand how delicate and fragile teachers' working lives are. In fact, we found that most teachers need four weeks to try out a new idea in their classroom. However, we also found that when meetings were less frequent than once a month, there was a definite loss of momentum. While school calendars create a number of constraints, having a regular pattern of meetings seems to be especially important. In particular, when teachers know there will be a meeting every month, improvement becomes part of the natural cycle of work in the school.

Rally the Herd: Make New Mistakes

For the previously mentioned strategy of following the bright spots, I suggested that schools should start with volunteers rather than conscripts. The danger of such an approach is that those who do not volunteer are left behind. Therefore, while following the bright spots is a good starting point, within four to six months, attention needs to be given to bringing nonvolunteers into the program. This, of course, is exactly what Jerry Sternin did in Vietnam—follow the bright spots—but then use those in the vanguard to bring others on board. We have found that those who have participated in the early stages of the program are the most persuasive advocates for bringing others on board and, of course, are likely to be more comfortable leading TLCs because they have been through the process already. As mentioned earlier, when experienced teachers start talking about mistakes they have made, and thus normalize the idea of taking risks even when they don't work out, this creates an ethos about the importance of experimentation. This was perhaps best summarized by Esther Dyson, who has pointed out that there's no excuse for making the same mistake over and over again, but there's no excuse for making no mistakes at all (recall the quote from Mario Andretti: "If everything seems under control, you're not going fast enough"). Esther Dyson's advice is, "Make new mistakes." When all the teachers in a school share the goal of making new mistakes, wonderful things are likely to happen.

Conclusion

This chapter has explored a number of features that appear to be especially important for effective teacher learning when the goal is to improve pedagogy. By engaging with thousands of teachers in hundreds of schools, we have found that five features appear to be particularly important in maximizing the effectiveness of teacher learning: giving teachers choice about which aspects of practice to develop, encouraging them to adapt formative assessment techniques to suit their local circumstances, requiring them to focus on a small number of changes to their practice, making them accountable to their peers for trying out these innovations, and providing the support they need. Since changing classroom practice is a process of habit change, this chapter has also reviewed the research on "how to change when change is hard," as Heath and Heath put it. Of course, no matter how well designed the teacher learning is, what really matters is the implementation, and that is the focus of the final chapter.

[*Chapter 7*]

Implementation

In previous chapters, I have argued that increased student achievement is vital both for our future economic prosperity and for allowing our young people the best chance possible of leading productive and fulfilled lives. While this does require some structural changes, such as ensuring a broad and balanced curriculum, the biggest impact on how much our students learn is the quality of teaching that students experience in classrooms. The quality of teaching is, in turn, influenced by factors such as class size, the quality of the curriculum, the resources teachers have available to them, the time they have to prepare instruction, and the support they receive from their colleagues. However, the most important factor influencing the quality of the teaching is the qualities that the individual teacher brings to the classroom. Improving teacher quality is therefore the key to improving education. Other changes have their role to play, of course, but any approach to improving our schools that does not embrace the idea of improving teachers will have, at best, a small impact.

As noted earlier, economists such as Eric Hanushek have shown that substantial increases in teacher quality can be achieved simply by raising the threshold for entry into the profession (Hanushek, 2004). Hiring at the 58th percentile rather than the 50th would, over time, lead to the United States having the best teaching force in the world. But it would take thirty to fifty years to get there, and schooling is a one-shot deal for our students. They can't wait. That is why I have argued that every single teacher needs to get better, even if he or she is already the best teacher in the state. Teachers need to improve because they can be even better, and when they do their jobs better, their students live longer, are healthier, and contribute more to society.

In subsequent chapters, I have shown why a focus on classroom formative assessment is likely to be the most powerful lever for improving student achievement and that the creation of building-based TLCs is likely to be the best way to support teachers in this process. In this final chapter, I discuss what we have learned about the practical difficulties of implementing, in schools and districts, the proposals made in earlier chapters.

An Overnight Success—in Twenty Years

Paul Black and I began working together on formative assessment in the mid-1990s, although each of us had been interested in the role of assessment to improve learning for many years before that. As we have worked together, what has been most interesting to me is that as we solved what we thought to be the major problems related to school improvement, the solutions to those problems created even more complex and seemingly intractable problems.

Between 1993 and 1998, we worked to synthesize the research on the role that assessment played in supporting learning, and this culminated in the publication of a major review article (Black & Wiliam, 1998a) and a companion booklet titled "Inside the Black Box" (Black & Wiliam, 1998b), which sought to draw out the implications of this work for policymakers and practitioners.

Looking back at the subsequent development of this work, it fits reasonably well into a series of Soviet-style five-year plans—although we hadn't thought the work would take this long. Indeed, if we had realized how long it would take, I doubt that either of us would have had the courage to begin.

The work we did between 1993 and 1998 in reviewing the research on formative assessment convinced us that this work should be a priority for schools, and so, from 1998 to 2003, we began working intensively with schools to see how they might be supported in making formative assessment a reality in classrooms. Working face to face with teachers in six schools, we found that they were able to incorporate the ideas into their practice (Black, Harrison, Lee, Marshall, & Wiliam, 2003) and that when they did so, their students achieved more, even when achievement was measured with standardized tests (Wiliam, Lee, Harrison, & Black, 2004).

The problem with such a model, of course, is that it cannot be scaled up. Although Paul Black and I have spoken face to face with literally tens of thousands of teachers, the sustained, practice-focused, job-embedded professional development that is needed to support teachers in their development of formative assessment is simply not viable if it requires face-to-face contact with professional developers.

For this reason, from 2003 to 2008, I worked with colleagues at the Educational Testing Service in Princeton, New Jersey, to explore ways that districts and schools could be supported in developing their use of classroom formative assessment.

In framing that work, we adopted a number of design constraints. The first was the idea of creating a framework that was "tight but loose" (Thompson & Wiliam, 2008). The idea behind the tight but loose framework is that it provides a way of managing a delicate balancing act between two conflicting requirements. The first is the need to ensure that the model is sufficiently flexible to allow it to be adapted to the local circumstances of the intervention, not only just to allow it to succeed, but also so that it can capitalize on any affordances present in the local context that will enhance the effectiveness of the intervention. The second is to design the model with sufficient rigidity to ensure that any modifications that do take place preserve sufficient fidelity to the original design to provide a reasonable assurance that the intervention does not undergo a lethal mutation, as described in the previous chapter.

Here is the definition:

> The Tight but Loose formulation combines an obsessive adherence to central design principles (the "tight" part) with accommodations to the needs, resources, constraints, and particularities that occur in any school or district (the "loose" part), *but only where these do not conflict with the theory of action of the intervention.* (Thompson & Wiliam, 2008, p. 35, original emphasis)

The second design constraint was that whatever we produced would have to be, in principle, capable of being scaled across an entire state or province. This did not mean that whatever we did had to be scalable at the outset, but it did mean that anything that could not in principle be scaled across a state or province would be ruled out.

For example, we had considered the possibility of training instructional coaches to play the role that Paul Black and I and our colleagues had played in face-to-face work with teachers, but concluded that this would not be viable for a number of reasons. First, we were not sure that skilled coaches would be available in sufficient numbers to make this a model that could, at least in principle, be scaled up across an entire state or province, let alone a country. Second, we thought the model would be too expensive for many districts to implement, given the vast difference in per-student expenditure across different districts. Third, even where it was possible to fund coaches in a district, the funding streams for such noncore activities are often regarded as discretionary and are therefore vulnerable to reductions in taxation revenue. That is why we decided to explore the potential of building-based professional learning communities—led by participating teachers rather than external facilitators—as a way of providing continuing support for teachers developing their practice of classroom formative assessment.

A third design principle was that the model would have to be the same model for all teachers working in a building. In our work with schools over the last twenty years or so, we have been dismayed to see how little coherence there is in the arrangements for teacher professional development, even in the same building. As noted in previous chapters, it is common to find mathematics teachers engaged in one set of professional development activities, the science teachers another, and the social studies and English language arts teachers doing something else entirely. Now of course this is perfectly understandable. Generic professional development has a rather poor track record in the United States, and there is ample evidence that to be most effective, professional development does need to engage with the actual content that teachers need to teach (Darling-Hammond, Wei, Andree, Richardson, & Orphanos, 2009). However, when there is no commonality in the professional development approaches being used by different groups of teachers in the same building, it is far more difficult to generate a coherent dialogue within the school about teaching and learning. The challenge was therefore to design a single model for a whole school, but one that also honored the specificities of age and school subject. Teaching five-year-olds is not the same as teaching ten-year-olds, and teaching mathematics is not the same as teaching history.

For those who are interested in further details of how we developed the model for effective, scalable teacher professional development described earlier in this book, these can be found in Thompson and Wiliam (2008). For the current discussion, the main point is that over a three-year period, we developed and implemented a number of different models that might be used. As noted in previous chapters, we tried different frequencies of meetings (from every two weeks to every six or seven weeks), different size groups (from fours and fives to meetings with twenty teachers or more), and different lengths of meetings (from 60 minutes to 120 minutes or longer).

As will of course be clear by now, one of the most important decisions we made was to use the idea of professional learning communities as the main mechanism for supporting teachers in their development of classroom formative assessment.

Working in groups, rather than individually, has become almost a panacea in education. In many ways, this is understandable, since for far too long, teachers have worked in isolation. Indeed, there can be few occupations where so much time is spent working in isolation from others. For that reason, teacher collaboration has been promoted as a solution to all educational ills, despite the clear evidence about the danger of groupthink, in which groups come to decisions that are more extreme than any individual would have reached alone (Myers & Lamm, 1976). In response to this, many point to *The Wisdom of Crowds* (Surowiecki, 2004) but fail to appreciate that the well-documented benefits of this phenomenon occur only when members of a large group reach decisions *independently*. Nevertheless, it appears that teacher collaboration is particularly useful in two circumstances—where problems are simply too challenging to be solved with a single perspective (Gibbons et al., 1994) and where self-knowledge is essential to progress.

The latter is especially important because there is now extensive literature on the inadequacy of self-reports, summarized in Figure 7.1.

Only 2 percent of high school seniors believe their leadership skills are below average (College Board, 1976) . . .
. . . and 25 percent of them believe they are in the top 1 percent in their ability to get along with others (College Board, 1976).
Ninety-three percent of Americans and 69 percent of Swedes think they are safer drivers than average (Svenson, 1981).
Ninety-four percent of college professors report doing above-average work (Cross, 1977).
People think they are at lower risk than their peers for heart attacks, stroke, cancer, food poisoning, etc. (Weinstein, 1980).
Strangers predict your IQ better than you do (Borkenau & Liebler, 1993).
People believe they are more accurate than their peers at accurate self-assessment (Pronin, Lin, & Ross, 2002).

Figure 7.1. Why people shouldn't work on their own.

The extensive research and development effort (although it would probably be more accurately described as development and research) resulted in a series of professional development resources that are being used all over the world (Northwest Evaluation Association, 2015; Wiliam & Leahy, 2014). Although at this stage, we do not have evidence from RCTs that prove the efficacy of this approach, its practical success does suggest that schools and teachers are finding the approach helpful. For example, the model is already being used in two-thirds of the elementary schools in Singapore (Lee, Oh, Ang, & Lee, 2014) and has been adopted state-wide in the state of South Australia. Work in the United States is less advanced, but preliminary work in Oregon shows that when schools use these materials, there is an impact on student engagement and learning (Thum, Tarasawa, Hegedus, Yun, & Bowe, 2015).

So, problem solved, surely? We had shown that formative assessment had a significant impact on student achievement, both in terms of the research literature and in practical experiments, and had found that schools, given the right tools, could reproduce the key experiences for teachers with reasonable fidelity. What we were not prepared for is how difficult it turns out to be to get schools to do what the research says will have the greatest impact on their students. In this final chapter, I will discuss what we have learned about the challenges of successfully implementing effective teacher learning in schools and districts.

Getting With the Program

The reason I have already discussed the development of the idea of TLCs in support of classroom formative assessment in such detail is that it is important to understand that the recommended model is not something that was just made up impulsively on the basis of our hunches about what might work. Indeed, what has been interesting—and sobering—is just how many things we got wrong to begin with. We started with groups that were too small, our meetings were too short, and we thought that the groups should consist of teachers with similar teaching assignments.

Because of the extensive trial and improvement process, involving much rapid prototyping, where models were developed, implemented, and revised many times each year, it is not surprising that schools and districts that have implemented the program as designed have found the program to be both effective and manageable. Given this, what is perhaps surprising is the number of schools and districts that believed they could get the benefit of the innovation by selecting a few elements of the program. Despite having attended presentations where the research basis for formative assessment was discussed at some length, and where it was shown that there was little or no research to support other innovations in learning that were attracting interest at the time (e.g., Brain Gym or learning styles), many schools reported that they liked the idea of TLCs but had decided to use them to support teachers in whatever was the school's current priority for professional development (e.g., differentiated instruction, personalization, learning styles). Other lethal mutations included having TLCs that met only two or three times per year or, as mentioned in the previous chapter, districts where principals chose for teachers which techniques they should develop or insisted on attending the meetings of the TLCs themselves. What was perhaps most surprising was that most of those who had transformed the innovation beyond recognition appeared to believe that they were implementing the materials *as intended*. They thought that the modifications they had made would not affect the likely effectiveness of the intervention.

Of course, in some ways, this modification of key messages is hardly surprising, impossible to prevent, and may even be very positive in its outcomes. Indeed, in designing a model that was designed to be, at least in principle, scalable across an entire state or province, we realized that districts and schools would have to change certain features of the model for the work to be feasible.

To this end, as part of the tight but loose framework, we were very clear in presenting this work to schools and districts about which aspects of the work could be modified (timings of meetings, size of groups), and which aspects our work had suggested really needed to be implemented as designed (frequency of meetings, teachers choosing for themselves what to work on). Nevertheless, even where certain aspects of the program were presented as features that really needed to be present for the innovation to be effective, schools routinely modified the program in ways that rendered it almost completely ineffective.

A Case Study in One District

Cannington is a school district in Greater London, covering an area of approximately ten square miles and serving a diverse population of approximately 200,000 residents, with three times as many of its residents from minority ethnic communities as the country as a whole.

In July 2007, a philanthropic organization made available some funds for the establishment of a research project designed to raise student achievement in mathematics, science, and modern foreign languages—subjects that administrators in the district had identified as priorities for development—although how this might be done was not identified at the time the philanthropic donation was made.

In November 2007, I gave a presentation at a meeting of the principals of the secondary schools in Cannington, proposing the establishment of three TLCs in each secondary school, one focusing on mathematics, one focusing on science, and the third on modern foreign languages, to provide support for teachers in their development of classroom formative assessment practices. I, and members of the project, attended monthly meetings of the principals of the secondary schools in Cannington for the remainder of the school year, and in July 2008, I ran three one-day workshops—one for each school subject—for teachers in the participating schools. The number of teachers from each school attending each of the events is shown in Table 7.1. Although the schools did not have to contribute to the costs of the training event, no funds were provided for substitute teachers, so each school had to arrange appropriate coverage for attending teachers from its own discretionary resources.

The training day consisted of a brief summary of the research on formative assessment, an overview of the five key strategies of formative assessment, and an introduction to approximately thirty of the techniques that teachers might use to implement formative assessment in their classrooms. The day concluded with details on the creation of the three subject-specific, school-based TLCs that would be established to provide ongoing support in each school. The training session also provided guidance on the role of the leader of each of the three TLCs to be established in each school.

Table 7.1. Number of Teachers Attending Each Training Event

	Number of teachers attending training event for:		
School	**Mathematics**	**Science**	**Modern languages**
Ashtree School	1	1	0
Cedar Lodge School	5	1	3
Hawthorne School	4	10	5
Hazeltree School	7	12	2
Larchtree School	1	0	0
Mallow School	6	7	3
Poplar School	11	3	1
Spruce School	7	8	5
Willowtree School	2	5	2
Totals	44	47	21

The reactions of the teachers to the training were extremely positive, and at the end of the training day, the participants from six of the nine schools appeared to have a firm plan for implementation. One school (Ashtree) had decided to delay participation in the project for a year, and Hazeltree School had earlier that month decided to create mixed-subject, rather than subject-specific, TLCs, as they felt that this was more in keeping with the professional development work that had already taken place at the school. However, because the charitable funding had been provided specifically for supporting the teachers of mathematics, science, and modern foreign languages, it was agreed that this would in effect mean that Hazeltree would be withdrawing from the project, although they continued to receive all materials necessary for supporting TLCs. Larchtree School had only sent a single teacher (to the mathematics session), but the teacher concerned appeared confident that she would be able to cascade the training to other teachers in the mathematics department, and possibly also to teachers of the other subjects.

While it was not possible for each teacher of mathematics, science, and modern foreign languages in each school to attend the one-day workshop, all teachers of these subjects in the secondary schools in Cannington were provided with a short (thirty-page) booklet outlining the major principles of formative assessment, together with specific details on how they could be applied in their subject (Black & Harrison, 2002; Hodgen & Wiliam, 2006; Jones & Wiliam, 2007), and a complete set of handouts for participants for each of the nine monthly meetings that were scheduled to take place over the coming year.

To provide a simple channel of communication between the teachers in the school and the project, six expert facilitators (two for each subject-specialism) were appointed. Their major role was not to drive the implementation of the program in the schools, but rather to respond to requests from TLC leaders and administrators within the school about how the materials should be used. Each facilitator kept a log of contacts with teachers at the school, which provided the main source of evidence on the extent to which the TLCs were functioning as intended.

Given the involvement of the principals of the school at each step of the process up to this point, and their investment in releasing significant numbers of teachers to attend the initial workshops, we expected the TLCs would be established quickly, but for a variety of reasons, adoption was extremely patchy.

At the end of seven months, logs provided by the facilitators were coded independently by two raters, with each rater being asked to rate the progress made by each TLC on a scale from 1 (little or no progress) to 4 (good progress). When the ratings were compared, in no case did the ratings differ by more than one point. The agreed-upon ratings are shown in Table 7.2.

Table 7.2. Extent of Progress of TLCs in Each School

School	Progress		
	Mathematics	Science	Modern languages
Ashtree School*	-	-	-
Cedar Lodge School	1	1	2
Hawthorne School	2	2	4
Hazeltree School*	-	-	-
Larchtree School	4	1	1
Mallow School	3	1	2
Poplar School	1	3	3
Spruce School	4	3	3
Willowtree School	1	1	4
Average	2.3	1.8	2.8

*Did not participate in project (Ashtree deferred for a year, Hazeltree implemented a different model—see text for explanation).

Perhaps the most surprising feature of the evidence presented in Tables 7.1 and 7.2 is that there does not appear to be any relationship between the investment made by the school, as measured by the number of teachers they released to attend workshops, and the progress made by the TLCs in the school. In fact, the correlation between the two is 0.01, which is shown more clearly in Figure 7.2.

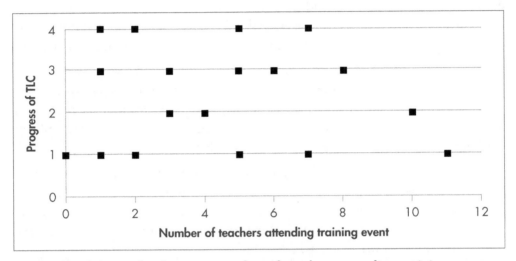

Figure 7.2. Relationship between number of teachers attending training events and progress of TLCs in Cannington.

Two additional features of these data are also worth noting. First, the greatest progress appears to have been made in modern foreign languages, which was the subject with the least-well-attended initial session. Second, with the exception of Spruce School, there does not appear to be any tendency for the best-progressing TLCs to be in the same school.

In the schools that were participating in the project, only nine of the twenty-one planned TLCs were making reasonable progress (defined as a rating of 3 or 4 in Table 7.2). A more careful analysis of the facilitator logs indicated that the major cause of the twelve TLCs making slow or no progress (defined as a rating of 2 or 1 in Table 7.2) was that the teachers had not been given time to meet. This was also the case for some of the more successful TLCs, where the members had decided to commit their own personal time to these meetings because of their interest in, and commitment to, the project. Where time within their contracted hours had been made available for members of TLCs to meet, the TLCs were going well, with considerable enthusiasm for the meetings, and in particular, the teachers appeared to value the opportunity to talk about practice in a structured way.

The difficulty that TLCs had in finding time to meet is, at first sight, rather surprising. While none of the schools in Cannington were on the list of approximately 600 schools in England designated at the time by the government as "National Challenge" schools for their failure to achieve the key benchmark of 30 percent of their students achieving proficiency (grade C or above) in five subjects in the national school-leaving examination for sixteen-year-olds, there is considerable pressure on all schools in England to improve results. Public transport links in Cannington are good, so students can easily travel from one side of the municipality to the other, and parents have a great deal of choice in secondary schools. This choice is at least informed, if not driven, by the publication of results achieved by students in the national school-leaving examinations. All the principals said that improving academic outcomes, as measured by success on national examinations taken at ages sixteen and eighteen, was one of their top priorities, and yet despite the research evidence suggesting that formative assessment could make more difference to these academic outcomes than anything else, it appears as if it was difficult for the principals and other school administrators to prioritize the development of formative assessment.

It is even more surprising when one considers that the principals had made a commitment to the program six months before its commencement, had been kept fully informed of the resource requirements necessary for the monthly meetings, and each school had made a considerable investment in the project by committing an average of twelve teacher days so that teachers could attend the introductory workshop.

When the principals of the participating schools were asked whether they were still committed to the project, they all said they were, and that, in fact, the establishment of TLCs remained a top priority. But of course, this was not the only top priority. Like every other school, the schools in Cannington had a number of important initiatives in place. All of the initiatives are good ideas, but when everything is a priority, nothing is.

This, of course, is the same idea that we encountered in the previous chapter. When there is little waste, the only way to improve the performance of an organization is to stop people doing good things to give them time to do even better things. As was stressed previously, if we spend our time looking for unproductive practices—things that do not help students to learn—we will produce very little change in our schools because most of what everyone does in schools is valuable. The only way we can improve schools, therefore, is to stop people doing good things—to give them time to do even better things. This is the uncomfortable reality behind the trite phrase "work smarter, not harder," and it is why change in schools is so hard.

It is this insight that lies behind a management technique called "Pareto analysis." Vilfredo Pareto (1848–1923) was an Italian engineer, economist, and, later in life, a sociologist and philosopher. In 1893, he was appointed as professor of political economy at the University of Lausanne. In his *Cours d'économie politique* (Pareto, 1896), he pointed out that the distribution of incomes followed a power law (a relationship where one variable varies as the power of another) and, more important, that the curve was roughly the same shape for most countries. In particular, he pointed out that in most countries, around 80 percent of the wealth was held by 20 percent of the population. Since this was noted, the same principle has been observed in many apparently unconnected areas, such as word frequency, citations of scientific papers, magnitudes of earthquakes, sizes of cities, and so on (Newman, 2006). In the late 1930s, Joseph Juran—a pioneer in the field of quality management—saw the same principle at work in many other areas, and he coined the idea of "the vital few and the trivial many," although in later years, he amended this to "the vital few and the useful many" to emphasize that all parts of the distribution were potentially important. In 1937, he named this idea "the Pareto principle" in honor of Pareto (Schroeder & Buckman, 2005, p. 36).

Although Pareto's name is today associated with the 80:20 rule, his most influential work was in the design of systems of taxation. He argued that governments should not increase taxation until they could demonstrate that the income they already had was being used in the most effective way. More important, he provided an operational definition of what this would mean in practice. Given an existing allocation of resources, if resources could be allocated in a different way that would make at least one person better off without making another person worse off, then that change—now called a Pareto improvement—should be made. When no further improvements can be made, an allocation of resources is described as Pareto optimal. Of course, as Amartya Sen (1999) has pointed out, there is nothing in this that guarantees that the allocation of resources will be fair or equitable, but for Pareto, that was precisely the point. If there are no more Pareto improvements to be made, then decisions cannot be made on economic grounds, and value considerations have to be made.

In education, most reforms are not Pareto improvements. For example, in the United States, the school year is shorter than the school year in many other countries, particularly those that do well in international comparisons (Organisation for Economic Co-operation and Development, 2014). For this reason, many commentators (e.g., Marcotte & Hansen, 2010) have suggested that the length of the school year should be increased. Such a change would not be a Pareto improvement. There are two ways an increase in the length of the school year could be introduced—paying teachers more for the longer school year or not paying teachers more. If teachers are paid more, then they will be no worse off (in economic terms at least), and the students will be better off (again in economic terms), but taxpayers would be worse off because taxes would have to increase to fund the higher teacher pay. If teachers are not paid more, then the situation of taxpayers is unchanged, but now teachers are worse off because they have to work longer hours for the same money.

As an example of something that could be a Pareto improvement, consider the idea of teaching larger classes in order to create more noncontact time for teachers. This is, in effect, what happens in Japan. The typical Japanese teacher is in front of students for only around 600 hours per year, which gives them time to engage in activities such as lesson study, as discussed in chapter 3. The trade-off is that they teach classes of forty students. The typical US teacher spends almost twice as much time in front of students, but this allows class sizes to be reduced to an average of twenty to twenty-five. The average student-teacher ratio in the two countries is reasonably similar, but the available resources are allocated in a different way. Of course, to make giving teachers less contact time with larger classes truly a Pareto improvement, a number of other changes would also need to be made, such as the amount of time spent grading. But the important point here is that a different distribution of the same resources might produce a better outcome for students, without any additional resources being provided.

Since school leaders rarely have any control over the amount of resources their schools are given, all leaders are, essentially, in the business of Pareto optimization: stopping people doing good things to give them time to do even better things. Time and time again, teachers and administrators tell me, "We haven't got time to do this." My response is, "You do; it's just that you're probably spending time on something else that contributes less to student achievement."

How Will We Know If It's Working?

Any educational reform must, ultimately, be validated by an impact on outcomes for learners. After educational experiences, we want students to be able to do things they could not do before or, occasionally, not do things they might have done before, such as taking drugs or becoming sexually active.

For some of these outcomes, whether things have gotten better is relatively clear. After an intervention, it is not that difficult to establish whether students are less obese or are less likely to become sexually active or take drugs (although of course establishing a causal link between the intervention and the outcome is often less straightforward). In other cases, we want students to learn more science, English, or mathematics, and although very few people believe that standardized tests capture all of the important aspects of these school subjects, the fact is that interventions that improve students' mathematical thinking as measured by problem-solving and other "authentic" forms of assessment tend also to increase their performance on standardized multiple-choice tests. More important, if districts had to choose between teaching for deep understanding on the one hand and raising test scores on the other, it would, in the current political climate, be very difficult to argue that the former should prevail over the latter. Therefore, while few would argue that our tests capture everything that's important, with the current state of US politics, raising test scores is a priority. Ultimately, any reform that does not increase student performance on state-mandated tests has little chance of being adopted and even less chance of being implemented with any fidelity.

This is a rather long-winded way of establishing that any educational intervention focused on academic outcomes should have, as its goal, improved student outcomes, even if we may not have perfect measures of these and may not find it easy to agree on what measures we do use. The problem is that changes in the ultimate goal—improved student outcomes—can take some years to materialize. While we have seen the use of classroom formative assessment increase student achievement within a single year (e.g., Wiliam et al., 2004), it is more common to find any significant impact on standardized test scores taking two or three years to materialize. The danger then is that schools give up on interventions that are working because they do not have an immediate impact on student achievement.

For this reason, especially where there is substantial pressure for rapid improvement, teachers and administrators may need some assurance that what they are doing is likely to lead to the desired impact on student outcomes. Test scores are examples of what economists call "lagging indicators." Unemployment is often regarded as a lagging indicator of the health of an economy because changes in employment tend to occur after changes in the underlying economy. Bond yields are thought by many to be a leading indicator of the stock market because bond traders try to anticipate trends in the economy. The point is that test scores will rise sometime after improvements in the quality of instruction in schools. What teachers and administrators need, in addition to lagging indicators, such as improved student test scores, are "leading indicators" of success—evidence that the elements needed for successful reform are in place.

Of course, there are many ways to develop such leading indicators, but one of the most powerful approaches is through the use of logic models, first developed in the 1970s by Carol Weiss (1972) and Joseph Wholey (1979).

Logic Models

While there are now many different views about the essential ingredients of a logic model, most authors seem to agree that it should lay out the activities, resources, processes, and intermediate outcomes of the proposed innovation and may also provide details of external influences that are relevant to the success of the innovation. Put another way, it represents the theory of action of the innovation—if it is successful, by what mechanisms will this success have been achieved? Because logic models identify intermediate outcomes, they can be useful in identifying things that will be happening if the innovation is proceeding as intended.

In the work on formative assessment done at Educational Testing Service between 2003 and 2006, Siobhán Leahy, Dawn Leusner, and Christine Lyon (2005) developed a series of logic models for a number of innovations in education. The logic model they produced for classroom formative assessment is shown in Figure 7.3 (Lyon & Leusner, 2009). In the logic model, the arrows indicate how a particular program—in this case the Keeping Learning on Track professional development program—is assumed to have its effect. Ultimately, of course, a professional development program such as Keeping Learning on Track would be validated by its impact on student achievement, but the arrows provide a way of presenting a prima facie argument that the program is likely to function as intended. In particular, it presents a convenient representation to help clarify which causal links are already well-enough established in the literature and which would require further research. For example, arrow 13 indicates a hypothesis that when students are more engaged in their learning, the result is improved student learning, which, of course, has been well established in the research literature for some time (e.g., Cobb, 1972; Hecht, 1978).

Obviously a logic model as complex as that presented in Figure 7.3 raises a very large number of potential research questions, and no school would have time to investigate them all. From our work with schools over the past ten years, however, we have identified six leading indicators that appear to be especially useful in providing evidence of progress with respect to developing formative assessment. Each of the six is discussed in turn.

Teachers Are Given Time to Meet, and Do So

This may seem like the most obvious thing of all, but, as is clear from the case study of Cannington above, this may actually be the hardest to secure. We have come across many examples like Cannington, where teachers have been promised time to meet, but, for one reason or another, the time they were promised never seems to materialize. On the other hand, we have come across no examples where teachers were given time to meet, used the recommended structure for regular monthly meetings of TLCs, and did not see improvements in the quality of instruction.

Teachers Increasingly Act as Critical Friends to Others

When we first started using TLCs to support teachers in their development of classroom formative assessment, we found that, in general, the conversations were polite but shallow. A teacher would describe what she or he had done, and the TLC leader would thank the teacher for his or her contribution and move on, even if what

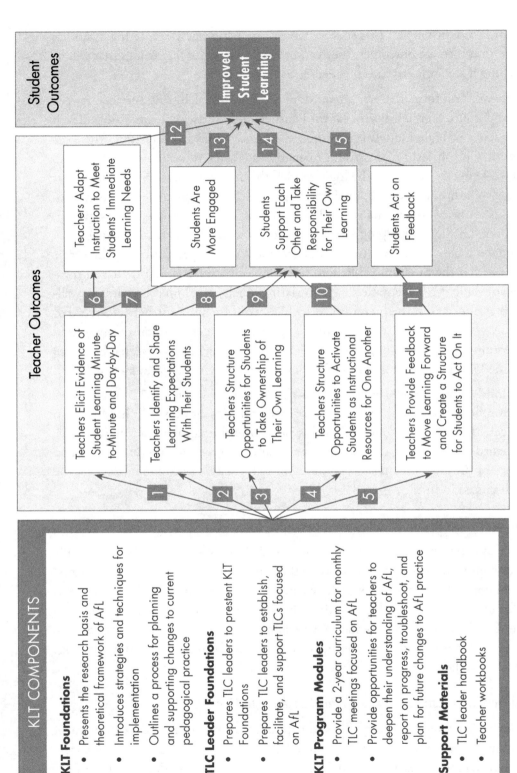

Figure 7.3. Logic model for Keeping Learning on Track.

Source: Educational Testing Service. Used with permission.

the teacher had said was not particularly appropriate. The reason, of course, is that, to avoid being seen as infringing on professional autonomy, teachers are reluctant to comment on something another teacher has done, even if it would be entirely appropriate to do so. To address this, we suggested that each TLC, at each meeting, appoint a challenger—someone whose task was to raise an objection every time someone said something that was not supported by evidence. We had come across the idea in the work of Neil Mercer and his colleagues in middle school science classrooms (Mercer, Dawes, Wegerif, & Sams, 2004), but it seemed to us that it would work equally well with adults. In fact, we were surprised how well it worked. By legitimating the role of the challenger—and sometimes even making it into a bit of a joke—TLCs found that their conversations rapidly became much more focused on deep aspects of practice.

Obviously there are many ways in which the development of the relationships within a TLC can be evaluated, but one useful framework comes from a study conducted by Pam Grossman and her colleagues. Grossman, Wineburg, and Woolworth (2000) studied a professional learning community of twenty-two English language arts and social studies teachers over a period of two and a half years. Their analysis identified four dimensions of development over the period of the study.

Forming group identity and norms of interaction. At the beginning of the project, teachers tended to identify with their own subgroups (e.g., English language arts teachers with other English language arts teachers). Individuals were seen as interchangeable and expendable, and members seemed to feel as if their own needs were more important than how well the community functioned as a group. As the group progressed, there was a greater sense of the need for civility in the group's interactions, so that norms for interactions were discussed and agreed upon. Toward the end of the project, there was greater awareness of the value of multiple perspectives and, associated with this, a noticeable sense of loss when individuals left the group.

Understanding difference / navigating fault lines. Initially, members of the group appeared to avoid conflict, with the result that conflict went backstage. However, as tensions built up, conflicts often flared up and interfered with the work of the group. Over time, however, conflict came to be seen as a natural, inevitable, and even productive aspect of the group's work and was dealt with openly and honestly.

Negotiating the essential tension. From the outset, members differed about the purpose of the group's work. Some saw it as a chance for continuing intellectual development in the subject they taught, while others saw it as being concerned with improved learning outcomes for their students. Over time, this developed into a grudging acceptance that different members could, legitimately, pursue different interests, but eventually, members of the group came to see teacher learning and student learning as inseparable.

Taking communal responsibility for individuals' growth. Most members began their work with the group with the view that intellectual growth was the responsibility of the individual teacher, whose primary duty was toward her or his students. Later, participants came to realize that others in the group could be useful resources for one's planning and, therefore, that participation was expected. Ultimately, members of the group embraced the idea of a commitment to the intellectual growth of one's colleagues, leading to an acceptance that membership entailed both rights and responsibilities.

These four dimensions of teacher community provide a useful framework for evaluating the progress of TLCs and, where progress appears to be halting or blocked, may also suggest what kinds of interventions may be appropriate. They may also prove useful in making clear to teachers that problems, disagreements, and setbacks are not only to be expected, but may also actually be useful in advancing the learning of the community.

The Prevalence of Classroom Formative Assessment Practices Is Increasing

Over the last twenty years, schools in the United States have made increasing use of instructional walk-throughs or learning walks (Ginsberg & Murphy, 2002). The idea that managers can learn a great deal about how to improve the performance of their organizations by getting out of their offices and seeing what is happening on the ground is probably as old as the whole idea of organizations. However, the idea was formalized by executives at Hewlett-Packard in the 1970s, and it was there that the phrase "management by wandering around" (or, alternatively, "management by walking around"/"management by wandering about") appears to have been first used (Mears, 2009). The idea came to much wider attention through its endorsement in *In Search of Excellence* (Peters & Waterman, 1982) and is now in widespread use in schools, as well as in business more generally. However, as Grissom, Loeb, and Master (2013) point out, there is little value in principals observing teaching unless they use the information in some way.

This creates a real problem for leaders. If leaders are regularly visiting classrooms, it seems as if the information should be used in some way to support teacher learning. However, short visits to classrooms are unlikely to be able to support decisions about what kinds of help a teacher might need. Moreover, any visit to a classroom that is likely to figure in decisions about teacher tenure or teacher deselection is likely to be the subject of intense negotiation with teacher unions. One way around this is for administrators to clearly distinguish between observations where the focus is on the teacher and those where the focus is intended as a sample of the learning that is taking place across the whole school.

Where the focus is on the latter, typically, administrators in a building decide to visit at least three or four classrooms in an hour and record any examples of formative assessment practice they see. Because of the limited amount of time each administrator spends in each classroom, no conclusions can be drawn about the extent to which an individual teacher is using formative assessment, but if each teacher is observed two or three times, then the results for the school are probably a good guide to the prevalence of classroom formative assessment across the building. The important point is that the record of the observation does not need to include the teacher's name, because the only conclusions that are intended are school-wide. Some suggestions for what might be included in an observation schedule are as follows:

- Clear, valuable learning intentions for lesson
- Success criteria understood by students
- Students chosen at random
- Questions that make students think
- Students, not teacher, dominate discussions
- At least 80 percent of students involved in answering questions
- All-student response system used
- Teacher waits three seconds after question
- Students support each other's learning
- Students take responsibility for their own learning
- Teacher gives oral formative feedback
- Evidence of comments that advance learning
- Teacher finds out what students learned
- Teaching adjusted after data collection

What kind of scale is used for each of these dimensions of classroom practice is obviously a matter for the school, but the schools that we have worked with have found the following rating scale useful:

Exemplary practice

Good practice

Seen, but weak

Nonexistent

Used inappropriately

Students Are More Engaged in Classrooms

One of the most common things we hear from students when their teachers are making greater use of classroom formative assessment is that lessons are more engaging, and time seems to fly by. One student summed it up like this: "It used to be a laid back sort of feel in some lessons, but now you've got to know the answer all the time because there's a chance you could get picked" (Wiliam & Leahy, 2015, p. 66). There are many ways that schools can measure student engagement. At one extreme, students can simply be asked whether they "count the minutes to the end of a lesson"—in one survey in England, up to 70 percent of students said they did so (Barber, 1994). A useful review of more formal instruments for surveying student engagement, from elementary through high school, has been produced by Fredricks et al. (2011).

Teachers Modify the Techniques in Appropriate Ways, Indicating an Understanding of the Underlying Theory

In this and the previous chapter, I have mentioned the importance of teachers adapting techniques to suit their own circumstances, but also pointed out the danger of lethal mutations—adaptations of techniques that rendered the innovation ineffective. These inappropriate adaptations occur most frequently when teachers have not understood the key ideas behind the technique and focus instead on surface features of techniques. Examples of these that we have already encountered include using exit passes for responses to single multiple-choice questions and entrance tickets where, at the beginning of the lesson, teachers give themselves the rather challenging task of reading twenty to thirty extended responses to questions, interpreting them, and then, on the fly, making any indicated adjustments in the lesson plan. A more extreme example occurred in a kindergarten classroom where the teacher was having difficulty getting her class to listen to her when she was giving instructions. She had heard about the use of ice-pop sticks as a way of creating student engagement. She decided to adapt the technique by attaching two "bunny ears" to each stick, and then giving the sticks back to the students, so that they could hold up the stick with the ears attached to show that they were listening. However, what is perhaps most interesting was that her colleagues in the TLC meeting did not let this go. They probed the teacher's rationale for the technique by asking her, "What's formative about that?" Through supportive but rigorous questioning, her colleagues got the teacher to see that the technique had been modified to the point where it was probably not helpful, and the teacher reverted to using ice-pop sticks in a more traditional way.

At the other extreme, in the previous chapter, we saw how Charlotte Kerrigan, an English language arts teacher, got her students to pay more attention to the comments she was giving them by providing feedback on strips of paper and asking groups of four students to match the comments to the essays. The point is that the ways that teachers modify these techniques, and in particular, the extent to which the modifications indicate an understanding of the underlying theory of formative assessment, can be used as an indicator of the extent to which teachers are acting their way into a new way of thinking.

There Is a Shift in the Ownership of the Reform

Cynthia Coburn (2003) mentions that taking reforms to scale involves three important dimensions:

1. *Depth.* Scaling up a reform involves moving beyond counts of the numbers of schools "reached by a reform" and instead focusing on the extent to which reforms "effect deep and consequential change in classroom practice" (p. 4).

2. *Sustainability.* Perhaps the most impressive feature of Jerry and Monique Sternin's work in Vietnam was not that the nutrition of children improved. It was that children who had not been born when the Sternins intervened were benefitting years later. As Coburn says, "Reforms can be adopted without being implemented, and can be implemented superficially only to fall into disuse" (p. 6). If a reform is not sustainable, it is probably not worth pursuing.

3. *Shift in reform ownership.* If the authority, impetus, and funding for a reform remains external to the school or the district, then not only is the reform vulnerable to changes in funding or policy, but it will require constant support from outside to be sustained. Over time, therefore, scalability requires a shift from "an externally understood and supported theory to an internally understood and supported theory-based practice" (Stokes, Sato, McLaughlin, & Talbert, 1997, p. 21).

The last of these is, perhaps, the most important, because, in a very real sense, it subsumes the other two dimensions. Almost by definition, when there is a shift in reform ownership, the reform becomes more sustainable because it becomes part of the regular work of the school. Similarly, reforms cannot, in any sense, be owned by practitioners without deep and lasting change in practice.

The two resource packs for supporting the development of classroom formative assessment with TLCs that I and my various colleagues have produced—Keeping Learning on Track (Northwest Evaluation Association, 2015) and *Embedding Formative Assessment* (Wiliam & Leahy, 2014)—contain enough materials for two years of monthly meetings. As a result, I am often asked when the materials for year three will be available. I reply that we have no intention of ever producing materials for year three because by the time participants have spent two years on the program, they ought to have understood the program well enough to produce their own materials for subsequent years (and if they have not, it probably indicates that they may need to revisit the materials for the first two years).

So, the willingness and capability of teachers to develop further materials to sustain their own professional learning is the last, and possibly the most important, leading indicator of success. If all these elements are in place, success, in the form of increased student achievement, is practically guaranteed. As has been argued repeatedly throughout this book, the hard part is not knowing what to do, but doing the things that we know we need to do—the knowing-doing gap.

In the previous chapter, I suggested that this was largely a problem of habit change, but it is also important to recognize that any change may be unwelcome—as one judge once remarked, "I will not countenance change. Things are bad enough as they are." Leaders are only ever successful through the work of others, and so as well as understanding the importance of habit change, leaders need to take key constituencies with them.

Taking People With You

There are many people whose involvement will be important in making any long-lasting changes in how schools work, and many of them have different priorities and different agendas. In this section, I discuss some ideas about how to engage with some of the most important groups of individuals.

Unions

Particularly in the United States, teachers' unions are perhaps the most important constituency in any school reform. The relative power of unions and districts varies considerably from state to state, partly influenced by whether school districts are based on states (e.g., Hawaii), counties (e.g., Florida, Maryland), or municipalities (e.g., Vermont, Washington), as well as the history of union organization in the state. However, the fundamental argument of this book—that teachers need to get better, not because they're not good enough, but because they can be even better—is entirely consistent with the position of all the main teacher unions. Indeed, the idea of continuous improvement is at the heart of the idea of teaching as a profession. At several places in the book, I have pointed out that the kinds of changes that I am seeking are designed to completely avoid the major flare points in education. Evaluating teaching is technically difficult, and right now, apart from distinguishing the very best teachers from the very worst, simply not possible. The upshot of this is that time spent evaluating teachers is highly unlikely to benefit students. That is why I have argued that the time currently spent evaluating teachers would be better spent helping all teachers improve—again, a point that has been made by the teachers' unions. Put simply, there is nothing in what I have argued in this book that is inconsistent with the positions of the main teachers' unions, and so, provided that unions are involved in all the discussions about how teachers will be supported in improving their practice, union objections should not be a significant issue.

Departmental Subcultures

In secondary schools, teachers often create their own subject subcultures. Because they have laboratories with preparation areas, science teachers often congregate in the science labs, and athletics staff hang out in the sports facilities. Therefore, teachers talk much more to those with similar assignments than they do to others. This has both strengths and weaknesses. Because there are real differences in how classroom formative assessment strategies play out in different school subjects, it is valuable for teachers to talk to others with similar assignments to get practical ideas for implementation. But if these are the only conversations teachers are having, the subject subcultures can quickly become a straitjacket. To counter this, it can be very valuable to build in opportunities for teachers to observe those with very different assignments.

In one district, we suggested to math teachers that they might find it valuable to observe physical education teachers. As we had predicted, they were not impressed by that suggestion—they thought that they would have nothing to learn from physical education teachers. For this reason, we did not ask the math teachers to look for techniques that they could use in the classrooms. Instead, we asked them to see if there were any techniques they observed physical education teachers using that they could modify to make them appropriate for use in a math classroom (this of course is just an application of the flexibility element discussed in the previous chapter). One of the math teachers spoke to me after visiting a physical education lesson and said, "We know why you started with math teachers. We're the remedial group, aren't we?" The math teachers had not realized how much formative assessment was routinely used by physical education teachers in their regular practice, and, to be fair, physical education teachers also learned a great deal by observing math teachers. When the message is "Copy what someone else is doing," there is likely to be little professional learning. However, when the message is, "How might this be adapted to make it relevant for your practice?" the experience is likely to be far more useful.

Teachers' Aides and Other Paraprofessionals

The role of teachers' aides in the implementation of classroom formative assessment depends on the roles that the aides undertake. In some schools, aides are involved with the preparation of material resources and reprographics, and it would not make sense to involve such individuals in TLCs. However, most teachers' aides are involved in helping students directly, and so it would be entirely appropriate for the aides to be full members of a TLC. Indeed, in my experience, there is no clear line between the teaching skill of aides and of qualified teachers. There are some aides who are better than some teachers. As long as an aide's job involves interaction with students, and they are trying to develop their practice so that they can do their job better, then they can be full members of a TLC, as can instrumental music teachers and specialist sports coaches.

Parents

In my experience, all parents care about their children's education. What they don't always have is the understanding of how to get involved and to support the school more effectively. We could regard this as the parents' problem—after all, plenty of parents do know how to support the work of the school, and so we could take the view that the others need to get with the program. However, where education is concerned, we are the professionals, and the parents are not. So if we make it too hard for the parents to support the work of the school, it seems to me that this is our problem rather than theirs. And it has to be remembered that parents have no idea what goes on in school, and children like it that way.

School (and specifically, the school bus) is generally the first place that children develop a personal identity outside the family home, so children are often uncommunicative about what goes on. That is why parents rely on students' notebooks and report cards as indicators of whether the school is doing its job. And if the school changes the way that feedback is given without explaining the changes to parents, the parents are likely to feel that the school is failing in its responsibilities. That is why schools must devote a considerable amount of time to communicating with parents. Some ideas for how this might be done, including sample letters to parents, are provided in Wiliam and Leahy (2015). Our experience has been that as soon as parents understand the reasons behind the changes, and as soon as they discover that they will still be informed about their children's progress and that they will still get grades at the end of sequences of learning, they are generally very positive about the kinds of ideas entailed in developing classroom formative assessment.

School Board Members and Community Leaders

What will almost certainly derail a school's attempt to develop its practice of classroom formative assessment is a school board that does not understand or support what it is the school is doing. That said, it is important to realize that the kinds of changes I am arguing for are evolutionary, rather that revolutionary. Indeed, if as recommended, each teacher works on one or two techniques of his or her own choosing for several months, it is unlikely that anyone would notice, except for an increasing sense of engagement in the students and gradual improvements in student achievement. What is radical here is not the idea of small, gradual improvements in teachers' practice. It is that the gradual improvements are focused on changes that are most likely to benefit students and that there are support mechanisms in place that mean that the improvements are sustained, rather than sporadic.

Nevertheless, it is worth engaging with school board members and the wider community so that when parents or others in the community raise issues about the changes they are seeing, the reasons behind the changes—and particularly the research evidence—are explained clearly.

Managing Setbacks and Disappointments

The argument being advanced in this book is that we are now in a position where what needs to be done is reasonably clear. While researchers will always say that "more research needs to be done," the basic elements of school improvement are known well enough to make further research less valuable than experience of practical implementation. We therefore need to get on with implementation and refine the innovations on the basis of real experience—summarized neatly in the phrase, "Ready. Fire. Aim." (attributed to, among others, the actor Michael Landon).

Along the way, there will, of course, be setbacks and disappointments, but as someone once said, "Success has been defined as the ability to go from failure to failure without losing enthusiasm" (Powers, 1953, p. 109). Indeed, one of the few things that I have found with almost all successful leaders in education is their almost unreasonable optimism about how much better things can be.

But there is a more important, deeper point here, and that is that failures are actually opportunities for learning, for strengthening the work of the organization. Nassim Nicholas Taleb (2014) indicates that the opposite of fragility is not robustness, but antifragility. The idea is that an organization or system that is antifragile actually gets stronger when stressed, while those that are simply robust will eventually break.

For example, most people know that air travel is relatively safe—and certainly much safer than most other methods of covering the same distance. But what most people fail to realize is that when aircraft crash, air travel actually gets safer because of the extraordinary efforts that go into finding out the causes of the crash. In the same way, significant advances in the safety of surgical procedures have been brought about by treating patient deaths during surgery as failures of systems, rather than as the fault of individuals. When organizations respond to failures by attempting to attach blame, the result is that individuals cover up to deflect blame. When organizations instead treat failures as chances to learn, then the truth, and how to prevent future failure, is far more likely to be revealed.

As McLaughlin and Talbert (2006) point out:

> On the topic of confronting failure, the organizational culture of schools and school districts stands in stark contrast to that of so-called high-performance organizations—team-based organizations such as nuclear power plants, hospitals, and aerospace that cannot afford failure. These organizations take evidence of failure as a signal of needed improvements, rather than cause for blame. Debra Meyerson (personal communication, April 18, 2005) encountered a vivid example of celebration of mistakes on a Gulf of Mexico oil platform. To reinforce the importance of learning, the platform crew had established the "$1 Million Dollar Club" in mocking reference to the corporate club of the same name. Unlike the corporate version established to recognize salespeople who sold one million dollars' worth of products, however, employees on the platform who were initiated into the club had made an error that cost the company one million dollars. The club and the playful ritual that accompanied it legitimated talking about mistakes so that employees could learn from them, and served as a visible symbol of the company's commitment to learning from experience. Likewise, the medical community has organized rituals to review errors and learn from them. The Morbidity and Mortality Conference, which usually takes place once a week in academic hospitals across the country, provides a place where doctors can talk frankly with one another about their mistakes and consider what to do differently (Gawande, 2000). Few districts have such norms or venues for candid examination of shortfalls and opportunity to learn from experience. (p. 118)

However, perhaps the most extreme example of a willingness to learn from mistakes comes from Tom Watson, Jr., CEO of IBM from 1956 to 1971, recounted by Paul Carroll (1993):

In the 1960s, an executive at IBM made a decision that ended up losing the company $10 million (about $70 million in 2009 dollars). The CEO of IBM, Tom Watson, summoned the offending executive to his office at corporate headquarters.

As the executive cowered, Watson asked, "Do you know why I've asked you here?" The man replied, "I assume I'm here so you can fire me." Watson looked surprised. "Fire you?" he asked. "Of course not. I just spent $10 million educating you." (p. 51)

Closely related to the idea of learning from mistakes is the idea that resistance to change, and complaints, are also opportunities for learning. Whenever I speak to teachers about changes they might make in their school, teachers often point out that what I am recommending will not work with their students, in their subject, or in their particular school. Some reformers treat this as evidence that teachers resist change, but as we saw in the previous chapter, it is far more likely that the teacher is trying to think through how this could be applied in his or her setting. In other words, it is a sign of *engagement*, not resistance. It would be much worse if teachers just let my words wash over them, knowing that "this too shall pass." So when teachers raise objections, this should be treated as a chance for learning, not as something to be overcome. Often, the objections will have merit.

For example, when Paul Black and I first started talking to teachers about the power of giving feedback in the form of comments rather than grades, math teachers said to us, "This is all very well in social studies and English language arts, and may even work in science, but it won't work in math. If you check fifteen equations as correct, and put a cross next to five others, the students can figure out for themselves that they've got 75 percent whether you tell them or not." This is, of course, a perfectly valid point, and it forced us to think through the really important idea more carefully, which is, of course, that feedback should lead to productive activity on the part of the learner (Kluger & DeNisi, 1996). In the end, we realized that telling the student, "Five of these are wrong; find them and fix them" would be likely to lead to useful responses by students. This, in turn, has led to the formulation of the more general principle "make feedback into detective work" (Wiliam & Leahy, 2015, p. 124).

The important point here, which connects to MacGregor's Theory X and Theory Y discussed in the previous chapter, is that pushback from others is a chance to develop deeper and more unifying ways of thinking about the changes that need to be made. If, following Theory X, we assume that pushback is caused by hostility and resistance, we miss the opportunity to learn, and, just as important, we will not change that person's mind. If, instead, we embrace Theory Y and assume that pushback is a sign of someone engaging with the challenge of implementing a new idea, then we may learn something, and the person raising the issues has been heard. In this context, it is worth noting that in many cases, even if they don't get their way, people feel much happier if they have had an opportunity to have their say. As noted before, Theory X isn't always wrong, and Theory Y isn't always right—sometimes people really are resisting—but Theory Y is invariably a better place to start the conversation.

This idea of listening is closely related to the idea of "service recovery" in the hospitality industry. Claus Møller points out that "a complaint is a gift" (Barlow & Møller, 1996). He describes one London hotel that gives each room attendant a budget for service recovery. The idea is that when something goes wrong with a guest's stay, the attendant can buy some flowers, some tickets for a show, or something similar as a gesture to show that the hotel understands how upsetting the hotel's service failure was for the guest and that the hotel wants to make a gesture by way of acknowledgment. What the hotel found is that the repeat booking rate from those for whom things go wrong is actually higher than for guests who have a perfect stay. A complaint is a chance to cement a lasting relationship.

The same goes for teachers, aides, unions, school board members, and the wider school community. When complaints are treated first as being legitimate—so that people know they are being heard—then response is likely to cement a deep and enduring relationship between the complainant and the administrators. Done well, it can even make the complainant into an advocate for the reforms.

So far in this chapter, I have dealt with a number of implementation issues that have arisen in the schools with whom we have worked over the years. None of the issues are trivial—they all represent real issues and concerns that need to be dealt with thoughtfully if teachers are to be given time, dispensation, and support to improve. But just as important, none of the issues are deal breakers. Handled appropriately, there is no reason that the ideas presented in this book should not be implemented into every single school.

What I have not yet touched upon—what some may regard as the elephant in the room—is the issue of the evaluation of teaching. Obviously how this is done varies radically across states and provinces, and so there cannot be a single plan for how the ideas in this book mesh with systems of teacher evaluation. That said, in the final section of the book, I want to show how the perspectives on student learning that are at the heart of classroom formative assessment can be used, in turn, for the formative evaluation of teaching.

The Formative Evaluation of Teaching

In chapter 4, the development of a framework for formative assessment began by identifying three processes in learning (where the learner is going, where the learner is right now, and how to get there) with three kinds of agents in the classroom (teacher, peer, learner), summarized in Figure 4.1. A similar approach can be used for the formative evaluation of teaching, by beginning with three key processes of teacher learning:

1. The goal for the teacher's learning

2. His or her current level of performance

3. The steps needed to reach the goal

We can then consider these three processes in conjunction with the roles of the various individuals involved in this process—the teacher, the teacher's peers, and those who are professionally responsible for that teacher's learning (for convenience here, termed *leaders*). Crossing these two dimensions leads to a 3x3 matrix of cells. The contents of each of the nine cells could be discussed individually, but, as with Figure 4.1, the model is considerably simplified if we group some of the cells together, as shown in Figure 7.4 (after Wiliam & Thompson, 2008). Each of the following five strategies is discussed in turn.

	Where the teacher is going	Where the teacher is right now	How to get there
Leader	Clarifying, understanding, and sharing learning intentions and criteria for success	Engineering effective situations, activities, and tasks that elicit evidence of development	Providing feedback that moves teachers forward
Peer		Activating teachers as learning resources for one another	
Teacher		Activating teachers as the owners of their own learning	

Figure 7.4. Aspects of formative assessment

Clarifying, Understanding, and Sharing Learning Intentions

Perhaps the most problematic aspect of formative evaluation of teaching performance relates to points made in chapter 2. Because we have little idea about the characteristics of effective teaching practice, it is difficult to make sure that the formative evaluation of teachers is appropriately directed. Put simply, if we don't know what good teaching looks like, how can we improve teachers? More important, given that, as shown in chapter 2, our observation frameworks capture only a small proportion of the variation in teacher quality, there is a real danger of establishing goals for teacher development that actually make teachers less effective.

In recent years, considerable attention has been focused on the use of rubrics to communicate standards to learners, both for school students and for teaching performance. All the main teacher evaluation models, such as Danielson's Framework for Teaching discussed in chapter 2 and the teacher evaluation model developed by Marzano and Toth (2013), present levels of teacher performance in the form of scoring rubrics that identify different levels of performance in the area in question. Presenting levels of performance in the form of a scoring rubric can undoubtedly be useful, but it is important to note that scoring rubrics may not be effective in communicating levels of performance to those who are not already able to demonstrate those levels of performance. Rubrics are often treated as if they were instructions about how to improve performance, but they are more often post hoc descriptions of quality. More important, while experts are often able to identify what they are doing with the descriptions contained in rubrics, *the contents of the rubrics are not used by experts in their performance.* As Michael Polanyi (1958) wrote:

> Maxims are rules, the correct application of which is part of the art which they govern. The true maxims of golfing or of poetry increase our insight into golfing or poetry and may even give valuable guidance to golfers and poets; but these maxims would instantly condemn themselves to absurdity if they tried to replace the golfer's skill or the poet's art. *Maxims cannot be understood, still less applied by anyone not already possessing a good practical knowledge of the art. They derive their interest from our appreciation of the art and cannot themselves either replace or establish that appreciation.* (pp. 31–32, my emphasis)

Rubrics may therefore provide a valuable starting point for conversations between teachers and their leaders, but slavish adherence to the text of the rubrics is unlikely to improve teaching. Because of the importance of context, it is likely that examples of actual practice, ideally on video, together with commentary that draws out significant features, is likely to be far more effective in communicating to teachers aspects of high-quality performance.

Engineering Effective Situations, Activities, and Tasks That Elicit Evidence of Development

The research on the generalizability of ratings of teacher performance discussed in chapter 2 suggests that any one observation of teaching performance is unlikely to yield robust evidence of a teacher's capabilities. This is obviously a significant problem for the accountability function of assessment since the performance observed on any one occasion is not a reliable indicator of the teacher's performance on another occasion. However, for the improvement function of assessment, the variability of teacher performance can be useful since observations of teaching can be scheduled for specific occasions when they are most likely to be beneficial for the teacher's development. In general, therefore, this suggests that it should be the teacher being observed who should choose the lesson to be observed. One important point to bear in mind is that all observations are theory dependent. Even in physics, as Werner Heisenberg noted, "What we learn about is not nature itself, but nature exposed to our methods of questioning" (Johnson, 1996, p. 147). For the observer of the teaching practice, it is likely to be helpful to have an opportunity to meet with the teacher before the lesson to understand what the teacher intends the students to learn and to have a significant period of time after the lesson to try to understand the teacher's own understanding of what happened in the lesson. The quotation from David Ausubel presented in chapter 4—that learning should start from where the learner is—would appear to be as true for the learning of teachers as it is for the learning of school students.

The idea that the teacher being observed should choose the lesson to be observed was a particularly significant feature of the My Teaching Partner coaching system (Allen, Pianta, Gregory, Mikami, & Lun, 2011), which focused attention on three aspects of teaching: emotional support for students (positive relationships, teacher sensitivity, and regard for adolescent perspectives), classroom organization (behavior management, maximizing learning time, and effective instructional formats), and instructional support (content understanding, analysis and problem solving, and quality of feedback). Every two weeks, participating teachers video recorded one lesson and uploaded the recording to a secure server where the coach could review the video and select a small number of short segments (one to two minutes in duration) for detailed discussion via telephone. After two years, students taught by teachers participating in the My Coaching Partner system were learning 50 percent more than those taught by matched teachers not participating in the program.

Providing Feedback That Moves Teachers Forward

As is clear from the research on feedback, the quality of the relationship between those giving and receiving feedback is crucial in determining whether feedback has a positive effect (Kluger & DeNisi, 1996). Leaders need to know their teachers so they know when to be critical and when to provide support. Just as important, teachers need to trust their leaders because unless the teacher believes that the leader has the teacher's best interests at heart, and unless the teacher believes the leader has credibility as a coach, the teacher is unlikely to invest the effort needed to improve practice (for more on this, see Tomsett, 2015). This means that there can be no simple recipe for effective feedback for teachers on their teaching performance, but a couple of principles derived from other research on feedback may be useful here.

The first is that feedback should cause thinking. Feedback that causes an emotional reaction, as is likely when the feedback compares an individual teacher's performance with that of other teachers, is unlikely to be helpful. Far more helpful is comparing a teacher's performance with his or her own previous performance (e.g., was this a personal best for the teacher?), which is likely to help the teacher adopt a growth mindset (Dweck, 2006). The second principle is that feedback should be more work for the recipient than the donor. The feedback event itself is likely to be relatively unimportant in improving teacher performance; what matters is the follow-up action taken by the teacher.

Activating Teachers as Learning Resources for One Another

Because, as noted above, the issue of trust between the donor and the recipient of feedback is crucial to the likely success of the feedback (Santiago & Benavides, 2009), it may be helpful to involve peers, rather than those with a formal leadership role within the school or district, in providing feedback to teachers. This is particularly important where leaders have a formal role in the accountability function because it can be difficult for leaders to separate out the two roles. Specifically, it can be very difficult for leaders to ignore evidence that might be relevant to the accountability function if they are meant to be focusing on the improvement function. Even if leaders *are* able to do this, ultimately the behavior of the teacher will depend not on whether the leader is able to separate these two roles clearly, but whether the teacher *believes* the leader is able to do so. If the teacher believes that evidence of weaknesses in practice revealed in an observation that is ostensibly intended to improve practice could also be used to affect the judgment made about the teacher's effectiveness, then the teacher is more likely to play safe so that the potential for the observation to improve practice is reduced. Where peers are involved in classroom observation, it can be particularly helpful to have a protocol for the lesson observation that makes clear that the teacher being observed:

- Specifies the focus of the observation
- Specifies the evidence to be collected
- Owns any notes made by the observer during the lesson

By making it clear that the teacher being observed owns the process, and the observation is clearly distinguished from observations for accountability purposes, it is easier for a trusting relationship to be developed.

Activating Teachers as the Owners of Their Own Learning

Ultimately, the amount of time for leaders and peers to observe practice will be limited, so if improvement is to occur, most of it will be generated by the teacher's own efforts to improve. Some have argued that this is best accomplished through systems of incentives, particularly financial incentives for teachers, but the evidence, both in the teaching profession and more widely, suggests that performance-related pay is not particularly successful in improving performance (Pfeffer, 1998; Springer et al., 2010). A more likely route for teacher improvement comes from engagement with the moral imperative identified in chapter 1 and the realization that, as shown in chapter 2, teachers can and do make a difference. While, as we saw in chapter 2, estimates of the relative magnitude of different influences on student learning are fraught with difficulties and may vary considerably from culture to culture and country to country, there is now substantial evidence that the impact of teacher effects at least rival, and may well exceed, the impact of family background and socioeconomic status (Rowe, 2003). As we have seen already, when teachers do their jobs better, their students live longer, are healthier, and contribute more to society. When all teachers embrace the idea that they can improve, not because they are not good enough, but because they can be even better, this creates a natural collegiality that supports all teachers in embracing the need for continuous improvement. As the research reviewed in chapter 5 shows, for most teachers after two or three years in the job, the rate of improvement slows down markedly, so the expertise research suggests that considerable improvements are possible if all teachers, rather than just the weakest, engage in continuous professional improvement.

Conclusion

In this chapter, I have discussed a number of issues that relate to putting the ideas raised in previous chapters into practice. Over twenty years ago, Paul Black and I began researching which of the many changes we could make in schools would produce the greatest benefits for students, and we were quite pleased to discover that there was—at least in terms of the currently available research evidence—a reasonably clear answer to that question: classroom formative assessment. We were even more pleased to discover that, with reasonable amounts of support, teachers were able to incorporate the key messages into their teaching, and when they did so, their students achieved more, even when achievement was measured using standardized tests and examinations.

To address issues of scale, we then explored how TLCs could provide the support that teachers needed and were again pleasantly surprised to discover that, with relatively inexpensive resources, groups of teachers could produce powerful learning communities in their own building, and over time, take ownership of the process so that it became self-regenerating.

What we were not prepared for—what in fact came as rather a shock—was that even though we knew exactly what needed to be done, it turned out to be extremely difficult to get schools and districts to give teachers the time to work on improvement—time, as Stephen Covey (1989) put it, "to sharpen the saw." We knew that time was a precious resource in schools, if not actually a constraint, but what we were surprised by was the extent to which school leaders who were under pressure to improve results were unable to create time for something that would take them a long way toward achieving their goals.

It could of course be that they were not convinced by the research evidence or thought that the gains promised by the research could be secured by selecting a few elements from the program they were offered, but, whatever the reason, it has become clear to me that the greatest challenge facing those who wish to help schools improve is what Mike Schmoker calls "Focus" (Schmoker, 2011)—the simple idea that, as noted earlier, when everything is a priority, nothing is.

Of course, focusing on a small number of priorities means giving less, or no, attention to things that are less important (not unimportant, just less important), and the idea that we are not doing something that might help our students achieve more is rather intimidating. That is why this chapter has also proposed a number of leading indicators of success so that even if student achievement—at least as measured by test scores—has not begun to improve, then leaders can have reasonable assurance that those improvements are on their way and that the improved results will follow.

The chapter has also discussed a number of other issues that will need attention if teachers are to be given the time to work on improving their classroom practice, including the views of key stakeholders. Finally, I have suggested that the process of formative assessment, so clearly effective for students, can also provide a powerful framework for supporting teachers.

Closing Thoughts

The task facing educational leaders today is daunting. Because of the changes in the world of work, and in society more generally, in order to have a reasonable chance at a good life, young people will need higher levels of education than have ever been achieved. Many—perhaps most—of the factors affecting the educational achievement of our students are things over which school and district leaders have little or no influence, such as poverty, staffing ratios, and so on. However, as the research reviewed in this book shows clearly, the most powerful factor—the quality of the teachers in a building—is something that leaders can do something about, not by replacing existing teachers with better ones but by helping existing teachers get better.

The idea of creating a culture of continuous improvement, in schools and other organizations, has of course been around for decades, but what is less widely appreciated is that it matters what gets improved. In education specifically, different interventions have widely different costs and widely different benefits, and this is where research evidence is so important. Research will never tell leaders what to do, but research can indicate which specific ways of developing teachers' practice will have the greatest benefit for their students and what the costs might be. Right now, as far as we know, there is nothing that teachers can develop in their practice that will have a bigger benefit for their students than making more use of classroom formative assessment, and the cost of doing this is actually quite modest.

The problem with developing classroom formative assessment is that it requires teachers to change what they do in classrooms when students are present. In other words, it requires changing habits, which requires a different approach to teacher professional development than is needed to give teachers new knowledge. Professional development must be job embedded, practice focused, and continued over a substantial period of time.

Some doubt that teachers can improve—they believe that teachers are born rather than made—but five decades of research on expertise suggests that while natural gifts matter a great deal in the beginning, over time, the influence of talent is dwarfed by the effects of practice. Moreover, the research on expertise in teaching shows that expertise in teaching is similar to expertise in other areas. This in turn suggests that the vast majority of teachers could be as good as the very best if their leaders provide the right learning environment for those they lead—creating a culture in which all teachers improve so that all students succeed.

References

Aaronson, D., Barrow, L., & Sander, W. (2007). Teachers and student achievement in the Chicago Public High Schools. *Journal of Labor Economics*, *25*(1), 95–135.

Abernethy, B. (1985). Cue usage in 'open' motor skills: A review of the available procedures. In D. G. Russell & B. Abernethy (Eds.), *Motor memory and control: The Otago symposium* (pp. 110–122). Dunedin, New Zealand: Human Performance Associates.

Abrami, P. C., Lenventhal, L., & Perry, R. P. (1982). Educational seduction. *Review of Educational Research*, *52*(3), 446–464.

Ackman, D. (2002, October 4). Excellence sought—and found. Retrieved from http://www .forbes.com/2002/10/04/1004excellent.html

ACT. (2014). *Technical manual: The ACT*. Iowa City, IA: ACT.

Adey, P. S., Fairbrother, R. W., Wiliam, D., Johnson, B., & Jones, C. (1999). *A review of research related to learning styles and strategies*. London, UK: King's College London Centre for the Advancement of Thinking.

Ainsworth, L. B., & Viegut, D. J. (Eds.). (2006). *Improving formative assessment practice to empower student learning*. Thousand Oaks, CA: Corwin.

Alberdi, E., Becher, J.-C., Gilhooly, K. E. N., Hunter, J. I. M., Logie, R., Lyon, A., . . . Reiss, J. A. N. (2001). Expertise and the interpretation of computerized physiological data: Implications for the design of computerized monitoring in neonatal intensive care. *International Journal of Human-Computer Studies*, *55*(3), 191–216. doi: http://dx.doi.org /10.1006/ijhc.2001.0477

Allal, L. (1988). Vers un élargissement de la pédagogie de maîtrise: processus de régulation interactive, rétroactive et proactive. In M. Huberman (Ed.), *Maîtriser les processus d'apprentissage: Fondements et perspectives de la pédagogie de maîtrise* (pp. 86–126). Paris, France: Delachaux & Niestlé.

Allen, J. P., Pianta, R. C., Gregory, A., Mikami, A. Y., & Lun, J. (2011). An interaction-based approach to enhancing secondary school instruction and student achievement. *Science*, *333*(6045), 1034–1037.

Amabile, T. M., & Kramer, S. J. (2011). *The progress principle: Using small wins to ignite joy, engagement and creativity at work*. Cambridge, MA: Harvard Business Review Press.

Amabile, T. M., Phillips, E., & Collins, M. A. (1994). Person and environment in talent development: The case of creativity. In N. Colangelo, S. G. Assouline, & D. L. Ambroson (Eds.), *Talent development: Proceedings of the 1993 Henry B. and Jocelyn Wallace National Research Symposium on Talent Development* (pp. 265–279). Dayton, OH: Ohio Psychology Press.

American Educational Research Association. (2006). Standards for reporting on empirical social science research in AERA publications. *Educational Researcher, 35*(6), 33–40.

American Educational Research Association, American Psychological Association, & National Council on Measurement in Education. (2014). *Standards for educational and psychological testing* (4th ed.). Washington, DC: American Educational Research Association.

American Statistical Association. (2014). *ASA statement on using value-added models for educational assessment.* Alexandria, VA: American Statistical Association.

Anderson, J. R. (1980). *Cognitive psychology and its implications.* San Francisco, CA: W. H. Freeman.

Anderson, L. M., & Stillman, J. A. (2013). Student teaching's contribution to preservice teacher development: A review of research focused on the preparation of teachers for urban and high-needs contexts. *Review of Educational Research, 83*(1), 3–69. doi: 10.3102/0034654312468619

Anderson, M. C., Bjork, R. A., & Bjork, E. L. (1994). Remembering can cause forgetting: Retrieval dynamics in long-term memory. *Journal of Experimental Psychology: Learning, Memory, and Cognition, 20*(5), 1063–1087. doi: 10.1037/0278-7393.20.5.1063

Antil, L. R., Jenkins, J. R., Wayne, S. K., & Vadasy, P. F. (1998). Cooperative learning: Prevalence, conceptualization and the relation between research and practice. *American Educational Research Journal, 35*(3), 419–454.

Aritomi, P., Coopersmith, J., & Gruber, K. (2009). *Characteristics of public school districts in the United States: Results from the 2007–08 Schools and Staffing Survey (first look).* Washington, DC: United States Department of Education National Center for Educational Statistics.

Aritzeta, A., Swailes, S., & Senior, B. (2007). Belbin's team role model: Development, validity and applications for team building. *Journal of Management Studies, 44*(1), 96–118. doi: 10.1111/j.1467-6486.2007.00666.x

Aspden, P., Wolcott, J., Boorman, J. L., & Cronenwett, L. R. (Eds.). (2007). *Preventing medication errors.* Washington, DC: National Academies Press.

Atteberry, A., Loeb, S., & Wyckoff, J. (2013). *Do first impressions matter? Improvement in early career teacher effectiveness.* Washington, DC: Center for Analysis of Longitudinal Data in Educational Research.

Ausubel, D. P. (1968). *Educational psychology: A cognitive view.* New York, NY: Holt, Rinehart & Winston.

Autor, D. H. (2014). Skills, education, and the rise of earnings inequality among the 'other 99 percent.' *Science, 344*(6186), 843–851. doi: 10.1126/science.1251868

Autor, D. H. (2015). Why are there still so many jobs? The history and future of workplace automation. *Journal of Economic Perspectives, 29*(3), 3–30. doi: 10.1257/jep.29.3.3

Autor, D. H., Katz, L. F., & Krueger, A. B. (1998). Computing inequality: Have computers changed the labor market? *The Quarterly Journal of Economics, 113*(4), 1169–1213. doi: 10.1162/003355398555874

Autor, D. H., Levy, F., & Murnane, R. J. (2003). The skill content of recent technological change: An empirical exploration. *The Quarterly Journal of Economics*, *118*(4), 1279–1333.

Baddeley, A. D. (1972). Selective attention and performance in dangerous environments. *British Journal of Psychology*, *63*(4), 537–546. doi: 10.1111/j.2044-8295.1972.tb01304.x

Bailey, A. L., & Heritage, M. (2008). *Formative assessment for literacy grades K–6*. Thousand Oaks, CA: Corwin.

Baker, E. L., Barton, P. E., Darling-Hammond, L., Haertel, E. H., Ladd, H. F., Linn, R. L., . . . Shepard, L. A. (2010). *Problems with the use of student test scores to evaluate teachers*. Washington, DC: Economic Policy Institute.

Balanced Assessment. (2007). Balanced assessment in mathematics. Retrieved from http://balancedassessment.concord.org/aboutprogram.html

Ballou, D. (2005). Value-added assessment: Lessons from Tennessee. In R. W. Lissitz (Ed.), *Value-added models in education: Theory and application* (pp. 272–297). Maple Grove, MN: JAI Press.

Bandura, A., & Schunk, D. H. (1981). Cultivating competence, self-efficacy, and intrinsic interest through proximal self-motivation. *Journal of Personality and Social Psychology*, *41*, 586–598.

Barber, M. (1994). *Young people and their attitudes to school: An interim report of a research project in the Centre for Successful Schools*. Keele, UK: University of Keele Institute of Education.

Barlow, J., & Møller, C. (1996). *A complaint is a gift: Recovering customer loyalty when things go wrong*. San Francisco, CA: Berrett-Koehler Publishers.

Barr, C. (2014). *How do teachers learn in a school-based Teacher Learning Community?* (Doctoral thesis, University of Sussex, Brighton, United Kingdom).

Barry, D., & Wiliam, D. (Writers), & Hardy, E. (Director). (2010). The classroom experiment (part 2) [TV]. In D. Barry (Producer), *The classroom experiment*. London, UK: BBC TV.

Bartlett, F. C. (1958). *Thinking: An experimental and social study*. New York, NY: Basic Books.

Baumert, J., Kunter, M., Blum, W., Brunner, M., Voss, T., Jordan, A., . . . Tsa, Y.-M. (2009). Teachers' mathematical knowledge, cognitive activation in the classroom, and student progress. *American Educational Research Journal*, *47*(1), 133–180.

BBC News. (2015, April 24). Valve expands video game 'mod' market. Retrieved from http://www.bbc.com/news/technology-32449141

Bédard, J., & Chi, M. T. H. (1993). Expertise in auditing. *Auditing: A Journal of Practice and Theory*, *12*(Supplement), 21–45.

Belbin, R. M. (1981). *Management teams: Why they succeed or fail*. Oxford, UK: Heinemann.

Bennett, C. M., Baird, A. A., Miller, M. B., & Wolford, G. L. (2014). Neural correlates of interspecies perspective taking in the post-mortem Atlantic Salmon: An argument for multiple comparisons correction. *Journal of Serendipitous and Unexpected Results*, *1*(1), 1–5.

Bennett, R. E. (2011). Formative assessment: A critical review. *Assessment in Education: Principles Policy and Practice*, *18*(1), 5–25.

Berliner, D. C. (1986). In pursuit of the expert pedagogue. *Educational Researcher*, *15*(7), 5–13. doi: 10.3102/0013189x015007007

Berliner, D. C. (1994). Expertise: The wonder of exemplary performances. In J. N. Mangieri, & C. C. Block (Eds.), *Creating powerful thinking in teachers and students: Diverse perspectives* (pp. 161–186). Fort Worth, TX: Harcourt Brace College.

Berliner, D. C., Stein, P., Saberrs, D., Brown Claridge, P., Cushing, K., & Pinnegar, S. (1988). Implications of research on pedagogical expertise and experience for mathematics teaching. In D. A. Grouws, T. J. Cooney, & D. Jones (Eds.), *Perspectives on research on effective mathematics teaching* (Vol. 1, pp. 67–95). Reston, VA: National Council of Teachers of Mathematics/Lawrence Erlbaum Associates.

Bernstein, W. (2013). Communication, power and the written word. *Econ Talk*. Retrieved December 31, 2014, from http://www.econtalk.org/archives/2013/05/bernstein_on_co.html

Biederman, I., & Shiffrar, M. M. (1987). Sexing day-olds chicks: A case study and expert systems analysis of a difficult perceptual learning task. *Journal of Experimental Psychology: Learning, Memory and Cognition, 13*(4), 640–645.

Bill and Melinda Gates Foundation. (2012a). *Asking students about teaching: Student perception surveys and their implementation.* Redmond, WA: Bill and Melinda Gates Foundation.

Bill and Melinda Gates Foundation. (2012b). *Ensuring fair and reliable measures of effective teaching: Culminating findings from the MET project's three-year study.* Redmond, WA: Bill and Melinda Gates Foundation.

Bjork, E. L., & Bjork, R. (2009). Making things hard on yourself, but in a good way: Creating desirable difficulties to enhance learning. In M. A. Gernsbacher, R. W. Pew, L. M. Hough, & J. R. Pomerantz (Eds.), *Psychology and the real world: Essays illustrating fundamental contributions to society* (pp. 56–64). New York, NY: Worth.

Black, H. (1986). Assessment for learning. In D. L. Nuttall (Ed.), *Assessing educational achievement.* (pp. 7–18). London: Falmer Press.

Black, P., & Harrison, C. (2002). *Science inside the black box: Assessment for learning in the science classroom.* London, UK: King's College London Department of Education and Professional Studies.

Black, P., Harrison, C., Lee, C., Marshall, B., & Wiliam, D. (2003). *Assessment for learning: Putting it into practice.* Buckingham, UK: Open University Press.

Black, P., Harrison, C., Lee, C., Marshall, B., & Wiliam, D. (2004). Working inside the black box: assessment for learning in the classroom. *Phi Delta Kappan, 86*(1), 8–21.

Black, P., & Wiliam, D. (2012). Developing a theory of formative assessment. In J. Gardner (Ed.), *Assessment and learning: practice, theory and policy* (2nd ed., pp. 206–229). London, UK: Sage.

Black, P. J., & Wiliam, D. (1998a). Assessment and classroom learning. *Assessment in Education: Principles, Policy and Practice, 5*(1), 7–74.

Black, P. J., & Wiliam, D. (1998b). Inside the black box: Raising standards through classroom assessment. *Phi Delta Kappan, 80*(2), 139–148.

Black, P. J., & Wiliam, D. (2009). Developing the theory of formative assessment. *Educational Assessment, Evaluation and Accountability, 21*(1), 5–31.

Blackburn, B. (2014). My beliefs about teaching. *The Eye on Education Blog.* Retrieved from http://www.routledge.com/eyeoneducation/blog/1681/

Blackwell, L. S., Dweck, C. S., & Trzesniewski, K. (2007). Implicit theories of intelligence predict achievement across an adolescent transition: A longitudinal study and an intervention. *Child Development, 78*(1), 246–263.

Blatchford, P., Basset, P., Brown, P., Koutoubou, M., Martin, C., Russell, A., . . . Rubie-Davies, C. (2009). *The impact of support staff in schools (results from strand 2, wave 2): Research report* (Vol. DCSF-RR148). London, UK: Department for Children, School and Families.

Bliesener, T. (1996). Methodological moderators in validating biographical data in personnel selection. *Journal of Occupational and Organizational Psychology, 69*(1), 107–120.

Blinder, A. S., & Krueger, A. B. (2011). Alternative measures of offshorability: A survey approach. *Journal of Labor Economics, 31*(2), S97–S128.

Bloom, B. S. (1969). Some theoretical issues relating to educational evaluation. In R. W. Tyler (Ed.), *Educational evaluation: New roles, new means: the 68th yearbook of the National Society for the Study of Education (part II)* (Vol. 68(2), pp. 26–50). Chicago, IL: University of Chicago Press.

Bloom, B. S. (1984). The 2-sigma problem: The search for methods of group instruction as effective as one-to-one tutoring. *Educational Researcher, 13*(6), 4–16.

Bloom, H. S., Hill, C. J., Black, A. R., & Lipsey, M. W. (2008). Performance trajectories and performance gaps as achievement effect-size benchmarks for educational interventions. *Journal of Research on Educational Effectiveness, 1*(4), 289–328.

Boaler, J. (2009). *What's math got to do with it? How parents and teachers can help children learn to love their least favorite subject.* New York, NY: Penguin.

Borenstein, M., Hedges, L. V., Higgins, J. P. T., & Rothstein, H. R. (2011). *Introduction to meta-analysis.* Chichester, UK: Wiley.

Borkenau, P., & Liebler, A. (1993). Convergence of stranger ratings of personality and intelligence with self-ratings, partner ratings, and measured intelligence. *Journal of Personality and Social Psychology, 65*(3), 546–553.

Borko, H., & Livingston, C. (1989). Cognition and improvisation: Differences in mathematics instruction by expert and novice teachers. *American Educational Research Journal, 26*(4), 473–498.

Boudett, K. P., City, E., & Murnane, R. (Eds.). (2013). *Data wise: A step-by-step guide to using assessment results to improve teaching and learning* (2nd ed.). Cambridge, MA: Harvard University Press.

Bowen, D. H., Buck, S., Deck, C., Mills, J. N., & Shuls, J. V. (2014). Risky business: An analysis of teacher risk preferences. *Education Economics, 23*(4) 1–11. doi: 10.1080/09645292.2014.966062

Brain Gym International. (2011a). Brain Gym studies. Retrieved from http://www.braingym.org/studies

Brain Gym International. (2011b). What is "Brain Gym"? Retrieved from http://www.braingym.org/about

Broadfoot, P. M., Daugherty, R., Gardner, J., Gipps, C. V., Harlen, W., James, M.,…Stobart, G. (1999). *Assessment for learning: beyond the black box.* Cambridge, UK: University of Cambridge School of Education.

Broadfoot, P. M., Daugherty, R., Gardner, J., Harlen, W., James, M., & Stobart, G. (2002). *Assessment for learning: 10 principles*. Cambridge, UK: University of Cambridge School of Education.

Brookhart, S. M. (2007). Expanding views about formative classroom assessment: A review of the literature. In J. H. McMillan (Ed.), *Formative classroom assessment: Theory into practice* (pp. 43–62). New York, NY: Teachers College Press.

Brousseau, G. (1997). *Theory of didactical situations in mathematics* (N. Balacheff, Trans. Vol. 19). Dordrecht, Netherlands: Kluwer.

Brown, A. L., & Campione, J. C. (1996). Psychological theory and the design of innovative learning environments: On procedures, principles, and systems. In L. Schauble & R. Glaser (Eds.), *Innovations in learning: New environments for education* (pp. 289–325). Hillsdale, NJ: Lawrence Erlbaum Associates.

Bryan, W. L., & Harter, N. (1899). Studies on the telegraphic language: The acquisition of a hierarchy of habits. *Psychological Review, 6*(4), 345–375. doi: 10.1037/h0073117

Brynjolfsson, E., & McAfee, A. (2014). *The second machine age: Work, progress, and prosperity in a time of brilliant technologies*. New York, NY: Norton.

Buckingham, M. (2007). *Now go put your strengths to work*. New York, NY: Simon & Schuster.

Bulkley, K. E., Christman, J. B., Goertz, M. E., & Lawrence, N. R. (2010). Building with benchmarks: The role of the district in Philadelphia's benchmark assessment system. *Peabody Journal of Education, 85*(2), 186–204. doi: 10.1080/01619561003685346

Bull, C., Yates, R., Sarkar, D., Deanfield, J., & de Leval, M. (2000). Scientific, ethical and logistical considerations in introducing a new operation: A retrospective cohort study from paediatric cardiac surgery. *British Medical Journal, 320*, 1168–1173.

Bureau of Labor Statistics. (2014). *Job openings and labor turnover – October 2014*. Washington, DC: Bureau of Labor Statistics.

Burnett, S., Sebastian, C., Kadosh, K. C., & Blakemore, S.-J. (2011). The social brain in adolescence: Evidence from functional magnetic resonance imaging and behavioural studies. *Neuroscience and Biobehavioral Reviews, 35*(8), 1654–1664.

Burns, M. K., Appleton, J. J., & Stehouwer, J. D. (2005). Meta-analytic review of responsiveness-to-intervention research: Examining field-based and research-implemented models. *Journal of Psychoeducational Assessment, 23*(4), 381–394. doi: 10.1177/073428290502300406

Button, K. S., Ioannidis, J. P. A., Mokrysz, C., Nosek, B. A., Flint, J., Robinson, E. S. J.,… Munafo, M. R. (2013). Power failure: Why small sample size undermines the reliability of neuroscience. *Nature Reviews Neuroscience*. Advance online publication. doi: 10.1038/nrn3475

Cajkler, W., Wood, P., Norton, J., & Pedder, D. (2014). Lesson study as a vehicle for collaborative teacher learning in a secondary school. *Professional Development in Education*, 1–19. doi: 10.1080/19415257.2013.866975

Calderwood, R., Klein, G. A., & Crandall, B. W. (1988). Time pressure, skill, and move quality in chess. *American Journal of Psychology, 101*(4), 481–493.

Campbell Collaboration. (2014). The Campbell Library: Published issues. *Campbell Systematic Reviews*. Retrieved from http://www.campbellcollaboration.org/lib/?go=browse_issues

Campbell, D. T. (1976). *Assessing the impact of planned social change* (Vol. 8). Hanover, NH: The Public Affairs Center, Dartmouth College.

Campitelli, G., & Gobet, F. (2008). The role of practice in chess: A longitudinal study. *Learning and Individual Differences, 18*(4), 446–458. doi: 10.1016/j.lindif.2007.11.006

Campitelli, G., & Gobet, F. (2011). Deliberate practice: Necessary but not sufficient. *Current Directions in Psychological Science, 20*(5), 280–285. doi: 10.1177/0963721411421922

Carnevale, A. P., Jayasundera, T., & Cheah, B. (2012). *The college advantage: Weathering the economic storm.* Washington, DC: Georgetown University.

Carnoy, M., & Rothstein, R. (2013). *What do international tests really show about U.S. student performance?* Washington, DC: Economic Policy Institute.

Carrell, S. E., & West, J. E. (2010). Does professor quality matter? Evidence from random assignment of students to professors. *Journal of Political Economy, 118*(3), 409–432.

Carroll, P. B. (1993). *Big Blues.* New York, NY: Crown.

Catalona, W. J., Smith, D. S., Ratliff, T. L., & Basler, J. W. (1993). Detection of organ-confined prostate cancer is increased through prostate-specific antigen-based screening. *Journal of the American Medical Association, 270*(8), 948–954.

Center for Research on Education Outcomes. (2013). *National charter school study 2013.* Stanford, CA: Center for Research on Education Outcomes.

Chait, R. (2010). *Removing chronically ineffective teachers: Barriers and opportunities.* Washington, DC: Center for American Progress.

Chalmers, I. (2005, September 20–23). *The scandalous failure of scientists to cumulate scientifically.* Paper presented at the Ninth World Congress on Health Information and Libraries, Salvador, Brazil. Retrieved from http://www.icml9.org/program/public/documents/Chalmers-131528.pdf

Charness, N., Krampe, R. T., & Mayr, U. (1996). The role of practice and coaching in entrepreneurial skill domains: An international comparison of life-span chess skill acquisition. In K. A. Ericsson (Ed.), *The road to excellence: The acquisition of expert performance in the arts and sciences, sports, and games* (pp. 51–80). Mahwah, NJ: Lawrence Erlbaum Associates.

Charness, N., Tuffiash, M. I., Krampe, R. T., Reingold, E., & Vasyukova, E. (2005). The role of deliberate practice in chess expertise. *Applied Cognitive Psychology, 19,* 151–165. doi: 10.1002/acp.1106

Chase, W. G., & Simon, H. A. (1973). Perception in chess. *Cognitive Psychology, 4*(1), 55–81.

Chetty, R., Friedman, J. N., & Rockoff, J. E. (2011). *The long-term impacts of teachers: Teacher value-added and student outcomes in adulthood* (Vol. w17699). Washington, DC: National Bureau of Economic Research.

Chetty, R., Friedman, J. N., & Rockoff, J. E. (2014). Measuring the impacts of teachers I: Evaluating bias in teacher value-added estimates. *American Economic Review, 104*(9), 2593–2632.

Chi, M. T. H., Feltovich, P. J., & Glaser, R. (1981). Categorization and representation of physics problems by experts and novices. *Cognitive Science, 5*(2), 121–152.

Choi, J. (2012). *Private tutoring and educational inequality: Evidence from a dynamic model of academic achievement in Korea.* Philadelphia, PA: University of Pennsylvania.

Cianciolo, A. T., Matthew, C., Sternberg, R. J., & Wagner, R. K. (2006). Tacit knowledge, practical intelligence, and expertise. In K. A. Ericsson, N. Charness, P. J. Feltovich, & R. R. Hoffman (Eds.), *The Cambridge handbook of expertise and expert performance* (pp. 613–632). Cambridge, UK: Cambridge University Press.

Cilley, M. (2014). 5-minute room rescue. Retrieved from http://www.flylady.net/d/getting -started/flying-lessons/decluttering-15-minutes/

Cobb, J. A. (1972). Relationship of discrete classroom behaviors to fourth-grade academic achievement. *Journal of Educational Psychology, 63*(1), 74–80. doi: 10.1037/h0032247

Coburn, C. (2003). Rethinking scale: Moving beyond numbers to deep and lasting change. *Educational Researcher, 32*(6), 3–12.

Cochrane, A. L. (1972). *Effectiveness and efficiency: Random reflections on health services.* London, UK: Nuffield Provincial Hospitals Trust.

Cochrane, A. L. (1979). 1931–1971: A critical review, with particular reference to the medical profession. In G. Teeling-Smith & N. Wells (Eds.), *Medicines for the year 2000* (pp. 1–11). London, UK: Office of Health Economics.

Cochrane Collaboration. (2014, October 6). About us. Retrieved from http://www.cochrane .org/about-us

Cochran-Smith, M., & Zeichner, K. M. (Eds.). (2005). *Studying teacher education: The report of the AERA Panel on Research and Teacher Education.* Mahwah, NJ: Lawrence Erlbaum Associates.

Coffield, F., Moseley, D., Hall, E., & Ecclestone, K. (2004). *Learning styles and pedagogy in post-16 learning: A systematic and critical review.* London, UK: Learning and Skills Development Agency.

Cohen, J. (1969). *Statistical power analysis for the behavioral sciences.* San Diego, CA: Academic Press.

Cohen, J. (1988). *Statistical power analysis for the behavioral sciences* (2nd ed.). Hillsdale, NJ: Lawrence Erlbaum Associates.

Cohen, J. (1992). A power primer. *Psychological Bulletin, 112*(1), 155–159.

College Board. (1976). *Student descriptive questionnaire.* Princeton, NJ: Educational Testing Service.

College Board. (2012). *2012 college-bound seniors: Total group profile report.* New York, NY: College Board.

College Board. (2014). *Test characteristics of the SAT®: Reliability, difficulty levels, completion rates.* New York, NY: College Board.

Collins, J. (2001). *Good to great: Why some companies make the leap...and others don't.* New York, NY: HarperBusiness.

Collins, J., & Porras, J. (1994). *Built to last: Successful habits of visionary companies.* New York, NY: HarperBusiness.

Colvin, G. (2009). *Talent is over-rated: What really separates world-class performers from everybody else.* New York, NY: Portfolio.

Commission for Architecture and the Built Environment. (2002). *Assessing secondary school design quality: Research report.* London, UK: Commission for Architecture and the Built Environment.

Cook, D. A., & Hatala, R. (2014). Got power? A systematic review of sample size adequacy in health professions education research. *Advances in Health Science Education, (20)*1, 78–83. doi: 10.1007/s10459-014-9509-5

Cordingley, P., Higgins, S., Greany, T., Buckler, N., Coles-Jordan, D., Crisp, B., . . . Coe, R. (2015). *Developing great teaching: Lessons from international reviews into effective professional development (full report)*. London, UK: Teacher Development Trust.

Covey, S. R. (1989). *The seven habits of highly effective people: Restoring the character ethic*. New York, NY: Simon & Schuster.

Cowen, T. (2013). *Average is over: Powering America beyond the age of the Great Stagnation*. New York, NY: Penguin.

Cowie, B., & Bell, B. (1999). A model of formative assessment in science education. *Assessment in Education: Principles Policy and Practice, 6*(1), 32–42.

Cox, W. M., & Alm, R. (2008). Creative destruction. *Concise Encyclopedia of Economics*. Retrieved from http://www.econlib.org/library/Enc/CreativeDestruction.html

Craig, J., Clanton, F., & Demeter, M. (2014). Reducing interruptions during medication administration: the White Vest study. *Journal of Research in Nursing, 19*(3), 248–261. doi: 10.1177/1744987113484737

Craven, A. An interview with Esther Dyson. *Emerald Management First*. Retrieved November 2, 2015, from http://first.emeraldinsight.com/interviews/pdf/dyson.pdf

Crawford, C., & Cribb, J. (2013) *Reading and maths skills at age 10 and earnings in later life: A brief analysis using the British Cohort Study* (Vol. REP03). London, UK: Institute for Fiscal Studies.

Cronbach, L. J. (1971). Test validation. In R. L. Thorndike (Ed.), *Educational measurement* (2nd ed., pp. 443–507). Washington, DC: American Council on Education.

Crooks, T. J. (1988). The impact of classroom evaluation practices on students. *Review of Educational Research, 58*(4), 438–481.

Cross, K. P. (1977). Not can but will college teaching be improved? *New Directions for Higher Education, (17)*, 1–15.

Crouch, C. H., & Mazur, E. (2001). Peer instruction: Ten years of experience and results. *American Journal of Physics, 69*(9), 970–977.

Cummings, K. L., Anderson, D. J., & Kaye, K. S. (2010). Hand hygiene noncompliance and the cost of hospital-acquired methicillin-resistant Staphylococcus aureus infection. *Infection Control and Hospital Epidemiology, 31*(4), 357–364. doi: 10.1086/651096

Dalton, D. R., Aguinis, H., Dalton, C. M., Bosco, F. A., & Pierce, C. A. (2012). Revisiting the file drawer problem in meta-analysis: An assessment of published and nonpublished correlation matrices. *Personnel Psychology, 65*(2), 221–249. doi: 10.1111/j.1744-6570.2012.01243.x

Damasio, A. R. (1994). *Descartes' error: Emotion, reason and the human brain*. London, UK: Picador.

Danielson, C. (1996). *Enhancing professional practice: A framework for teaching*. Alexandria, VA: ASCD.

Danielson, C. (2014). *The framework for teaching evaluation instrument: 2013 edition*. Princeton, NJ: Danielson Group.

Darling-Hammond, L. (2014). One piece of the whole: Teacher evaluation as part of a comprehensive system for teaching and learning. *American Educator, 38*(1), 4–13, 44.

Darling-Hammond, L., Wei, R. C., Andree, A., Richardson, N., & Orphanos, S. (2009). *A status report on teacher development in the United States and abroad.* Dallas, TX: National Staff Development Council.

Dawes, R. M. (1994). *House of cards: Psychology and psychotherapy built on myth.* New York, NY: Free Press.

Day, C. (1999). *Developing teachers: The challenges of lifelong learning.* London, UK: Falmer.

de Groot, A. D. (1965/1978). *Thought and choice in chess.* Amsterdam, Netherlands: Amsterdam University Press.

Della Sala, S., & Anderson, M. (Eds.). (2011). *Neuroscience in education: The good, the bad, and the ugly.* Oxford, UK: Oxford University Press.

Dickersin, K., & Min, Y.-I. (1993). NIH clinical trials and publication bias. *Online Journal of Current Clincal Trials, 50*(April 28).

Dickerson, A., & Popli, G. (2012). *Persistent poverty and children's cognitive development* (Vol. 2/12). London, UK: Institute of Education, University of London.

Dorsey, D. (2000, November 30). Positive deviant. *Fast Company.* Retrieved from http://www .fastcompany.com/42075/positive-deviant

Dreyfus, H. L., Dreyfus, S. E., & Anathanasiou, T. (1986). *Mind over machine: The power of human intuition and expertise in the era of the computer.* New York, NY: Free Press.

Duckworth, A., & Gross, J. J. (2014). Self-control and grit: Related but separable determinants of success. *Current Directions in Psychological Science, 23*(5), 319–325.

Duffy, L. J., Baluch, B., & Ericsson, K. A. (2004). Dart performance as a function of facets of practice amongst professional and amateur men and women players. *International Journal of Sport Psychology, 35,* 232–245.

Duflo, E., Hanna, R., & Ryan, S. P. (2012). Incentives work: Getting teachers to come to school. *American Economic Review, 102*(4), 1241–1278. doi: 10.1257/aer.102.4.1241

DuFour, R. (2004). What is a professional learning community? *Educational Leadership, 61*(8), 6–11.

DuFour, R., DuFour, R., Eaker, R., & Karhanek, G. (2004). *Whatever it takes: How professional learning communities respond when kids don't learn.* Bloomington, IN: Solution Tree.

DuFour, R., DuFour, R., Eaker, R., & Many, T. (2005). *Learning by doing: A handbook for professional learning communities at work.* Bloomington, IN: Solution Tree.

DuFour, R., Eaker, R., & DuFour, R. (2005). Closing the knowing-doing gap. In R. DuFour, R. Eaker, & R. DuFour (Eds.), *On common ground: The power of professional learning communities* (pp. 225–254). Bloomington, IN: National Education Service.

Duhatschek, E. (2014, January 14). In the City of Angels, NHL mends fences with The Great One. *Los Angeles Globe and Mail.* Retrieved from http://www.theglobeandmail.com /sports/hockey/duhatschek-in-the-city-of-angels-nhl-mends-fences-with-the-great-one /article16320423/

Dweck, C. S. (2006). *Mindset: The new psychology of success.* New York, NY: Random House.

Dweck, C. S. (2012). Mindsets and human nature: Promoting change in the Middle East, the schoolyard, the racial divide, and willpower. *American Psychologist, 67*(8), 614–622. doi: 10.1037/a0029783

Economist. (2013, October 26). Hard times. *Economist.* Retrieved from http://www.economist.com/news/china/21588402-how-young-criminals-are-treated-says-much-about-urban-rural-gap-hard-times

Economist. (2014, February 15). Sunstroke. *Economist.* Retrieved from http://www.economist.com/news/business/21596583-cirque-du-soleil-may-be-struggling-cluster-around-it-thriving-sunstroke

Eddington, A. S. (1935/1959). *New pathways in science.* Cambridge, UK: Cambridge University Press.

Education Endowment Foundation. (2013). Teaching and learning toolkit. Retrieved from http://educationendowmentfoundation.org.uk/toolkit/

Education Endowment Foundation. (2015). Teaching and learning toolkit. Retrieved from https://educationendowmentfoundation.org.uk/toolkit/toolkit-a-z/

Educational Testing Service. (2010). *ETS item bank: Measuring student success.* Princeton, NJ: Educational Testing Service.

Eisenhardt, K. M. (1990). Speed and strategic choice: How managers accelerate decision making. *California Management Review, 32*(3), 39–54.

Eisenstadt, M., & Kareev, Y. (1979). Aspects of human problem solving: The use of internal representations. In D. A. Norman, & D. E. Rumelhart (Eds.), *Explorations in cognition* (pp. 308–346). San Francisco, CA: Freeman.

Eisner, E. W. (1985). *The educational imagination: On the design and evaluation of school programs* (2nd ed.). New York, NY: Macmillan.

Elo, A. (1978). *The rating of chessplayers, past and present.* New York, NY: Arco.

English, L. D., Jones, G., Lesh, R., Tirosh, D., & Bussi, M. B. (2002). Future issues and directions in international mathematics education research. In L. D. English (Ed.), *Handbook of international research in mathematics education* (pp. 787–812). Mahwah, NJ: Lawrence Erlbaum Associates.

Epstein, D. (2013). *The sports gene: Inside the science of extraordinary athletic performance.* New York, NY: Penguin.

Epstein, S. A. (1991). *Wage labor and guilds in medieval Europe.* Chapel Hill, NC: University of North Carolina Press.

Ericsson, K. A. (2004). Deliberate practice and the acquisition and maintenance of expert performance in medicine and related domains. *Academic Medicine, 79*(10 Supplement), S70–S81.

Ericsson, K. A. (2006). The influence of experience and deliberate practice on the development of superior expert performance. In K. A. Ericsson, N. Charness, P. J. Feltovich, & R. R. Hoffman (Eds.), *The Cambridge handbook of expertise and expert performance* (pp. 683–703). Cambridge, UK: Cambridge University Press.

Ericsson, K. A., Krampe, R. T., & Tesch-Römer, C. (1993). The role of deliberate practice in the acquisition of expert performance. *Psychological Review, 100*(3), 363–406.

Feltovich, P. J., Prietula, M. J., & Ericsson, K. A. (2006). Studies of expertise from psychological perspectives. In K. A. Ericsson, N. Charness, P. J. Feltovich, & R. R. Hoffman (Eds.), *The Cambridge handbook of expertise and expert performance* (pp. 41–67). Cambridge, UK: Cambridge University Press.

Ferguson, R. F. (2008). *The TRIPOD Project framework.* Cambridge, MA: Harvard University.

Fitzpatrick, M. D., Grissmer, D., & Hastedt, S. (2011). What a difference a day makes: Estimating daily learning gains during kindergarten and first grade using a natural experiment. *Economics of Education Review, 30*(2), 269–279.

Flynn, J. R. (1984). The mean IQ of Americans: Massive gains 1932 to 1978. *Psychological Bulletin, 95*(1), 29–51.

Flynn, J. R. (2012). *Are we getting smarter? Rising IQ in the twenty-first century.* Cambridge, UK: Cambridge University Press.

Flyvbjerg, B. (2001). *Making social science matter: Why social inquiry fails and how it can succeed again.* Cambridge, UK: Cambridge University Press.

Franco, A., Malhotra, N., & Simonovits, G. (2014). Publication bias in the social sciences: Unlocking the file drawer. *Science, 345*(6203), 1502–1505. doi: 10.1126/science.1255484

Fredricks, J., McColskey, W., Meli, J., Mordica, J., Montrosse, B., & Mooney, K. (2011). *Measuring student engagement in upper elementary through high school: A description of 21 instruments.* Washington, DC: National Center for Education Evaluation and Regional Assistance.

Frey, C. B., & Osborne, M. A. (2013). *The future of employment: How susceptible are jobs to computerisation?* Oxford, UK: University of Oxford.

Friedman, T. L. (2005). *The world is flat: A brief history of the twenty-first century.* New York, NY: Farrar, Straus & Giroux.

Fuchs, L. S., & Fuchs, D. (1986). Effects of systematic formative evaluation—A meta-analysis. *Exceptional Children, 53*(3), 199–208.

Fullan, M., & Stiegelbauer, S. (1991). *The new meaning of educational change.* London, UK: Cassell.

Furberg, C. D. (1983). Effect of antiarrhythmic drugs on mortality after myocardial infarction. *American Journal of Cardiology, 52*(6), 32C–36C.

Furnham, A., Steele, H., & Pendleton, D. (1993). A psychometric assessment of the Belbin Team-Role Self-Perception Inventory. *Journal of Occupational and Organizational Psychology, 66*(3), 245–257. doi: 10.1111/j.2044-8325.1993.tb00535.x

Gabrielsen, P. (2014). Teach science through argument. Retrieved from https://ed.stanford.edu/spotlight/teach-science-through-argument

Gawande, A. (2007). *Better: A surgeon's notes on performance.* London, UK: Profile Books.

Gersten, R., Taylor, M. J., Keys, T. D., Rolfhus, E., & Newman-Gonchar, R. (2014). *Summary of research on the effectiveness of math professional development approaches.* Washington, DC: National Center for Education Evaluation and Regional Assistance.

Ghemawat, P. (2011). *World 3.0: Global prosperity and how to achieve it.* Cambridge, MA: Harvard Business Press.

Gibbons, M., Limoges, C., Nowotny, H., Schwartzman, S., Scott, P., & Trow, M. (1994). *The new production of knowledge: The dynamics of science and research in contemporary societies.* London, UK: Sage.

Gilbert, R., Salanti, G., Harden, M., & See, S. (2005). Infant sleeping position and the sudden infant death syndrome: Systematic review of observational studies and historical review of recommendations from 1940 to 2002. *International Journal of Epidemiology, 34*(4), 874–887. doi: 10.1093/ije/dyi088

Ginsberg, M. B., & Murphy, D. (2002). How walkthroughs open doors. *Educational Leadership, 59*(8), 34–36.

Gladwell, M. (2008). *Outliers: The story of success.* New York, NY: Little, Brown.

Gladwell, M. (2008, December 15). Most likely to succeed. *New Yorker,* 36–42.

Glass, G. V. (1976). Primary, secondary, and meta-analysis of research. *Educational Reseacher, 5*(10), 3–8.

Glenberg, A. M., & Epstein, W. (1987). Inexpert calibration of comprehension. *Memory and Cognition, 15*(1), 84–93.

Goe, L., & Bridgeman, B. (2006). *Effects of Focus on Standards on academic performance.* Princeton, NJ: Educational Testing Service.

Goldacre, B. (2012). *Bad pharma.* London, UK: Fourth Estate.

Goldhaber, D., Grout, C., & Huntington-Klein, N. (2014). *Screen twice, cut once: Assessing the predictive validity of teacher selection tools.* Seattle, WA: University of Washington Bothell.

Goldhaber, D. D., Goldschmidt, P., & Tseng, F. (2013). Teacher value-added at the high-school level: Different models, different answers? *Educational Evaluation and Policy Analysis, 35*(2), 220–236. doi: 10.3102/0162373712466938

Goldin, C., & Katz, L. F. (2009). The future of inequality: The other reason education matters so much. *Milken Institute Review, 11*(Third Quarter), 26–33.

Goldstein, H. (1987). *Multilevel models in educational and social research.* London, UK: Griffin.

Gollwitzer, P. M. (1999). Implementation intentions: Strong effects of simple plans. *American Psychologist, 54,* 493–503.

Gollwitzer, P. M., & Brandstätter, V. (1997). Implementation intentions and effective goal pursuit. *Journal of Personality and Social Psychology, 73*(1), 186–199.

Good, T. L., Grouws, D. A., Mason, D. A., Slavings, R. L., & Cramer, K. (1990). An observational study of small-group mathematics instruction in elementary schools. *American Educational Research Journal, 27*(4), 755–782.

Goos, M., & Manning, A. (2003). *Lousy and lovely jobs: The rising polarization of work in Britain.* London, UK: London School of Economics and Political Science.

Grabner, R. H., Stern, E., & Neubauer, A. C. (2007). Individual differences in chess expertise: A psychometric investigation. *Acta Psychologica, 124*(3), 398–420. doi: 10.1016/j.actpsy .2006.07.008

Green, S., Higgins, J. P. T., Alderson, P., Clarke, M., Mulrow, C. D., & Oxman, A. D. (2008). Introduction. In J. P. T. Higgins & S. Green (Eds.), *Cochrane handbook for systematic reviews of interventions* (pp. 1–10). Chichester, UK: Wiley.

Greenwald, A. G. (1997). Validity concerns and usefulness of student ratings of instruction. *American Psychologist, 52*(11), 1182–1186. doi: 10.1037/0003-066X.52.11.1182

Gretzky, W., & Reilly, R. (1990). *Gretzky: An autobiography.* New York, NY: HarperCollins.

Grissom, J. A., & Loeb, S. (2013, April). *What effective principals do: Longitudinal evidence from school leader observations.* Paper presented at the Annual Meeting of the American Educational Research Association, San Francisco, CA.

Grissom, J. A., Loeb, S., & Master, B. (2013). Effective instructional time use for school leaders: Longitudinal evidence from observations of principals. *Educational Researcher, 42*(8), 433–444. doi: 10.3102/0013189x13510020

Grossman, P., Greenberg, S., Hammerness, K., Cohen, J., Alston, C., & Brown, M. (2009). *Development of the Protocol for Language Arts Teaching Observation (PLATO).* Paper presented at the Annual Meeting of the American Educational Research Association, San Diego, CA.

Grossman, P., Loeb, S., Hammerness, K., Wyckoff, J., Boyd, D., & Lankford, H. (2010). *Measure for measure: The relationship between measures of instructional practice in middle school English language arts and teachers' value-added scores.* Cambridge, MA: National Bureau of Economic Research.

Grossman, P., Wineburg, S. S., & Woolworth, S. (2000). *What makes teacher community different from a gathering of teachers?* Seattle, WA: University of Washington Center for the Study of Teaching and Policy.

Gutman, L. M., & Midgley, C. (2000). The role of protective factors in supporting the academic achievement of poor African American students during the middle school transition. *Journal of Youth and Adolescence, 29*, 223–248.

Gzowski, P. (1981). *The game of our lives.* Toronto, Canada: McClelland & Stewart.

Hagen, U. (1973). *Respect for acting.* New York, NY: Macmillan.

Haidt, J. (2005). *The happiness hypothesis: Finding modern truth in ancient wisdom.* New York, NY: Basic Books.

Hall, T., Strangman, N., & Meyer, A. (2011). *Differentiated instruction and implications for UDL implementation.* Wakefield, MA: National Center on Accessing the General Curriculum.

Hambrick, D. Z., & Engle, R. W. (2002). Effects of domain knowledge, working memory capacity, and age on cognitive performance: An investigation of the knowledge-is-power hypothesis. *Cognitive Psychology, 44*(4), 339–387. doi: http://dx.doi.org/10.1006/cogp.2001.0769

Hamre, B. K., & Pianta, R. C. (2005). Can instructional and emotional support in the first-grade classroom make a difference for children at risk of school failure? *Child Development, 76*(5), 949–967. doi: 10.1111/j.1467-8624.2005.00889.x

Hancock, P. A. (1996). The effect of skill on performance under an environmental stressor. *Aviation, Space, and Environmental Medicine, 57*(1), 59–64.

Hanninen, G. (1985). *Do experts exist in gifted education?* Tucson, AZ: University of Arizona College of Education.

Hanushek, E. A. (1971). Teacher characteristics and gains in student achievement: Estimation using micro data. *American Economic Review, 61*(2), 280–288.

Hanushek, E. A. (2004). *Some simple analytics of school quality* (Vol. W10229). Cambridge, MA: National Bureau of Economic Research.

Hanushek, E. A., & Wößmann, L. (2010). *The high cost of low educational performance: The long-run impact of improving PISA outcomes*. Paris, France: Organisation for Economic Co-operation and Development.

Harcombe, Z., Baker, J. S., Cooper, S. M., Davies, B., Sculthorpe, N., DiNicolantonio, J. J.,...Grace, F. (2015). Evidence from randomised controlled trials did not support the introduction of dietary fat guidelines in 1977 and 1983: A systematic review and meta-analysis. *Open Heart*, *2*(1). doi: 10.1136/openhrt-2014-000196

Harris, D. N. (2009). Would accountability based on teacher value added be smart policy? An examination of the statistical properties and policy alternatives. *Education Finance and Policy*, *4*(4), 319–350. doi: 10.1162/edfp.2009.4.4.319

Harris, D. N., & Sass, T. R. (2007). *Teacher training, teacher quality and student achievement*. Washington, DC: National Center for Analysis of Longitudinal Data in Education Research.

Haselkorn, D., & Harris, L. (2001). *The essential profession: American education at the crossroads. A national survey of public attitudes toward teaching, educational opportunity, and school reform*. Belmont, MA: Recruiting New Teachers, Incorporated.

Hattie, J. (2008). *Visible learning*. London, UK: Routledge.

Heath, C., & Heath, D. (2010). *Switch: How to change things when change is hard*. New York, NY: Broadway Books.

Heathcote, A., Brown, S., & Mewhort, D. J. K. (2000). The power law repealed: The case for an exponential law of practice. *Psychonomic Bulletin & Review*, *7*(2), 185–207.

Hecht, L. W. (1978). Measuring student behavior during group instruction. *Journal of Educational Research*, *78*(5), 283–290.

Hedesstrom, T., & Whitley, E. A. (2000, July). *What is meant by tacit knowledge? Towards a better understanding of the shape of actions*. Paper presented at the European Conference on Information Systems, Vienna, Austria. Retrieved from http://aisel.aisnet.org/cgi/viewcontent.cgi?article=1020&context=ecis2000

Hill, A. B. (1965). The environment and disease: Association or causation? *Proceedings of the Royal Society of Medicine*, *58*(5), 295–300.

Hill, H. C., Blunk, M. L., Charalambous, C. Y., Lewis, J. M., Phelps, G. C., Sleep, L.,... Ball, D. L. (2008). Mathematical knowledge for teaching and the mathematical quality of instruction: An exploratory study. *Cognition and Instruction*, *26*(4), 430–511. doi: 10.1080/07370000802177235

Hill, H. C., Charalambous, C. Y., & Kraft, M. A. (2012). When rater reliability is not enough: Teacher observation systems and a case for the generalizability study. *Educational Researcher*, *41*(2), 56–84.

Hill, H. C., Rowan, B., & Ball, D. L. (2005). Effects of teachers' mathematical knowledge for teaching on student achievement. *American Educational Research Journal*, *42*(2), 371–406.

Hill, N. M., & Schneider, W. (2006). Brain changes in the development of expertise: Neuroanatomical and neurophysiological evidence about skill-based adaptations. In K. A. Ericsson, N. Charness, P. J. Feltovich & R. R. Hoffman (Eds.), *The Cambridge handbook of expertise and expert performance* (pp. 653–682). Cambridge, UK: Cambridge University Press.

Hodgen, J., & Wiliam, D. (2006). *Mathematics inside the black box: Assessment for learning in the mathematics classroom.* London, UK: NFER-Nelson.

Howard, J. (1991). *Getting smart: The social construction of intelligence.* Waltham, MA: The Efficacy Institute.

Huebner, T. A. (2010). What research says about...differentiated learning. *Educational Leadership, 67*(5), 79–81.

Hunt, L., Fleming, P., Golding, J., & ALSPAC Study Team. (1997). Does the supine sleeping position have any adverse effects on the child? I. Health in the first six months. *Pediatrics, 100*(1), e11. doi: 10.1542/peds.100.1.e11

Husén, T. (Ed.). (1967). *International study of achievement in mathematics: A comparison of twelve countries* (Vol. 1). New York, NY: John Wiley & Sons.

Hyatt, K. J. (2007). Brain Gym®: Building stronger brains or wishful thinking? *Remedial and Special Education, 28*(2), 117–124. doi: 10.1177/07419325070280020201

Ioannidis, J. P. A. (2005). Why most published research findings are false. *PLoS Medicine, 2*(8), e124.

Ioannidis, J. P. A. (2011). Excess significance bias in the literature on brain volume abnormalities. *Archives of General Psychiatry, 68*(8), 773–780. doi: 10.1001/archgenpsychiatry.2011.28

International Review Panel on the Structure of Initial Teacher Education Provision in Ireland. (2012). *Report.* Dublin, Ireland: Department of Education and Skills.

Jacob, B. A., & Lefgren, L. (2005). *Principals as agents: Subjective performance measurement in education.* Cambridge, MA: National Bureau of Economic Research.

Jacob, B. A., & Rockoff, J. E. (2011). *Organizing schools to improve student achievement: Start times, grade configurations, and teacher assignments* (Vol. 2011-08). Washington, DC: Brookings Institution.

James, M. (1992, April). *Assessment for learning.* Paper presented at the Annual Meeting of the American Educational Research Association, New Orleans, LA.

Jansma, J. M., Ramsey, N. F., Slagter, H. A., & Kahn, R. S. (2001). Functional anatomical correlates of controlled and automatic processing. *Journal of Cognitive Neuroscience, 13*(6), 730–743.

Jee, B., Wiley, J., & Griffin, T. (2006). Expertise and the illusion of comprehension. In R. Sun & N. Miyake (Eds.), *Proceedings of the 28th Annual Conference of the Cognitive Science Society* (pp. 419–424). Mahwah, NJ: Lawrence Erlbaum Associates.

Jerrim, J. (2014). *Why do East Asian children perform so well in PISA? An investigation of Western-born children of East Asian descent.* London, UK: Institute of Education, University of London.

Johnson, D. W., & Johnson, R. T. (2009). An educational psychology success story: Social interdependence theory and cooperative learning. *Educational Researcher, 38*(5), 365–379.

Johnson, G. (1996). *Fire in the mind: Science, faith and the search for order.* London, UK: Viking.

Jones, J., & Wiliam, D. (2007). *Modern foreign languages inside the black box: Assessment for learning in the modern foreign languages classroom.* London, UK: Granada.

Jørgensen, H. (1997). Time for practising? Higher level music students' use of time for instrumental practising. In H. Jørgensen & A. C. Lehmann (Eds.), *Does practice make perfect? Current theory and research on instrumental music practice* (pp. 123–139). Oslo, Norway: Norges Musikkhøgskole [Norwegian State Academy of Music].

Kahl, S. (2005, 21 September). Where in the world are formative tests? Right under your nose! *Education Week, 25*(4), 11.

Kane, T. J., McCaffrey, D., Miller, T., & Staiger, D. O. (2013). *Have we identified effective teachers? Validating measures of effective teaching using random assignment.* Seattle, WA: Bill & Melinda Gates Foundation.

Kaplan, R. S., & Norton, D. P. (2006). *Alignment: Using the balanced scorecard to create corporate synergies.* Cambridge, MA: Harvard Business School Press.

Keck, J. W., Arnold, L., Willoughby, L., & Calkins, V. (1979). Efficacy of cognitive/ noncognitive measures in predicting resident-physician performance. *Journal of Medical Education, 54*(10), 759–765.

Kennedy, E. (2002). Higher education and Pell grants. *Congressional record: Proceedings and debates of the 107th Congress second session* (Vol. 148 part 7, pp. 9355–9358). Washington, DC: United States Government Printing Office.

Kida, N., Oda, S., & Matsumura, M. (2005). Intensive baseball practice improves the Go/ Nogo reaction time, but not the simple reaction time. *Cognitive Brain Research, 22*(2), 257–264. doi: http://dx.doi.org/10.1016/j.cogbrainres.2004.09.003

Kingston, N. M., & Nash, B. (2011). Formative assessment: A meta-analysis and a call for research. *Educational Measurement: Issues and Practice, 30*(4), 28–37.

Kingston, N. M., & Nash, B. (2015). Erratum. *Educational Measurement: Issues and Practice, 34*(1), 55.

Kirschner, P. A., Sweller, J., & Clark, R. E. (2006). Why minimal guidance during instruction does not work: An analysis of the failure of constructivist, problem-based, experiential, and inquiry-based teaching. *Educational Psychologist, 41*(2), 75–86.

Klein, G., Wolf, S., Militello, L., & Zsambok, C. (1995). Characteristics of skilled option generation in chess. *Organizational Behavior and Human Decision Processes, 62*(1), 63–69. doi: http://dx.doi.org/10.1006/obhd.1995.1031

Klein, H. A., & Klein, G. A. (1981, May). *Perceptual/cognitive analysis of proficient cardiopulmonary resuscitation (CPR) performance.* Paper presented at the Annual Meeting of the Midwestern Psychological Association, Detroit, MI.

Klenowski, V. (2009). Assessment for learning revisited: An Asia-Pacific perspective. *Assessment in Education: Principles, Policy and Practice, 16*(3), 263–268.

Kluger, A. N., & DeNisi, A. (1996). The effects of feedback interventions on performance: A historical review, a meta-analysis, and a preliminary feedback intervention theory. *Psychological Bulletin, 119*(2), 254–284.

Konstantopoulos, S. (2006). *The power of the test in three-level designs* (Vol. DP 2412). Bonn, Germany: Forschungsinstitut zur Zukunft der Arbeit (Institute for the Study of Labour).

Kooijman, J. D. G., Meijaard, J. P., Papadopoulos, J. M., Ruina, A., & Schwab, A. L. (2011). A bicycle can be self-stable without gyroscopic or caster effects. *Science, 332*(6027), 339–342. doi: 10.1126/science.1201959

Kotter, J. P., & Cohen, D. S. (2002). *The heart of change*. Boston, MA: Harvard Business School Press.

Kurzweil, R. (1999). *The age of spiritual machines: When computers exceed human intelligence*. New York, NY: Viking Penguin.

Laby, D. M., Davidson, J. L., Rosenbaum, L. J., Strasser, C., Mellman, M. F., Rosenbaum, A. L., ...Kirschen, D. G. (1996). The visual function of professional baseball players. *American Journal of Ophthalmology, 122*(4), 476–485. doi: 10.1016/S0002-9394(14)72106-3

Ladd, H. F., & Sorensen, L. C. (2015). *Returns to teacher experience: Student achievement and motivation in middle school*. Washington, DC: Center for Analysis of Longitudinal Data in Educational Research.

Lagemann, E. C. (2000). *An elusive science: The troubling history of education research*. Chicago, IL: Chicago University Press.

LaMore, R., Root-Bernstein, R., Root-Bernstein, M., Schweitzer, J. H., Lawton, J. L., Roraback, E., . . . Fernandez, L. (2013). Arts and crafts: Critical to economic innovation. *Economic Development Quarterly, 27*(3), 221–229. doi: 10.1177/0891242413486186

Lavy, V., Ebenstein, A., & Roth, S. (2014). *The long run human capital and economic consequences of high-stakes examinations*. Cambridge, MA: National Bureau of Economic Research.

Le, Q. V., Ranzato, M. A., Monga, R., Devin, M., Chen, K., Corrado, G. S., . . . Ng, A. Y. (2012). Building high-level features using large scale unsupervised learning. In J. Langford & J. Pineau (Eds.), *Proceedings of the 29th International Conference on Machine Learning* (pp. 81–88). New York, NY: Omnipress.

Leahy, S., Leusner, D. M., & Lyon, C. J. (2005). *Providing a research basis for ETS products*. Princeton, NJ: Educational Testing Service.

Leahy, S., Lyon, C., Thompson, M., & Wiliam, D. (2005). Classroom assessment: Minute-by-minute and day-by-day. *Educational Leadership, 63*(3), 18–24.

Leape, L. L., Bates, D. W., Cullen, D. J., Cooper, J., Demonaco, H. J., Gallivan, T., . . . Edmondson, A. (1995). Systems analysis of adverse drug events. *Journal of the American Medical Association, 274*(1), 35–43. doi: 10.1001/jama.1995.03530010049034

Lebergott, S. (1957). Annual estimates of unemployment in the United States, 1900–1954. In Universities-National Bureau Committee for Economic Research (Ed.), *The measurement and behavior of unemployment* (pp. 211–242). Princeton, NJ: Princeton University Press.

Lee, C., Oh, P. S., Ang, A., & Lee, G. (2014, May). *Holistic assessment implementation in Singapore primary schools part I: Using assessment to support the learning and development of students*. Paper presented at the Annual Meeting of the International Association for Education Assessment, Singapore.

Leigh, A. (2010). Estimating teacher effectiveness from two-year changes in students' test scores. *Economics of Education Review, 29*(3), 480–488.

Leinhardt, G., & Greeno, J. G. (1986). The cognitive skill of teaching. *Journal of Educational Psychology, 78*(2), 75–95. doi: 10.1037/0022-0663.78.2.75

Lenth, R. V. (2006, August 14). Java applets for power and sample size. Retrieved April 20, 2015, from http://homepage.stat.uiowa.edu/~rlenth/Power/

Lesgold, A. M., & Resnick, L. B. (1982). How reading difficulties develop: Perspectives from a longitudinal study. In J. P. Das, R. F. Mulcahy & A. E. Wall (Eds.), *Theory and research in learning disabilities* (pp. 155–187). New York, NY: Plenum.

Lesgold, A. M., Rubinson, H., Feltovich, P. J., Glaser, R., Klopfer, D., & Wang, Y. (1988). Expertise in a complex skill: Diagnosing x-ray pictures. In M. T. H. Chi, R. Glaser & M. J. Farr (Eds.), *The nature of expertise* (pp. 311–342). Hillsdale, NJ: Lawrence Erlbaum Associates.

Levin, T., & Long, R. (1981). *Effective instruction*. Washington, DC: Association for Supervision and Curriculum Development.

Levine, J. (2011, April 11). Finnishing school. *TimeLife, 177*(14).

Levitt, S. D. (2008, July 28). From good to great...to below average. *Freakonomics*. Retrieved from http://freakonomics.com/2008/07/28/from-good-to-great-to-below-average/

Levy, F., & Murnane, R. J. (2004). *The new division of labor: How computers are creating the next job market*. Princeton, NJ: Princeton University Press.

Levy, F., & Murnane, R. J. (2013). *Dancing with robots: Human skills for computerized work*. Washington, DC: Third Way.

Li, M., Ruiz-Primo, M. A., Yin, Y., Liaw, Y.-L., & Morozov, A. E. (2013, April). *Identifying characteristics of effective feedback practices: A literature synthesis of feedback studies in STEM education*. Paper presented at the Annual Meeting of the American Educational Research Association, San Francisco, CA.

Light, R. J., & Pillemer, D. B. (1984). *Summing up: The science of reviewing research*. Cambridge, MA: Harvard University Press.

Lipsey, M. W., Puzio, K., Yun, C., Hebert, M. A., Steinka-Fry, K., Cole, M., . . . Busick, M. D. (2012). *Translating the statistical representation of the effects of education interventions into more readily interpretable forms*. Washington, DC: United States National Center for Special Education Research.

Livingston, C., & Borko, H. (1990). High school mathematics review lessons: Expert-novice distinctions. *Journal for Research in Mathematics Education, 21*(5), 372–387.

Looney, J. (Ed.). (2005). *Formative assessment: Improving learning in secondary classrooms*. Paris, France: Organisation for Economic Co-operation and Development.

Lou, Y., Abrami, P. C., Spence, J. C., Poulsen, C., Chambers, B., & d'Apollonia, S. (1996). Within-class grouping: A meta-analysis. *Review of Educational Research, 66*(4), 423–458. doi: 10.3102/00346543066004423

Love, J. F. (1995). *McDonalds: Behind the golden arches*. New York, NY: Bantam.

Loveless, T. (2010). *The 2010 Brown Center report on American education: How well are American students learning? With sections on NAEP trends, the persistence of school test scores, and conversion charter schools*. Washington, DC: Brookings Institution.

Loveless, T. (2014). *The 2014 Brown Center report on American education: How well are American students learning? With sections on the PISA-Shanghai controversy, homework, and the common core.* Washington, DC: Brookings Institution.

Lunn, J. H. (1946). Chick sexing. *American Scientist, 36*(2), 280–287.

Lyon, C. J., & Leusner, D. M. (2009). *Product efficacy argument for the Keeping Learning on Track® program* (Vol. PEAr-09-02). Princeton, NJ: Educational Testing Service.

Lyon, C. J., Wylie, E. C., & Goe, L. (2006, April). *Changing teachers, changing schools.* Paper presented at the Annual Meeting of the American Educational Research Association, San Francisco, CA.

Lyons, B. D., Hoffman, B. J., & Michel, J. W. (2009). Not much more than g? An examination of the impact of intelligence on NFL performance. *Human Performance, 22*(3), 225–245. doi: 10.1080/08959280902970401

Mackintosh, U. A. T., Marsh, D. R., & Schroeder, D. G. (2002). Sustained positive deviant child care practices and their effects on child growth in Viet Nam. *Food and Nutrition Bulletin, 23*(4 [supplement]), 16–25.

Mandel, M. (2013, July 8). 752,000 app economy jobs on the 5th anniversary of the App Store [Web log post]. Retrieved from http://www.progressivepolicy.org/slider/752000-app -economy-jobs-on-the-5th-anniversary-of-the-app-store/

Mankiw, N. G., & Swagel, P. (2006). *The politics and economics of offshore outsourcing.* Cambridge, MA: National Bureau of Economic Research.

Marcotte, D. E., & Hansen, B. (2010). Time for school? *Education Next, 10*(1), 52–59.

Marshall, B., & Wiliam, D. (2006). *English inside the black box: Assessment for learning in the English classroom.* London, UK: NFER-Nelson.

Marzano, R. J. (2003). *What works in schools: Translating research into action.* Alexandria, VA: ASCD.

Marzano, R. J., & Toth, M. D. (2013). *Teacher evaluation that makes a difference: A new model for teacher growth and student achievement.* Alexandria, VA: ASCD.

Maslow, A. H. (1966). *The psychology of science: A renaissance.* New York, NY: Joanna Cotler Books.

Mauboussin, M. J. (2012). *The success equation: Untangling skill and luck in business, sports, and investing.* Boston, MA: Harvard Business Review Press.

McCartney, F. J., Spiegelhalter, D. J., & Rigby, M. L. (1987). Medical management. In R. H. Anderson, F. J. McCartney, E. A. Shinebourne & M. Tynan (Eds.), *Paediatric cardiology* (2nd ed., pp. 421–442). Edinburgh, UK: Churchill Livingstone.

McGrath, C. (1997, March 23). Elders on ice. *New York Times Magazine.* Retrieved from http://www.nytimes.com/1997/03/23/magazine/elders-on-ice.html

McGraw, K. O., & Wong, S. P. (1992). A common language effect size statistic. *Psychological Bulletin, 111*(2), 361–365. doi: 10.1037/0033-2909.111.2.361

McGregor, D. M. (1960). *The human side of enterprise.* New York, NY: McGraw-Hill.

McGugin, R. W., Gatenby, J. C., Gore, J. C., & Gauthier, I. (2012). High-resolution imaging of expertise reveals reliable object selectivity in the fusiform face area related to perceptual performance. *Proceedings of the National Academy of Sciences, 109*(42), 17063–17068. doi: 10.1073/pnas.1116333109

McLaughlin, M. W., & Talbert, J. E. (2006). *Building school-based teacher learning communities: Professional strategies to improve student achievement.* New York, NY: Teachers College Press.

McMillan, J. H., & Foley, J. (2006). Reporting and discussing effect size: Still the road less traveled? *Practical Assessment, Research & Evaluation, 16*(14).

Mears, M. (2009). *Leadership elements: A guide to building trust.* Bloomington, IN: iUniverse.

Mercer, N., Dawes, L., Wegerif, R., & Sams, C. (2004). Reasoning as a scientist: Ways of helping children to use language to learn science. *British Educational Research Journal, 30*(3), 359–377.

Micklewright, J., & Schnepf, S. V. (2006). *Response bias in England in PISA 2000 and 2003.* London, UK: Department for Education and Skills.

Mills College Lesson Study Group. (2014). Lesson Study Group at Mills College. Retrieved from http://www.lessonresearch.net

Milton, J., Solodkin, A., Hlustík, P., & Small, S. L. (2007). The mind of expert motor performance is cool and focused. *NeuroImage, 35*(2), 804–813.

Moore, G. E. (1965). Cramming more components onto integrated circuits. *Electronics, 38*(8), 114–117. doi: 10.1109/jproc.1998.658762

Moore, T. J. (1995). *Deadly medicine: Why tens of thousands of heart patients died in America's worst drug disaster.* New York, NY: Simon & Schuster.

Moravec, H. (1988). *Mind children: The future of robot and human intelligence.* Cambridge, MA: Harvard University Press.

Mullis, I. V. S., Martin, M. O., Foy, P., & Arora, A. (2012). *TIMSS 2011 international results in mathematics.* Boston, MA: Boston College.

Myers, D. G., & Lamm, H. (1976). The group polarization phenomenon. *Psychological Bulletin, 83*(4), 602–627. doi: 10.1037/0033-2909.83.4.602

Naftulin, D. H., Ware, J. E., & Donnelly, F. A. (1973). The Doctor Fox lecture: A paradigm of educational seduction. *Journal of Medical Education, 48*(7), 630–635.

National Alliance for Public Charter Schools. (2015). The public charter schools dashboard: A comprehensive data resource from the National Alliance for Public Charter Schools. Retrieved from http://dashboard.publiccharters.org/dashboard/schools/year/2014

National Assessment of Educational Progress. (2006). *The nation's report card: Mathematics 2005* (Vol. NCES 2006-453). Washington, DC: Institute of Education Sciences.

National Endowment for Science, Technology and the Arts. (2014, August 18). 'Benefit of the doubt' is the basis for prescribing antibiotics, finds Longitude survey. Retrieved from http://www.nesta.org.uk/news/benefit-doubt-basis-prescribing-antibiotics-finds-longitude-survey

Natriello, G. (1987). The impact of evaluation processes on students. *Educational Psychologist, 22*(2), 155–175.

Newman, D., Finney, P. B., Bell, S., Turner, H., Jaciw, A. P., Zacamy, J. L.,…Gould, L. F. (2012). *Evaluation of the effectiveness of the Alabama Math, Science, and Technology Initiative (AMSTI): Final report* (Vol. NCEE 2012-4008). Washington, DC: Institute of Education Sciences.

Newman, M. E. J. (2006). Power laws, Pareto distributions and Zipf's law. *Contemporary Physics, 46*(5), 323–351.

Nguyen, D. (2013). The first mention of "computer" in the *New York Times* [Web log post]. Retrieved from http://danwin.com/2013/02/the-first-mention-of-computer-in-the-new -york-times/

Noice, H., & Noice, T. (1993). The effects of segmentation on the recall of theatrical material. *Poetics, 22*, 51–67.

Northwest Evaluation Association. (2015). Keeping Learning on Track: Discover how to assess student learning. Retrieved from https://www.nwea.org/professional-development /keeping-learning-on-track/

Nyquist, J. B. (2003). *The benefits of reconstruing feedback as a larger system of formative assessment: A meta-analysis* (Master's thesis).Vanderbilt University, Nashville, TN.

Organisation for Economic Co-operation and Development. (2014). *Education at a glance.* Paris, France: Organisation for Economic Co-operation and Development.

Organisation for Economic Co-operation and Development. (2014). OECD Better Life index: Finland. Retrieved from http://www.oecdbetterlifeindex.org/countries/finland/

Ost, B. (2014). How do teachers improve? The relative importance of specific and general human capital. *American Economic Journal: Applied Economics, 6*(2), 127–151. doi: 10.1257/app.6.2.127

Panitz, T. (1999). Collaborative versus cooperative learning: A comparison of the two concepts which will help us understand the underlying nature of interactive learning. Retrieved from http://files.eric.ed.gov/fulltext/ED448443.pdf

Papay, J. P., & Kraft, M. A. (2015). Productivity returns to experience in the teacher labor market: Methodological challenges and new evidence on long-term career improvement. *Journal of Public Economics.*

Papp, K. K., Polk, H. C., & Richardson, J. D. (1997). The relationship between criteria used to select residents and performance during residency. *American Journal of Surgery, 173*(4), 326–329. doi: 10.1016/S0002-9610(96)00389-3

Pareto, V. (1896). *Cours d'économie politique professé à l'Université de Lausanne [Course in political economy taught at the University of Lausanne].* Geneva, Switzerland: Librairie Droz.

Partanen, A. (2011, December 29). What Americans keep ignoring about Finland's school success. *Atlantic.* Retrieved from http://theatlantic.com/national/archive/2011/12 /what-americans-keep-ignoring-about-finlands-school-success/250564/

Pashler, H., McDaniel, M., Rohrer, D., & Bjork, R. A. (2008). Learning styles: Concepts and evidence. *Psychological Science in the Public Interest, 9*(3), 105–119.

Penuel, W. R. (2006). Implementation and effects of one-to-one computing initiatives. *Journal of Research on Technology in Education, 38*(3), 329–348. doi: 10.1080/15391523 .2006.10782463

Perrenoud, P. (1998). From formative evaluation to a controlled regulation of learning. Towards a wider conceptual field. *Assessment in Education: Principles, Policy and Practice, 5*(1), 85–102.

Perry, R., & Lewis, C. C. (2011). Improving the mathematical content base of lesson study: Summary of results. Retrieved from http://www.lessonresearch.net/IESAbstract10.pdf

Persing, J., James, H., Swanson, J., Kattwinkel, J., & Committee on Practice and Ambulatory Medicine. (2003). Prevention and management of positional skull deformities in infants. *Pediatrics, 112*(1), 199–202.

Peters, T. J., & Waterman, R. H. (1982). *In search of excellence*. London, UK: HarperCollins.

Pfeffer, J. (1998). Seven practices of successful organizations. *California Management Review, 40*(2), 96–124.

Pittenger, D. J. (2005). Cautionary comments regarding the Myers-Briggs Type Indicator. *Consulting Psychology Journal: Practice and Research, 57*(3), 210–221. doi: 10.1037/1065 -9293.57.3.210

Polanyi, M. (1958). *Personal knowledge*. London, UK: Routledge & Kegan Paul.

Polanyi, M. (1966/2009). *The tacit dimension*. Chicago, IL: University of Chicago Press.

Popham, W. J. (2001). Standardized achievement tests: Misnamed and misleading. *Education Week, 21*(3), 46.

Popham, W. J. (2008). *Transformative assessment*. Alexandria, VA: ASCD.

Powers, D. G. (1953). *How to say a few words*. New York, NY: Doubleday.

President's Committee on the Arts and the Humanities. (2011). *Reinvesting in arts education: Winning America's future through creative schools*. Washington, DC: President's Committee on the Arts and the Humanities.

PricewaterhouseCoopers. (2003). *Building better performance: An empirical assessment of the learning and other impacts of schools capital investment*. London, UK: Department for Education and Skills.

Programme for International Student Assessment. (2001). *Knowledge and skills for life: First results from PISA 2000*. Paris, France: Organisation for Economic Co-operation and Development.

Programme for International Student Assessment. (2004). *Learning for tomorrow's world: First results from PISA 2003*. Paris, France: Organisation for Economic Co-operation and Development.

Programme for International Student Assessment. (2013). *PISA 2012 results: What students know and can do. Student performance in mathematics, reading and science (volume 1)*. Paris, France: Organisation for Economic Co-operation and Development.

Pronin, E., Lin, D. Y., & Ross, L. (2002). The bias blind spot: Perceptions of bias in self versus others. *Personality and Social Psychology Bulletin, 28*, 369–381.

Quetelet, L. A. J. (1835). *Sur l'homme et le developpement de ses facultés, essai d'une physique sociale [On man and the development of his faculties, an essay on social physics]*. London, UK: Bossange & Co.

Quilici, J. L., & Mayer, R. E. (1996). Role of examples in how students learn to categorize statistics word problems. *Journal of Educational Psychology, 88*(1), 144–161. doi: 10.1037 /0022-0663.88.1.144

Randel, B., Beesley, A. D., Apthorp, H., Clark, T. F., Wang, X., Cicchinelli, L. F.,…Williams, J. M. (2010). *Classroom assessment for student learning: Impact on elementary school mathematics in the central region* (Vol. NCEE 2011-4005). Denver, CO: Mid-continent Research for Education and Learning (McREL).

Raudenbush, S. W., & Bryk, A. S. (1988). Methodological advances in analyzing the effects of schools and classrooms on student learning. In E. Z. Rothkopf (Ed.), *Review of research in education* (Vol. 15, pp. 423–475). Washington, DC: American Educational Research Association.

Redmond, G. (1993). *Wayne Gretzky: The Great One*. Toronto, Canada: ECW Press.

Richardson, J. (2013). The Finnish way. *Phi Delta Kappan, 94*(5), 76–77.

Ritter, S., Anderson, J. R., Koedinger, K. R., & Corbett, A. (2007). Cognitive Tutor: Applied research in mathematics education. *Psychonomic Bulletin & Review, 14*(2), 249–255.

Rivkin, S. G., Hanushek, E. A., & Kain, J. F. (2005). Teachers, schools and academic achievement. *Econometrica, 73*(2), 417–458.

Roberts, K. H. (1990). Some characteristics of one type of high reliability organization. *Organization Science, 1*(2), 160–176. doi: 10.1287/orsc.1.2.160

Robinson, K. (2009). *Out of our minds: Learning to be creative*. Chichester, UK: Capstone.

Rosenthal, R. (1979). The "file drawer problem" and tolerance for null results. *Psychological Bulletin, 86*(3), 638–641.

Rosson, M. B. (1985). The role of experience in editing. In B. Shackel (Ed.), *Proceedings of INTERACT '84 IFIP Conference on Human-Computer Interaction* (pp. 45–50). New York, NY: Elsevier.

Rowe, K. J. (2003, October). *The importance of teacher quality as a key determinant of students' experiences and outcomes of schooling*. Paper presented at the ACER Research Conference, Melbourne, Australia. Retrieved from https://www.det.nsw.edu.au/proflearn/docs/pdf /qt_rowe2003.pdf

Roza, M., & Miller, R. (2009). *Separation of degrees: State-by-state analysis of teacher compensation for master's degrees*. Washington, DC: Center on Reinventing Public Education.

Ruiz-Primo, M. A., Shavelson, R. J., Hamilton, L., & Klein, S. (2002). On the evaluation of systemic science education reform: Searching for instructional sensitivity. *Journal of Research in Science Teaching, 39*(5), 369–393.

Ryle, G. (1949). *The concept of mind*. London, UK: Hutchinson.

Sabers, D. S., Cushing, K. S., & Berliner, D. C. (1991). Differences among teachers in a task characterized by simultaneity, multidimensionality, and immediacy. *American Educational Research Journal, 28*(1), 63–88. doi: 10.2307/1162879

Sadler, D. R. (1989). Formative assessment and the design of instructional systems. *Instructional Science, 18*, 119–144.

Sahlberg, P. (2011). *Finnish lessons: What can the world learn from educational change in Finland?* New York, NY: Teachers College Press.

Sahlberg, P. (2014). The brainy questions on Finland's only high-stakes standardized test. *Washington Post*. Retrieved from http://www.washingtonpost.com/blogs/answer-sheet /wp/2014/03/24/the-brainy-questions-on-finlands-only-high-stakes-standardized-test/

Santiago, P., & Benavides, F. (2009). *Teacher evaluation: A conceptual framework and examples of country practices*. Paris, France: Organisation for Economic Co-operation and Development.

Sartain, L., Stoelinga, S. R., Brown, E. R., Luppescu, S., Matsko, K. K., Miller, F. K.,... Glazer, D. (2011). *Rethinking teacher evaluation in Chicago: Lessons learned from classroom observations, principal-teacher conferences, and district implementation.* Chicago, IL: Consortium on Chicago School Research.

Saunders, W. M., Goldenberg, C. N., & Gallimore, R. (2009). Increasing achievement by focusing grade level teams on improving classroom learning: A prospective, quasi-experimental study of title 1 schools. *American Educational Research Journal, 46*(4), 1006–1033.

Schleicher, A. (2008). *The critical policy focus on learning: Seeing school systems through the prism of international comparisons.* Paris, France: Organisation for Economic Co-operation and Development.

Schloss, D. F. (1891). Why working-men dislike piece-work. *Economic Review, 1*(3), 312–326.

Schmoker, M. (2010, September 29). When pedagogic fads trump priorities. *Education Week, 30*(5), 22–23.

Schmoker, M. (2011). *Focus: Elevating the essentials to radically improve student learning.* Alexandria, VA: ASCD.

Schneider, W. (1996). The effects of expertise and IQ on children's memory: When knowledge is, and when it is not enough. *International Journal of Behavioral Development, 19*(4), 773–796. doi: 10.1080/016502596385578

Schneider, W., Körkel, J., & Weinert, F. E. (1989). Domain-specific knowledge and memory performance: A comparison of high- and low-aptitude children. *Journal of Educational Psychology, 81*(3), 306–312.

Schön, D. (1983). *The reflective practitioner: How professionals think in practice.* New York, NY: Basic Books.

Schroeder, R., & Buckman, J. (2005). The Juran Center for Leadership in Quality. In P. O'Mara (Ed.), *Juran, quality, and a century of improvement* (pp. 31–54). Milwaukee, WI: Quality Press.

Schueneman, A. L., Pickleman, J., & Freeark, R. J. (1985). Age, gender, lateral dominance, and prediction of operative skill among general surgery residents. *Surgery, 98*(3), 506–515.

Schumpeter, J. A. (1942). *Capitalism, socialism and democracy.* New York, NY: Harper & Row.

Scriven, M. (1967). The methodology of evaluation. In R. W. Tyler, R. M. Gagné & M. Scriven (Eds.), *Perspectives of curriculum evaluation* (Vol. 1, pp. 39–83). Chicago, IL: Rand McNally.

Sedlmeier, P., & Gigerenzer, G. (1989). Do studies of statistical power have an effect on the power of studies? *Psychological Bulletin, 105*(2), 309–316. doi: 10.1037/0033-2909.105.2.309

Selden, S. (1999). *Inheriting shame: The story of eugenics and racism in America* (Vol. 23). New York, NY: Teachers College Press.

Sen, A. (1999). The possibility of social choice. *American Economic Review, 89*(3), 349–378.

Sharpe, T. L., & Hawkins, A. (1993). Expert and novice elementary specialists: A comparative analysis. *Journal of Teaching in Physical Education, 12*(1), 55–75.

Sheeran, P., Milne, S., Webb, T. L., & Gollwitzer, P. M. (2005). Implementation intentions and health behaviors. In M. Conner & P. Norman (Eds.), *Predicting health behavior: Research and practice with social cognition models* (2nd ed., pp. 276–323). Buckingham, UK: Open University Press.

Shepard, L. A. (2008). Formative assessment: Caveat emptor. In C. A. Dwyer (Ed.), *The future of assessment: Shaping teaching and learning* (pp. 279–303). Mahwah, NJ: Lawrence Erlbaum Associates.

Shepard, L. A. (2010). What the marketplace has brought us: Item-by-item teaching with little instructional insight. *Peabody Journal of Education, 85*(2), 246–257.

Shepard, L. A., Hammerness, K., Darling-Hammond, L., Rust, F., Snowden, J. B., Gordon, E., . . . Pacheco, A. (2005). Assessment. In L. Darling-Hammond & J. Bransford (Eds.), *Preparing teachers for a changing world: What teachers should learn and be able to do* (pp. 275–326). San Francisco, CA: Jossey-Bass.

Shim, H. S., & Roth, G. L. (2008). Sharing tacit knowledge among expert teaching professors and mentees: Considerations for career and technical education teacher educators. *Journal of Industrial Teacher Education, 44*(4), 5–28.

Shulman, L. (1986). Those who understand: Knowledge growth in teaching. *Educational Researcher, 15*(1), 4–14.

Shute, V. J. (2008). Focus on formative feedback. *Review of Educational Research, 78*(1), 153–189.

Siegel, L. S. (1989). IQ is irrelevant to the definition of learning disabilities. *Journal of Learning Disabilities, 22*(8), 469–478.

Siegel, L. S. (2006). Perspectives on dyslexia. *Paediatrics and Child Health, 11*(9), 581–587.

Simonsohn, U., Nelson, L. D., & Simmons, J. P. (2014). *P*-curve: A key to the file-drawer. *Journal of Experimental Psychology: General, 143*(2), 534–547. doi: 10.1037/a0033242

Slavin, R. E. (1987). Best-evidence synthesis: An alternative to meta-analytic and traditional reviews. *Educational Researcher, 15*(9), 5–11. doi: 10.3102/0013189x015009005

Slavin, R. E., Hurley, E. A., & Chamberlain, A. M. (2003). Cooperative learning and achievement. In W. M. Reynolds & G. J. Miller (Eds.), *Handbook of psychology volume 7: Educational psychology* (pp. 177–198). Hoboken, NJ: Wiley.

Sloboda, J. A., Davidson, J. W., Howe, M. J. A., & Moore, D. G. (1996). The role of practice in the development of performing musicians. *British Journal of Psychology, 87*(2), 287–309. doi: 10.1111/j.2044-8295.1996.tb02591.x

Smarter Scotland. (2012, February 13). PISA 2012—Representing your country. Retrieved from https://www.youtube.com/watch?v=-lohprRZnoU

Snow, P. B., Smith, D. S., & Catalona, W. J. (1994). Artificial neural networks in the diagnosis and prognosis of prostate cancer: A pilot study. *Journal of Urology, 152*(5 part 2), 1923–1926.

Sonnentag, S. (1998). Expertise in professional software design: A process study. *Journal of Applied Psychology, 83*(5), 703–715. doi: 10.1037/0021-9010.83.5.703

Spilich, G. J., Vesonder, G. T., Chiesi, H. L., & Voss, J. F. (1979). Text processing of domain-related information for individuals with high and low domain knowledge. *Journal of Verbal Learning and Verbal Behavior, 18*(3), 275–290. doi: http://dx.doi.org/10.1016/S0022-5371(79)90155-5

Spock, B. (1956). *The common sense guide to baby and child care*. New York, NY: Duell, Sloan, and Pearce.

Springer, M. G., Ballou, D., Hamilton, L., Le, V.-N., Lockwood, J. R., McCaffrey, D., . . . Stecher, B. M. (2010). *Teacher pay for performance: Experimental evidence from the project on incentives in teaching*. Nashville, TN: National Center on Performance Incentives at Vanderbilt University.

Squire, D., Giachino, A. A., Profitt, A. W., & Heaney, C. (1989). Objective comparison of manual dexterity in physicians and surgeons. *Canadian Journal of Surgery, 32*(6), 467–470.

Stiggins, R. J. (2005). From formative assessment to assessment FOR learning: A path to success in standards-based schools. *Phi Delta Kappan, 87*(4), 324–328.

Stiggins, R. J., Arter, J. A., Chappuis, J., & Chappuis, S. (2004). *Classroom assessment for student learning: Doing it right—using it well*. Portland, OR: Assessment Training Institute.

Stiglitz, J. E. (2007). *Making globalization work*. New York, NY: Norton.

Stokes, L. M., Sato, N. E., McLaughlin, M. W., & Talbert, J. E. (1997). *Theory-based reform and problems of change: Contexts that matter for teachers' learning and community (R97-7)*. Stanford, CA: Stanford University.

Stringfield, S. (1995). Attempting to improve students' learning through innovative programs: The case for schools evolving into high reliability organisations. *School Effectiveness and School Improvement, 6*(1), 67–96. doi: 10.1080/0924345950060104

Surowiecki, J. (2004). *The wisdom of crowds*. New York, NY: Doubleday.

Sutton, R. (1995). *Assessment for learning*. Salford, UK: RS Publications.

Svenson, O. (1981). Are we all less risky and more skillful than our fellow drivers? *Acta Psychologica, 47*(2), 143–148.

Syed, M. (2010). *Bounce: Mozart, Federer, Picasso, Beckham, and the science of success*. New York, NY: HarperCollins.

Taleb, N. N. (2014). *Antifragile: Things that gain from disorder*. New York, NY: Random House.

Tanaka, J. W. (2001). The entry point of face recognition: Evidence for face expertise. *Journal of Experimental Psychology: General, 130*(3), 534–543. doi: 10.1037/0096-3445.130.3.534

Tanaka, J. W., & Taylor, M. (1991). Object categories and expertise: Is the basic level in the eye of the beholder? *Cognitive Psychology, 23*(3), 457–482. doi: http://dx.doi.org/10.1016/0010-0285(91)90016-H

Taylor, S. E. (2010). Mechanisms linking early life stress to adult health outcomes. *Proceedings of the National Academy of Sciences, 107*(19), 8507–8512.

Teo, K. K., Yusuf, S., & Furberg, C. D. (1993). Effects of prophylactic antiarrhythmic drug therapy in acute myocardial infarction: An overview of results from randomized controlled trials. *JAMA, 270*(13), 1589–1595. doi: 10.1001/jama.1993.03510130095038

Tetlock, P. E. (2005). *Expert political judgement. How good is it? How can we know?* Princeton, NJ: Princeton University Press.

Thomas, J. R., Gallagher, J., & Lowry, K. (2003, June). *Developing motor and sport expertise: Meta-analytic findings.* Paper presented at the Annual Meeting of the North American Society for the Psychology of Sport and Physical Activity Conference, Savannah, GA.

Thompson, E. (2007, August 22). That which we sell as a jelly bean by the same label would taste as sweet. *The Gazette.* Retrieved from http://www.canada.com/montrealgazette/story .html?id=912825b6-34a7-4d26-a1fd-4ea6ee67286b#__federated=1

Thompson, M., & Wiliam, D. (2008). Tight but loose: A conceptual framework for scaling up school reforms. In E. C. Wylie (Ed.), *Tight but loose: Scaling up teacher professional development in diverse contexts* (Vol. RR-08-29, pp. 1–44). Princeton, NJ: Educational Testing Service.

Thum, Y. M., Tarasawa, B., Hegedus, A., Yun, X., & Bowe, B. (2015). *Keeping Learning on Track: A case-study of formative assessment practice and its impact on learning in Meridian School District.* Portland, OR: Northwest Evaluation Association.

Tomlinson, C. A. (2004). Sharing responsibility for differentiating instruction. *Roeper Review, 26*(4), 188–120.

Tomsett, J. (2015). *This much I know about love over fear: Creating a culture of truly great teaching.* Carmarthen, UK: Crown House.

Torrance, H. (1993). Formative assessment: Some theoretical problems and empirical questions. *Cambridge Journal of Education, 23*(3), 333–343.

Treu, R. M. (2014). *Judgment in the case of Vergara vs. State of California.* Los Angeles: Superior Court of the State of California.

Tullock, G. (2001). A comment on Daniel Klein's 'A plea to economists who favor liberty'. *Eastern Economic Journal, Spring 2001, 27*(2), 203–207.

United Nations Statistics Division. (2013, December 16). Gross value added by kind of economic activity at current prices—US dollars. *National Accounts Estimates of Main Aggregates.* Retrieved from http://data.un.org/Data.aspx?d=SNAAMA&f=grID%3a201 %3bcurrID%3aUSD%3bpcFlag%3a0%3bitID%3a12

Voss, J. F., Greene, T. R., Post, T. A., & Penner, B. C. (1983). Problem solving skill in the social sciences. In G. H. Bower (Ed.), *The psychology of learning and motivation* (Vol. 17, pp. 165–203). New York, NY: Academic Press.

Voss, J. F., Tyler, S. W., & Yengo, L. A. (1983). Individual differences in the solving of social science problems. In R. F. Dillon & R. R. Schmeck (Eds.), *Individual differences in cognition* (Vol. 1, pp. 205–232). New York, NY: Academic Press.

Vygotsky, L. S. (1978). Interaction between learning and development. In M. Gauvain & M. Cole (Eds.), *Readings on the development of children* (pp. 29–36). New York, NY: W. H. Freeman.

Wagner, R. K., & Steinberg, R. J. (1985). Practical intelligence in real-world pursuits: The role of tacit knowledge. *Journal of Personality and Social Psychology, 49*(2), 436–458. doi: 10.1037/0022-3514.49.2.436

Wainer, H. (2011). *Uneducated guesses: Using evidence to uncover misguided education policies.* Princeton, NJ: Princeton University Press.

Wald, A. (1943). *A method of estimating plane vulnerability based on damage of survivors.* New York, NY: Columbia University Statistics Research Group.

Wanzel, K. R., Hamstra, S. J., Anastakis, D., Matsumoto, E. D., & Cusimano, M. D. (2002). Effects of visual-spatial ability on learning of spatially-complex surgical skills. *Lancet, 359*(9302), 230–231.

Wanzel, K. R., Hamstra, S. J., Caminiti, M. F., Anastakis, D., Grober, E. D., & Reznick, R. K. (2003). Visual-spatial ability correlates with efficiency of hand motion and successful surgical performance. *Surgery, 134*(5), 750–757.

Weinstein, N. D. (1980). Unrealistic optimism about future life courses. *Journal of Personality and Social Psychology, 39*(5), 806–820.

Weiss, C. H. (1972). *Evaluation research: Methods of assessing program effectiveness.* Englewood Cliffs, NJ: Prentice Hall.

Wenglinsky, H. (2005/2006). Technology and achievement: The bottom line. *Educational Leadership, 63*(4), 29–32.

Wholey, J. S. (1979). *Evaluation: Promise and performance.* Washington, DC: Urban Institute.

Wijekumar, K., Hitchcock, J., Turner, H., Lei, P. W., & Peck, K. (2009). *A multisite cluster randomized trial of the effects of Compass Learning Odyssey Math on the math achievement of selected grade 4 students in the Mid-Atlantic Region (NCEE 2009-4068).* Washington, DC: National Center for Education Evaluation and Regional Assistance.

Wiliam, D. (1992). Special needs and the distribution of attainment in the national curriculum. *British Journal of Educational Psychology, 62*, 397–403.

Wiliam, D. (1999a). Formative assessment in mathematics part 1: Rich questioning. *Equals: Mathematics and Special Educational Needs, 5*(2), 15–18.

Wiliam, D. (1999b). Formative assessment in mathematics part 2: Feedback. *Equals: Mathematics and Special Educational Needs, 5*(3), 8–11.

Wiliam, D. (2000). Formative assessment in mathematics part 3: The learner's role. *Equals: Mathematics and Special Educational Needs, 6*(1), 19–22.

Wiliam, D. (2007). Keeping learning on track: Classroom assessment and the regulation of learning. In F. K. Lester Jr. (Ed.), *Second handbook of mathematics teaching and learning* (pp. 1053–1098). Greenwich, CT: Information Age Publishing.

Wiliam, D. (2008). International comparisons and sensitivity to instruction. *Assessment in Education: Principles, Policy and Practice, 15*(3), 253–257.

Wiliam, D., & Black, P. J. (1996). Meanings and consequences: A basis for distinguishing formative and summative functions of assessment? *British Educational Research Journal, 22*(5), 537–548.

Wiliam, D., & Leahy, S. (2014). *Embedding formative assessment professional development pack.* West Palm Beach, FL: Learning Sciences International.

Wiliam, D., & Leahy, S. (2015). *Embedding formative assessment: Practical techniques for K–12 classrooms.* West Palm Beach, FL: Learning Sciences International.

Wiliam, D., Lee, C., Harrison, C., & Black, P. J. (2004). Teachers developing assessment for learning: Impact on student achievement. *Assessment in Education: Principles, Policy and Practice, 11*(1), 49–65.

Wiliam, D., & Thompson, M. (2008). Integrating assessment with instruction: What will it take to make it work? In C. A. Dwyer (Ed.), *The future of assessment: Shaping teaching and learning* (pp. 53–82). Mahwah, NJ: Lawrence Erlbaum Associates.

Williams, A. M., & Davids, K. (1995). Declarative knowledge in sport: A by-product of experience or a characteristic of expertise? *Journal of Sport and Exercise Psychology, 17*(3), 259–275.

Williams, A. M., & Davids, K. (1998). Visual search strategy, selective attention, and expertise in soccer. *Research Quarterly for Exercise and Sport, 69,* 111–128.

Williams, A. M., Davids, K., Burwitz, L., & Williams, J. G. (1993). Cognitive knowledge and soccer performance. *Perceptual and Motor Skills, 76*(2), 579–593. doi: 10.2466/pms.1993.76.2.579

Wimber, M., Alink, A., Charest, I., Kriegeskorte, N., & Anderson, M. C. (2015). Retrieval induces adaptive forgetting of competing memories via cortical pattern suppression. *Nature Neuroscience, 18*(4), 582–589. doi: 10.1038/nn.3973

Winner, E. (1996). The rage to master: The decisive case for talent in the visual arts. In K. A. Ericsson (Ed.), *The road to excellence: The acquisition of expert performance in the arts and sciences, sports and games* (pp. 271–301). Hillsdale, NJ: Lawrence Erlbaum Associates.

Wolf, M. (2007). *Proust and the squid: The story and science of the reading brain.* New York, NY: Harper.

Wood, R. (1987). Your chemistry equals my French. In R. Wood (Ed.), *Measurement and assessment in education and psychology* (pp. 40–44). London, UK: Falmer.

Woods, T. (2001). *How I play golf.* New York, NY: Grand Central Publishing.

World Chess Federation. (2014). FIDE rating list. Retrieved from http://ratings.fide.com/advseek.phtml

Wylie, E. C., & Wiliam, D. (2006, April). *Diagnostic questions: Is there value in just one?* Paper presented at the Annual Meeting of the National Council on Measurement in Education, San Francisco, CA.

Wylie, E. C., & Wiliam, D. (2007, April). *Analyzing diagnostic questions: What makes a student response interpretable?* Paper presented at the Annual Meeting of the National Council on Measurement in Education, Chicago, IL.

Yates, J. F., Klatzky, R. L., & Young, C. A. (1995). Cognitive performance under stress. In R. S. Nickerson (Ed.), *Emerging needs and opportunities for human factors research* (pp. 262–290). Washington, DC: National Academies Press.

York, B. N., & Loeb, S. (2014). *One step at a time: The effects of an early literacy text messaging program for parents of preschoolers.* Cambridge, MA: National Bureau of Economic Research.

Zeitz, C. M. (1997). Some concrete advantages of abstraction: How experts' representations facilitate reasoning. In P. J. Feltovich, K. M. Ford & R. R. Hoffman (Eds.), *Expertise in context: Human and machine* (pp. 43–65). Menlo Park, CA: AAAI/MIT Press.

Zhang, W. (2014). The demand for shadow education in China: Mainstream teachers and power relations. *Asia Pacific Journal of Education, 34*(4), 436–454. doi: 10.1080/02188791.2014.960798

Zhang, Y. (2011). *The determinants of national college entrance exam performance in China—With an analysis of private tutoring.* (Doctoral dissertation). Retrieved from http://academiccommons.columbia.edu/catalog/ac%3A131438

Index

CPSIA information can be obtained
at www.ICGtesting.com
Printed in the USA
LVHW050045221222
735709LV00005B/326